A Lawyer's Life

A Lawyer's Life

JOHNNIE COCHRAN

with David Fisher

THOMAS DUNNE BOOKS/ST. MARTIN'S GRIFFIN ☙ NEW YORK

THOMAS DUNNE BOOKS.
An imprint of St. Martin's Press.

www.stmartins.com

Book design by Susan Yang

Library of Congress Cataloging-in-Publication Data

Cochran, Johnnie, L., 1937–
    A lawyer's life / Johnnie Cochran, with David Fisher.
        p. cm.
    ISBN 0-312-27826-8 (hc)
    ISBN 0-312-31967-3 (pbk)
    1. Cochran, Johnnie L., 1937– 2. Lawyers—United States—Biography.
  3. African American lawyers—Biography. I. Fisher, David, 1946– II. Title.

KF373.C59 A35 2002
340'.092—dc21
  [B]   2002072061

10 9 8 7 6 5 4 3

This book is dedicated to all of those lawyers, past, present, and future, who spend their lives seeking justice for others, especially those who have used the law to change society for the better. Among these people are Charles Hamilton Houston, Thurgood Marshall, Leon Higginbotham, Damon Keith, Constance Baker Motley, and Revius Ortique, as well as Peter Neufeld and Barry Scheck of the Innocence Project.

A Lawyer's Life

ONE

If it may please the reader . . .

There is a young California Highway Patrol officer who begins work each night at almost exactly ten o'clock and finishes at 6:15 A.M. That's known as the graveyard shift; he chooses to work through the night because by that time the worst of Southern California's daily traffic jams have faded into the sunset and the job becomes the most interesting.

During his eight and a half hours in the black-and-white patrol car he'll cover several hundred miles of Los Angeles freeway, mostly the 10 and the 110, upholding the law of the land. His patrol car is equipped to respond to a range of emergencies; there are ample medical supplies in the trunk and a shotgun in the back.

There is no such thing as a typical shift on this job. A single serious accident might fill up most of his time, or he can drive smoothly through the night making as many as twenty different and very routine stops. But on this job the next minute is always one brimming with possibilities; the unexpected is what makes it intriguing. Usually, though, the first couple of hours are pretty routine. Traffic is light. The officer and his partner will assist drivers with disabled vehicles. They'll write some tickets, mostly for speeding. But in the early morning the bars around town close and the drunk drivers hit the road. It's during those three or four hours in the middle of the night that damage will be done.

This particular young man became a law enforcement officer in

1

1998. He was studying microbiology at UCLA, thinking about becoming a doctor, when his best friend joined the Highway Patrol. The job is exciting, his best friend reported, it's different. Try it. And so he did. He had been on the job only a few months the first time he saw a traffic fatality. A man driving home one night had a flat tire and parked on the side of the freeway to change it. It was nothing, a simple flat tire. But another driver wasn't paying attention, his car drifted onto the apron, just close enough to hit the man changing his tire. He had been killed instantly. The result of a ton of metal traveling at high speed hitting a human being was brutal, the young officer remembered, the victim's body was ripped up pretty badly. It was a serious welcome to the work.

The uniform the officer wears is tan, with a blue stripe running down the seam of his trousers. His badge is a gold star. He has a campaign hat, the familiar Smokey the Bear model, but never wears it on the road. It's mostly for show, for dress occasions.

It is still early in his career and he's been fortunate thus far. He's never had to draw his weapon; he's never been threatened. He's only been in three or four hot pursuits and each of them ended quickly and safely.

He has been pleasantly surprised to discover that most of the people he has stopped for traffic infractions have treated him politely. Several speeders have told him they were racing home to go to the bathroom. Only occasionally have drivers reacted to the stop with anger. Three or four people have accused him of stopping them only because they are African-American, and to each of them he politely pointed out that it was night and the windows of their car were tinted, making it impossible for him to see who was inside. Several times the drivers of cars he had stopped warned him that they knew influential people, that they could cause problems in his career. Two people told him they were "personal friends of Johnnie Cochran."

Obviously they failed to read this young officer's name tag. It reads "J. E. Cochran." Jonathan Eric Cochran. My son.

• • •

Most people are quite surprised to learn that my only son is a police officer. Truthfully, when he called me from college and told me about this decision I was surprised, too. Surprised, but supportive. I've spent much of my life around law enforcement officers. Among my best friends is the former chief of police of Los Angeles, Bernard Parks. My brother-in-law and my friend for more than forty years, Bill Baker served in the L.A. Sheriff's Department for more than thirty years, rising to the rank of chief. At two different times in my life I served as a prosecutor in Los Angeles, for three years being the third-highest-ranking attorney in the L.A. County District Attorney's office. So there are few people in this nation with more respect for law enforcement officers—and the law— than me.

That statement may surprise many people, too, particularly those people who most associate me with the criminal trial for murder and the acquittal on all charges of O.J. Simpson. The Simpson trial changed the lives of every person who participated in that trial. As advertised, it was indeed the "Trial of the Century." It had all the elements of great drama: a beloved black athlete was accused of murdering his estranged white wife; it had money and sex, race and gore; it had intrigue and mystery and showcased a cast of diverse and fascinating characters. The trial dominated the popular culture in almost all of its forms for more than a year. It was probably the subject of more conversations and arguments than any subject since the Vietnam War. And, most importantly, it was televised around the world.

At the end of that trial not one of the participants walked out of that courthouse the same person he had been only months earlier. Our lives, too, had been changed forever.

Prior to the Simpson trial I was among the best-known and respected attorneys in Southern California. During my legal career

I had been involved in literally thousands of cases, ranging from prosecuting dangerous drivers to defending accused killers. I am the only attorney to have been honored in Los Angeles as both Civil Trial Lawyer of the Year and Criminal Trial Lawyer of the Year. I had represented victims and their families in some of the most notorious cases in Los Angeles history. I'd won several of the largest judgments in police negligence cases ever paid by the city. I'd prosecuted or represented people of all races and religions and from every social stratum. Among the many celebrities I'd represented—this was long before the O. J. Simpson case—were Michael Jackson and football Hall of Famer Jim Brown. I represented former child TV star Todd Bridges in an attempted murder case in which he was positively identified by the victim. And in the case that spanned several decades of my professional career, I represented Geronimo Pratt, a member of the Black Panther Party who had been wrongly convicted of murder. In the community of Los Angeles I served on the boards of several charities, I was active in civic organizations, and was a member of the Los Angeles Airport Commission—during the massive rebuilding of LAX—for almost thirteen years.

I had an interesting and extremely successful legal practice, a strong marriage to a very bright and beautiful woman, I enjoyed a position of prestige and power within my community, and I had all the material possessions I needed to make me a very happy man. Life was good.

So the Simpson trial was the sea change of my life. It changed my life drastically and forever in ways impossible to even imagine. It obscured everything I had done previously. Everything. As I later understood, being in the middle of the trial was somewhat like being in the eye of a great hurricane; living there in the center it was impossible to truly appreciate the magnitude of the winds swirling around me. Unlike other famous trials of the past, throughout the Simpson trial the television cameras allowed viewers to become emotionally invested in its outcome. At some point for many people it ceased being a trial in which the prosecutors and the defense followed long-established guidelines to determine an accused man's guilt or innocence, and instead became some sort of legal soap opera. My participation as the head of Simpson's successful defense team had made me one of the most easily recognized—and controversial—people in this country. I was loved and I was vilified. I received countless requests and offers—at times I got as many as five hundred phone calls a day—as well as hate letters and threats on my life and that of my family too numerous to count.

Most of America, most of the world actually, came to know me and define me only by my work in that trial. I was the man who had told the jury, "If the glove doesn't fit, you must acquit." I was the attorney who pulled a knitted cap over my head and questioned its value as a disguise. But much more than anything else, I was the attorney accused of "playing the race card." I was accused of using the fact that O. J. Simpson was a black man to convince black jurors to vote to acquit him—not because he might be innocent of the crime, but rather because it was time in America for African-Americans to take retribution for the legal crimes that had been committed against them for almost three centuries.

The attacks on me personally were voluminous and ferocious. In a column in *The New York Times*, best-selling author Gay Talese described me as "a peerless exponent of racism as a weapon of defense." In a best-selling book, author Dominick Dunne wrote, "[Johnnie Cochran's] gotten rich over the years suing the LAPD for infractions against black people..." *Infractions*, I suppose, like breaking into an innocent young black man's apartment and killing him, or *infractions* like stopping an innocent young black man for speeding while he was driving his pregnant wife to the hospital and killing him.

And then, when I was retained in New York City by Abner Louima, a man who had been beaten and sodomized with a plunger by a policeman in a police station while other policemen stood guard, an hysterical columnist in the conservative *New York Post* wrote about me, "The man who cynically turned West Coast justice on its ear in service of the guilty is now poised to do a similar number on the city of New York."

This columnist added, "(H)istory reveals that he will say or do just about anything to win, typically at the expense of the truth." This columnist's ignorance about my career, my "history," did not surprise me. Obviously she had not taken the time necessary to understand what had happened in that Los Angeles courtroom. I sued the newspaper for libel, but the case was dismissed as the column was judged to be "protected opinion."

But I also received considerable acclaim for my work in the Simpson case. People of all races approached me on the street to congratulate me. In restaurants people would send over champagne. One perk I most definitely enjoyed was that my wife, Dale, and I didn't have to stand in long lines at local movie theaters, the manager simply invited us inside. African-Americans in particular were extremely supportive. Extremely. They were very proud that a black man proved that he was among the leading attorneys in the nation, that a black professional could compete successfully on the highest level.

More significantly than that, until the Simpson verdict, many people in the majority community believed that the legal system in this country functioned properly. Guilty people were convicted and innocent people went free. Well, for members of that majority it did, but for the many African-Americans and other minorities, the justice system often had failed to provide justice. Sometimes it seemed to me that I'd spent too many hours of my life defending the rights—and the reputations—of people who had been shot, beaten, or choked by police officers. The reality that the system failed to protect minorities was sort of our national secret, the dirt swept under the rug. The absolutely ecstatic reaction to the Simpson verdict by so many people from the minority communities surprised and probably shocked a great number of people in the majority; and the fact that it did was simply an indication of how great is the division between the races in America.

I'm not sure that even I truly appreciated the extraordinary impact of the Simpson verdict until my wife and I visited South Africa. By that time I was used to being recognized in America. But one day in South Africa we visited the black township of Soweto. Until recently in South Africa, blacks had been forced to live in ghettos. So a township had become a small city in which lived people of every income level—but all of them black. We drove into Soweto in two vans and stopped at a small restaurant. As I got out of the car I saw a child look at me, then start running toward me. Almost immediately he was followed by other children and adults. It seemed like we were surrounded by the whole neighborhood. And they started saying my name, and they sang a song about me, a song that had been written about me. I was astonished. As we ate lunch there that day people came up to me with pictures for me to sign. It was stunning. These were people who didn't even have television sets, yet somehow they knew who I was. What had happened in that courtroom in Los Angeles had resonated with people of color literally throughout the world.

Before becoming involved in the Simpson case I'd seriously considered retiring—though admittedly Dale never for even a moment took me seriously—but at least the thought was in my mind. But my success in the Simpson case provided me with the kind of high-profile celebrity and visibility few attorneys have ever enjoyed. Court TV hired me to cohost a nightly TV show. Characters in movies made reference to me; in one of the *Lethal Weapon* movies, for example, Chris Rock warned a suspect after reading him his Miranda rights, "... and if you get Johnnie Cochran I'll kill you." In *Jackie Brown* Samuel L. Jackson told a compatriot that the lawyer he was hiring was so good, "He's my own personal Johnnie Cochran. As a matter of fact, he kicks Johnnie Cochran's ass." I appeared as myself in the Robert De Niro/Eddie Murphy film *Showtime*. I appeared often as a guest on shows ranging from the very serious *Nightline* to Larry King's show to sitcoms like *The Hughleys*. *Saturday Night Live* and *Seinfeld* parodied me. I was at the center of the uniquely American celebrity blitz.

It was fun. At times it was a lot of fun. And I knew that accepting it good-naturedly, even participating in it, helped soothe some of the angry feelings from the Simpson case.

But I never forgot who I was, what I believed to be my purpose in life, and those things that I had fought for my entire professional career. As a result of my efforts in the Simpson case I was given the extraordinary opportunity to express those views publicly, loudly, and often. And the attention that I received caused me to get involved in some of the most interesting and significant cases of my career. Cases that involved exactly the same institutionalized injustice I had been fighting for decades. In New York City, for example, in addition to Abner Louima's family, I represented the family of a man named Patrick Dorismond, a black man who said no to a drug deal offered by undercover police and was shot and killed. I represented, for a time at least, the family of Amadou Diallo, an unarmed African immigrant who was shot nineteen times—nineteen times— by police officers. Working with my friends and co-counsel from the Simpson case, Peter Neufeld and Barry Scheck, we were able to cause significant changes to be made in the basic policies of the NYPD.

In Buffalo an upscale mall permitted buses full of tourists from across the border to pull directly in front of the shops, but buses from the surrounding minority neighborhoods were not permitted to enter the mall. They had to stop on the far side of a major thoroughfare. The mall management made some ridiculous explanations for this policy, but its real purpose was obvious. As a result a teenage mother named Cynthia Wiggins, who had just been trying to get to her minimum-wage job at the mall, was run down and killed by a truck. An excellent Buffalo attorney named Bob Perk asked me to join him in this civil case, in which we set out to send a strong message to all businesses that still find indirect means to discriminate against minorities.

In New Jersey, Peter, Barry, and I represented several young black and brown men driving on the New Jersey Turnpike to college who were stopped by state troopers for absolutely no reason— except that they fit an illegal law enforcement profile. When their van apparently started rolling backward the state troopers started shooting. This enabled us to focus national attention on the heinous practice of racial profiling, one of the core problems affecting race relations in this country.

And we represent Dantae Johnson, a black teenager who was afraid of New York City cops, so when two officers stopped to question him he ran away. Dantae Johnson was suspected of no crime, there was no emergency, yet the sight of a young black man running away was enough for a police officer to believe he must have done something wrong. The officer chased him in his squad car, pulled his gun, and while attempting to apprehend Johnson shot him. After six months in the hospital Johnson partially recovered. Peter, Barry, and I set out not just to guarantee his financial future—that is the easiest part—but also to make sure this kind of irresponsible shooting never happened again. Additionally, we took a personal interest in Dantae Johnson, and set out to help him put together a new life.

Although I had vowed that the Simpson case would be my last criminal trial, and most certainly my last celebrity criminal trial, I defended Sean "Puffy" Combs, the rap star–entrepreneur accused of firing a gun in a nightclub and possession of a weapon found in the SUV in which he fled the scene. I can't recall another case in which charges similar to these had resulted in a two-month trial. In most jurisdictions this case would have been settled with a fine; in California this would have been a misdemeanor. But Puffy Combs was an extremely successful young black man. To me, this was an example of the system trying to knock down a very successful black man, as well as an opportunity for an ambitious prosecutor to make a reputation for himself. I couldn't turn the case down.

The Simpson case gave me the platform to try to change some of those things that need to be changed in this country. Many of the cases I accepted were vehicles to force those changes to be made. They were not all racial discrimination cases, some of the most important civil cases concerned basic property rights, for example. But whatever the dispute, it was the Simpson case that put me squarely in a position to make a difference. And that was precisely the reason I had become an attorney.

I am a black man. I am the great-grandson of slaves, the grandson of a sharecropper, the son of a hardworking businessman. I am at least a fourth-generation American: This is my heritage and my country and I am so very proud of it. I believe in the goodness of this nation even when I have been so often exposed to the worst part of it. I believe completely in the legal system as it was designed to function by the Founding Fathers, although I know from my experience that too often it doesn't work that way. Many of my battles in American courtrooms have been a simple attempt to extend the benefits of that system to those people who for so long have been excluded. My career did not begin—nor did it end—with the trial of O. J. Simpson. I didn't create myself to try that case and no one can truly know who I am merely by virtue of my work in his defense.

I am also an attorney. A lawyer. Just about as long as I can remember the only thing I wanted to do with my life was practice law. My mother wanted me to be a doctor, but I wanted to be a lawyer. That was probably the first case I won; my parents supported me in pursuit of my dream. I can't remember the precise reason that I decided on the law, but I know that it had much to do with the fact that I liked to argue. Liked to argue? I loved it, I absolutely loved it. In high school I excelled in debate. I don't remember a single question we debated, but the questions didn't matter as I was able to take either side of almost any reasonable statement. But I do remember that incredible surge of power and satisfaction I felt when I made a strong argument and dragged people over to my side of the question.

I learned to defend my ideas and beliefs at the Cochran family dinner table. My father, Johnnie L. Cochran Sr., set the intellectual standard for his children. He had been the valedictorian of his class at Central Colored High when he was only fourteen years old. He expected us to work as hard as was necessary to reach our fullest potential. And he seemed to think our fullest potential was always a little fuller than we did.

My mother, Hattie B. Cochran, was the disciplinarian. If we did something wrong, if we got out of line, it was mostly my mother who would apply the punishment. One time I talked back to my mother and the next thing I knew my parents had packed a small bag for me and were taking me to reform school. Reform school! I hadn't even said anything bad, I just answered back to her. If I close my eyes I can see my two sisters, Pearl and Jean, sadly waving good-bye to me as I left for that reform school. Fortunately, my parents gave me a second chance. I learned in that house in the projects of Alameda, California, the value of the English language and the importance of using it correctly to make myself heard. I had to just survive.

I do remember with great clarity the day of May 17, 1954, one of the most important days of my life. I was sixteen years old, in the eleventh grade at L.A. High School. On that day the Supreme Court of the United States issued its decision in the case of *Brown v. the Board of Education of Topeka, Kansas.* The court ruled that the long-accepted practice of "separate but equal" that had legally permitted segregated facilities to exist in this country was unconstitutional. "Separate but equal" was inherently unequal. This decision marked the beginning of the end of legalized racial discrimination.

And the man who had made that happen was a black lawyer named Thurgood Marshall, the only man besides my father that I idolized, who later became the first black justice on the Supreme Court. I didn't know too much about what a lawyer did, or how he worked, but I knew that if one man could cause this great stir, then the law must be a wondrous thing. I read everything I could find about Thurgood Marshall and confirmed that a single dedicated man could use the law to change society.

When I was growing up, first in Shreveport, Louisiana, and later Los Angeles, the law was not a profession easily accessible to "Negroes." Black people were considered qualified mostly for blue-collar work. Service jobs. Labor. A few black men, like my father who was an insurance salesman, worked for black-owned companies serving the black community. Black men rarely were able to enter elite professions like medicine or the law. In fact, the only black lawyer most people knew about was Algonquin J. Calhoun, a bumbling caricature from the *Amos 'N Andy Show*.

So I became a lawyer to change society for the better. I wanted to be like my idol Thurgood Marshall. In retrospect that seems pretty audacious, but I truly believed that if I worked hard enough, if I was smart enough, if I wasn't afraid to stand up and say loudly to the whole world what I knew to be true, I could do that. Me, Johnnie Cochran, the great-grandson of slaves, I could cause society to change.

It has taken society just a little bit longer than I originally anticipated to make some of those changes. And truthfully the world still has many more changes to make before I'll be satisfied. With tremendous optimism and perhaps slightly less realism, I began my personal efforts to change the world after graduating from the Loyola Marymount University School of Law in 1962, becoming a member of the California bar in January 1963.

There was not a lot of opportunity in the legal profession for aggressive young black lawyers in 1963. This was even before corporate, criminal, or general practice law firms began hiring a "token black." Most law firms were what was called "lily white." In fact, four decades later—four decades—there are still astonishingly few black partners at America's major law firms. During law school I became the first black law clerk to work in the Los Angeles City Attorney's Office. I was assigned to represent the great city of Los Angeles in disputes involving less than $200. There is no lower place to start a career in the legal profession than small claims court. I defended the city in cases involving everything from potholes to puddles. After passing the bar I was offered a staff job. So I began my career as a deputy city attorney, one of only three African-American attorneys in the Los Angeles City Attorney's Office. As there was no shortage of young black men being prosecuted, it seemed to make good sense to have young black men prosecute them.

I made $608 monthly. My first day on the job I prosecuted thirty traffic tickets. I won fifteen or sixteen cases in a row. I was pretty pleased with myself. I must be pretty good, I thought. While I wasn't exactly changing the world, at least I was making the streets of Los Angeles a little safer. And then I lost my first case. I probably lost two cases that day. As I learned very quickly, any attorney who claims to have never lost a case simply hasn't tried enough cases. Any attorney who has spent considerable time in a courtroom has lost cases. And they *should* lose some cases, because not every suspect accused of a crime is guilty and not every paying client is innocent. The facts aren't always as they initially appear to be.

There probably were less than a thousand black lawyers in the entire country. While there were no laws against black men becoming lawyers, there certainly were some very high barriers placed in their way. I had been raised to believe that the secret to success was simply preparation, preparation, and preparation. But I saw that no matter how prepared black attorneys seemed to be, they never got the opportunity to prove their ability. They never got the high-profile cases. When they did succeed the media rarely reported it, which might have led to more work.

I never tried to compete against white attorneys; rather, I competed against the standards. All I ever asked for was the opportunity to prove that black professionals were the equal of men—there weren't very many women in the professions, either—of any ethnic background. I wasn't interested in being a crusader, I had no intention of waving a big sign around, I just intended to do my job successfully every day. If I did that, I knew, it would be difficult to ignore me.

For several months I successfully prosecuted cases in traffic court. And I was good at it. If you received a traffic ticket, you did not want to be prosecuted by young Johnnie Cochran. Many defendants pleaded guilty in exchange for reduced fines, but when an individual fought the ticket we had to have a jury trial. I'm sure it would be difficult for those millions of people watching the Simpson trial to visualize me in front of a jury fighting as vigorously, but certainly without the resources and experience, to convict a driver of speeding. It probably was that long ago in my career that I first fell in love with juries. I have stood in front of several hundred juries; no two juries have ever been alike. I have always loved the concept that six or twelve men and women who don't know each other and often have very little in common can come together for a brief period of time, listen to the evidence presented, and work together to reach a conclusion. I've lost cases in front of juries, and I may have disagreed with the verdict, but rarely have I been disappointed by the efforts of a jury to reach a verdict based on the evidence presented to them.

In my traffic court if you got caught speeding, it's money you'd be needing. Obviously as a young lawyer, I also had a lot of work to do on my courtroom rhymes.

Eventually I began prosecuting a wider range of cases. Too

often, though, the defendants would arrive in court bruised and beaten, with broken arms and noses. Most of the time the police officers were white and the defendants would be young black men. And it would be my assignment to prosecute these young men for resisting arrest or interfering with an officer performing his duty. "Flunking the attitude test," as the police officers referred to it. Often the defendants would be crying. Their lawyers would be crying. And almost inevitably the defendants' mothers would be sitting in the rear of the courtroom crying.

Day after day police officers would get on the stand and respond to my questions by testifying that reasonable force was used while making the arrest; that the defendants' faces came into contact with the sidewalk when they resisted.

On any given day it would look to an observer that the law was being upheld, that the system was functioning. The problem was that any given day could have been almost any day. The same testimony was repeated over and over as if the police officer were reading from a script. The defendants always, always had resisted. The police officers never, never had used anything but reasonable force. And my job was to stand up there and make it all look as if it was true.

A system was working, just not the legal system. This was theater. This was a gentlemen's arrangement that had evolved over time. Everybody knew their lines, the police officer, the judge— and me. It took me a while to understand the reason for this charade; by proving the defendant had resisted arrest or interfered with a police officer the city would not be liable for any injuries that the defendant had suffered. The theory was that since it was his fault he had been injured, he couldn't sue the city for the actions of the LAPD.

I started to feel like a pawn. What could appear to be more fair than having a black man prosecuting black criminals? There are moments when I look back on my career and I wonder, I wonder, how could I have done some of the things that I did? But I had been raised to believe in the American system of justice and it took some time for me to accept the fact that the system had more to do with promoting social issues and the public convenience than justice. In fact, it didn't even matter much if the defendant was white. The general belief was that if the police officer arrested him, he must have been doing something wrong, even if the evidence presented did not support the specific charge. It was accepted by the white majority that police officers did not lie; and it was pretty much accepted by the black minority that there wasn't too much that could be done about it when they did.

It appeared as though I was doing an excellent job, I won almost all of my cases, but these cases were difficult to lose. We were all playing roles in a carefully crafted play. We knew it, but we didn't admit it. The only one who didn't know his lines was the defendant. If he couldn't afford counsel and was assigned an over-worked public defender he had almost no chance at all. The public defenders had their role in this play, too. If the defendant could afford a private lawyer he at least had a reasonable chance of getting a hung jury and walking out of the courtroom.

Finally I just couldn't take it anymore. I couldn't continue to go along to get along. At that time I could not intellectually explain what I was feeling; it took me a long time to understand it. William Edward Burghardt Du Bois was an American black writer, editor, educator, and impassioned public speaker who spent his life crusading for black rights, finally renouncing his citizenship and living in Ghana. The Harvard-educated Du Bois, who had called upon black soldiers returning from World War I to "marshal every ounce of our brain and brawn to fight the forces of hell in our own land," wrote a book in 1903 entitled *The Souls of Black Folks*. In this book he explained that African-Americans have a dual consciousness. We are both black and American, or "Negro" and American, as he wrote. But black Americans had two souls, two ways of thinking, two unreconciled strivings in one dark body. And often these two souls are at war with each other, with only dogged strength keeping black people from being torn asunder.

What he was describing was a racial split personality. That is exactly the way I started to feel. And as W.E.B. Du Bois had written half a century earlier, it was tearing me apart. I was prosecuting bad guys, but most of the bad guys were black. And maybe, just maybe, some of them weren't really so bad. Maybe what they were saying, day after day, was true. Maybe they were telling the truth and the Los Angeles police officers were lying. Maybe these defendants were coming into contact with the cement sidewalk not while resisting arrest, but rather when police officers slammed them into the ground.

It became obvious to me that these police officers were lying, that the judges knew they were lying and willingly accepted it, and that I had become an active participant in this charade. I decided to stop. I told my boss I refused to prosecute any more police abuse cases. This wasn't quite a declaration of personal independence, it was just one young lawyer calmly telling a senior deputy city attorney that he didn't want to prosecute these cases anymore.

Fine, he said. That was perfectly acceptable and I was assigned other cases.

But inside me a passion had been born. I don't think I verbalized it at that time, I can't remember discussing it with anyone, but I knew that these suspects were not being properly represented, that they were being beaten and abused by public servants charged with protecting them, and I knew that I wanted to move to the other side of the courtroom to try to stop this injustice.

I left the City Attorney's Office in 1965 and joined the private practice of a black criminal lawyer named Gerald Lenoir. We became Lenoir & Cochran. He was a fine lawyer, a very intense man, and he had built a successful practice. There was no shortage of black men who needed a criminal lawyer. And every one of his clients was black. When I started he told me, "Johnnie, we are going to make money backwards!" I wasn't quite sure what he meant, but I did like the sound of it. I had always been able to earn enough money to survive, but I aspired to more than that. I did want to make a difference in this world, but admittedly I also wanted to make money doing it.

Gerald Lenoir helped complete my education in the practice of law. He emphasized the fact that we were doing the business of law. I had great confidence in my ability, but I had little practical experience. He taught me how to run a private law practice. While working for the city I had won most of my cases; but in private practice I learned how difficult it really was to beat the city.

Gerald Lenoir had two beautiful daughters and two fine sons whom he loved with all his heart. His daughters were students at the University of Wisconsin and each fall he would drive them halfway across the country to Madison, Wisconsin. On August 11, 1965, while Gerald was on his way to Wisconsin, two young black brothers, Marquette and Ronald Frye, were stopped by police for reckless driving in the Watts section of Los Angeles. Watts was the heart of the black ghetto. This stop was the type of thing that happened there every day, and a crowd gathered around the police car to watch. The boys' mother arrived and an argument began. Eventually all three Fryes were arrested and the police apparently used excessive force—they began hitting the brothers with their wooden batons—to get them into a squad car.

The crowd began to close in and the police called for reinforcements. When more cops arrived the crowd broke up into small groups. The anger and frustration that had been building in the inner cities of America for decades finally exploded into violence. The Watts riots lasted six days. When it ended thirty-four people had been killed and 856 people had been injured. The fires that burned through Watts destroyed 209 buildings and hundreds more were damaged. Property loss was estimated to be more than $100 million. Four thousand people were arrested for loitering, looting, and basically just being black.

Four thousand people. And every one of them needed an attorney. Our phones started ringing and long lines began forming outside our office. We had more clients than I had ever imagined possible. People were coming early in the morning till after midnight. This was the most intensive on-the-job training course anyone ever got. But having been part of the system, I knew how it worked and I was able to do a good job for many of my clients. The Watts riots marked the beginning of the racial explosion that would shake America over the next few years. But for me professionally, business could not possibly have been better. At night I would come home with my pockets filled with cash. We were making as much as $8,000 a day. Obviously that wasn't all my money, but enough of it was—and only a few weeks earlier I'd been earning considerably less than a thousand dollars a week.

By the end of that year I felt ready to open my own practice. I was nervous about it, but I was ambitious; I had confidence in my ability and I had very large aspirations. I decided to lease an office in the Union Bank Building at the intersection of Wilshire Boulevard and Western Avenue. It was a prestigious building in the perfect location for me. I wanted to be on Wilshire Boulevard because it was a major east-west street and ran right through the heart of the white business district. Western Avenue ran north-south and I wanted to be on that street because the poor people I would be representing could take the bus up that street right from the black neighborhoods to the stop outside my office.

The building wasn't *exclusive* or *restricted*, code words meaning blacks were not allowed, but there was not a single black tenant in that building. In fact, there was only one black lawyer on Wilshire Boulevard. The Los Angeles Club, a well-known men's club, was on the top floor of the Union Bank Building. I knew I couldn't be a member of that club, but I didn't care about that, I just wanted to be in that building. There were several vacant offices, but the management was reluctant to rent space to me.

I was not a racial activist at that time. I hadn't been brought up to be bitter or angry about the racism that had closed most avenues of opportunity to African-Americans. Throughout my childhood, racial discrimination had not been part of my experience. I don't remember ever feeling that my race was holding me back; a reason for that, I long ago understood, was that my father did not want any of his children using racism as an excuse for failure. So as a child I learned to integrate easily. Only thirty of almost two thousand students at Los Angeles High School were black, for example. But that was never an issue with me. I had several close white friends and would often spend time at their houses. And at their homes I was exposed to those things that success could buy. It was only after I became part of the system that I began to understand what it so often meant to be a black man in America.

Don't misunderstand me; I love this country. I am so very proud to be an American. I believe with all my heart in the words of the Constitution. But for African-Americans it is impossible to ignore the reality of racism. It was while working in the City Attorney's Office that I fully realized how the system actually worked to curtail the rights of black Americans.

I was very naïve. The fact that the building management did not want me as a tenant because I was an African-American was not the first thought that came into my mind. A few years earlier they might have been able to get away with it. But the civil rights movement was making substantial progress and the management needed a legitimate reason to keep me out of the building. "You've never been in business," they explained. "You have no experience." Finally, though, they agreed to rent office space to me—on the condition that my father co-sign my lease.

The Cochran Firm today consists of more than 120 attorneys. We have offices in eight states and have received verdicts valued at more than a billion dollars. It is the largest and most successful plaintiff firm in this country—and growing. But that's not the way I started out. My first office in the Union Bank Building might correctly be described as humble. It was suite 1219. The word *suite* conveys an image a bit grander than reality. Closet 1219 probably brings up a more accurate image. My staff consisted of one lovely young woman who sat out in the reception area. We had ordered furniture but it hadn't arrived, so we put her typewriter on a folding TV tray. But I never doubted that I would be successful. The possibility of failure just didn't occur to me.

I was busy from the day I opened my office. Many young lawyers focus on a specific area of the law; they become criminal lawyers or corporate lawyers, they specialize in mergers and contract disputes, they limit their practice to divorces or bankruptcies, they handle real estate transactions or accidents and injuries, there are First Amendment experts, there are criminal lawyers who do endless drug cases. New specialties like space law or international patent law emerge to meet growing needs. I specialized in any case that came through the door.

Initially most of my cases were referrals from my father's insurance clients. Over many years they had learned to trust him, so they knew they could trust his son. I became their liaison with the legal system, doing whatever they needed done. I made out wills, I handled adoptions, I did divorces. I loved adoptions, I hated divorce cases. These weren't major cases; my clients getting divorced weren't fighting over estates, they were fighting over who got the pots and pans. Literally. I had some truly unusual cases. One of my clients, for example, was a twelve-year-old boy who did an excellent imitation of Ava Gardner on the telephone. Over a three-month period he successfully convinced merchants to deliver items ranging from television sets to tickets to the Academy Awards to her "godson." He even managed to convince California governor Ronald Reagan to send him a Polaroid camera so he could take pictures at the Emmy Awards, for which he had also successfully gotten tickets. His ruse was discovered when bills sent to Ava Gardner were not paid. He was taken into custody by juvenile authorities. We managed to make sure he got the counseling he needed.

But from the day I opened my own practice, the majority of my cases concerned police brutality. It was a very good business, since in those days the Los Angeles Police Department was brutal. Under Chief of Police William Parker, L.A. cops were permitted to use as much force as they deemed necessary to keep the streets under their control. When the riots were finally subdued, Parker jubilantly announced, "We've got them dancing like monkeys in a cage."

Parker was a racist who died in office of a heart attack not long after the riots ended, but his influence lived long after him. A year after his death the LAPD's Administration Building was named in his honor and the William Parker Los Angeles Police Foundation was started "so that his name and influence would live on in the community and the Los Angeles Police Department."

As recent events have proven, unfortunately that was exactly what happened.

In October 2000 two police officers responded to complaints about a noisy Halloween party in Benedict Canyon. The officers were invited into the mansion, but were asked to wait while a security guard got the owner. Instead, one of the officers went outside and began walking around the house. In a back room an African-American actor named Anthony Dewain Lee was with several friends. When the police officer shined his flashlight into the room, Lee and the others turned in the direction of the bright light. Everyone agrees that Lee was holding a fake pistol. The officer, who is also

African-American, claimed that Lee aimed the pistol at him. Feeling his life was in jeopardy the officer fired nine shots, *nine* shots, through a glass door. Four of the bullets hit Lee, killing him.

The problem with that scenario was that according to autopsy reports Lee was shot once in the back of the head and three times in the back. He could not possibly have had the time to withdraw a gun and point it at an officer and then have been shot four times in the back. It's very difficult to understand how the officer could have fired in self-defense.

I don't believe that those police officers went to that house intending to kill Anthony Dewain Lee. In fact, they were not charged with a crime. But it should not have happened. After all these years, it should not have happened. This was a Halloween party. Many guests were still wearing their costumes. The system failed Anthony Dewain Lee, just as it failed Amadou Diallo and Patrick Dorismond and so many others. So many others. But to me, the real horror of the Lee shooting was that it wasn't particularly unusual.

I've spent so much of my career dealing with white police officers who've shot innocent African-Americans, most of the time getting away with it. Early in my career a nineteen-year-old boy named William Anthony Leonard was earning some extra money baby-sitting. He was in a rear room, opening a window. A white police officer standing outside saw him inside the house and assumed he was a burglar. He shot inside the house and killed him. The boy's only crime was trying to open a window. Would this shooting have happened if the victim had been white? There are people who would claim that we will never know, but I feel the answer is no.

I can close my eyes and see his parents sitting across my desk from me. His father was a short, dark man. His mother, I remember, was an attractive woman with great dignity. Looking at her, I was reminded of many other mothers of slain children who always find the inner strength to bury their children with dignity.

There had been many similar shootings in the history of the LAPD, but the city had never admitted negligence nor paid any money to the families of the victims. The city had been able to justify every shooting or at least explain how it had happened. Most often the victim supposedly had done something to cause the officer to react. But this time there was no reasonable justification for the shooting. I filed a lawsuit against the city and I expected to take this case to trial and win a substantial judgment for the family.

For the first time in Los Angeles's history the city offered to settle the case. According to the offer, the value of the life of a black teenager in Los Angeles in the late 1960's was $25,000. I wanted to try this case. I wanted to make the police department accountable for its actions. But $25,000 was a substantial amount of money. While the city was adamant that this was not a criminal act by the policeman, for the first time city officials were willing to pay a substantial sum to settle a case based on the actions of a Los Angeles police officer. I told Mr. and Mrs. Leonard that I was confident of winning at trial, but that I couldn't guarantee it. At that time it was considerably easier to exclude minorities from juries and all-white juries rarely voted against the police for a black victim. I recommended strongly that they accept the offer and they agreed.

I remember holding up the check for photographers. I remember handing it to his mother and father. Our picture was on the front page of the *Los Angeles Sentinel*. It was at best a very bittersweet victory. We'd moved the system just a little bit, but it had cost an innocent life to accomplish that. And I remember knowing, knowing, that this was only the beginning for me, that I would have many other opportunities to challenge the LAPD.

When I think of all the police abuse cases I've tried during my career, I like to believe that substantial progress has been made. But then I look at the Leonard and Lee cases, just about thirty-five years apart, and I know how much more progress has to be made.

At about the same time I settled the Leonard case, I represented a twenty-five-year-old pregnant widow named Barbara Deadwyler at a coroner's inquest, an official hearing into the cause of death of her husband. Many of the people who watched the Simpson trial believed they knew everything they needed to know about me by watching my work in his defense; it is impossible to know anything at all about me without knowing about this coroner's inquest. If one case could be said to have shaped my career, it was the investigation into the death of Leonard Deadwyler.

When Barbara Deadwyler, who was eight months pregnant, told her husband she was going into labor, the couple began racing to the hospital. Having moved to Los Angeles from Georgia about a year earlier, Leonard tied a white piece of cloth to his antenna, a signal recognized in Georgia to mean that the driver needed assistance. He raced at a very high speed through black neighborhoods toward the hospital. When a police car started following him, its siren wailing, he probably assumed the officer had seen the white cloth and was helping clear traffic. Only when the patrol car pulled alongside and an officer aimed a gun at him did Leonard Deadwyler understand he was being pursued, not assisted.

Leonard Deadwyler pulled his car to the side of the road. Police Officer Jerold Bova approached the car with his gun drawn. According to Barbara Deadwyler, as Bova leaned into the car, her husband asked him if he could take them to General Hospital. And then Bova's gun went off at point-blank range. Leonard Deadwyler said, "But she's having a baby," and fell onto his wife's lap and died.

The black community was outraged. Absolutely outraged. Leonard Deadwyler's only crime was speeding through a residential neighborhood. Coming only months after the Watts riots, city officials were terrified this death might lead to new riots. The Congress of Racial Equality telegraphed Governor Edmund Brown that "the flames of violence in Los Angeles" have been reignited.

I was asked to meet Barbara Deadwyler by a UCLA classmate, Dr. Herbert Avery, who was treating her at General Hospital. I told

Mrs. Deadwyler I would do everything possible to see that real justice was done and she asked me to represent her.

Rather than convening a secret grand jury to determine the culpability of the police officer, as would be done now, District Attorney Evelle Younger asked for a public coroner's inquest to establish the reason Leonard Deadwyler had died. Younger wanted all the facts out in public, which would take a great deal of pressure off the elected officials. It was an astute decision, but the smartest decision Younger made was to allow Channel 5, KTLA, to broadcast the hearing live. This was the first legal proceeding in California history to be broadcast live. Three decades before viewers throughout the world would become accustomed to seeing me defending Simpson, the people of Los Angeles watched me represent Leonard and Barbara Deadwyler.

A coroner's inquest is not a trial, it's an investigation to determine the cause of death. Rather than a judge, a hearing officer presides over the investigation. After listening to all the evidence, a jury determines why the victim died. They decide if anyone was responsible for that death. However, their verdict is not binding on the district attorney, who must then decide whether or not to take legal action. Normally a deputy district attorney questions all the witnesses, but as the representative of the African-American community I was seated next to Deputy DA John Provenzano. I spoke through him. I told him which witnesses I wanted called and he called them. I couldn't argue or object to testimony, but I told him the questions I wanted to ask and he asked them. It was as if he were a foreign language interpreter. He introduced each question by stating, "Mr. Cochran wants to know . . ."

Mr. Cochran wants to know . . . Mr. Cochran wants to know . . . That phrase was repeated countless times during the hearing and became as well known in Los Angeles as would my simple rhyme about the black glove in the Simpson case decades later.

In a harbinger of what was to happen those many years later

when Judge Lance Ito permitted cameras in his courtroom, *Life* magazine columnist Shana Alexander reported about this hearing, "The full-face camera close-ups on TV revealed tiny facial nuances—a bobbing Adam's apple, a shifty glance, a faintly tightening jaw, which could not have been noticeable in the actual courtroom, not even from the jury box, the viewer began to feel like a member of the jury . . .

"You find yourself trusting some people and mistrusting others for no logical reason. You develop favorites. My own was an ambulance attendant named Walter Hoof, who wore a zippered jacket. I have no idea why I believed him; perhaps it was the jacket . . ."

It was an extremely volatile proceeding. On the first day it had to be moved from the inquest room to a much larger courtroom to accommodate the hundreds of people who wanted to be there. Occasional fights broke out between deputies and spectators.

As it turned out, Mr. Cochran wanted to know a lot. A total of forty-nine witnesses testified. When the first witness to the shooting, Mary Jones, was asked if she could identify the officer who fired his weapon, she replied, "All policemen look the same to me with their hats on." But later she added, "You know, I think it was cold-blooded murder."

Many of the claims made by the state seemed suspicious to me. Supposedly Deadwyler had a blood-alcohol level of .35, meaning he was very drunk. But Barbara Deadwyler denied that he was intoxicated—and a blood level that high would have made it very difficult for him to function, much less drive safely at high speed. And yet he even stopped at one red light. The police officer also claimed the gun went off when Deadwyler's car lurched forward, but Deadwyler's car was stopped behind another vehicle, which would have made it difficult to move forward. The deputy medical examiner, Thomas Noguchi, told reporters that Deadwyler had puncture marks on his forearm similar to those found on narcotics addicts. Then he added that the scars were "over six weeks or could even be a year" old. Barbara Deadwyler testified that those scars had been on his arm for at least eight years and her husband did not use narcotics. Noguchi did not test for the presence of narcotics.

But the overall portrait of Leonard Deadwyler created by the city of Los Angeles was that he was driving drunk, he was a drug addict, and it was his fault that the police officer's gun accidentally discharged. This was the introduction of a tactic I was to encounter many times during my career in police abuse cases—an attempt to "dirty up" the victim, to find any kind of reason the police might have acted as they did. After killing Amadou Diallo, for example, police frantically searched his apartment for any evidence of drugs or other illegal activities that might have given them a flimsy excuse for the shooting. When Patrick Dorismond was killed, New York City mayor Rudy Giuliani, referring to a juvenile record that by law was supposed to be sealed, said, "He was no choirboy." In fact, Dorismond, who had committed no crime, actually *had* been an altar boy in his church. Somehow Leonard Deadwyler's death was supposed to be his own fault. He was drunk. His car moved forward, causing the killing. As Deadwyler's mother explained, "It appeared that my son was on trial rather than the man who shot him."

The nine-person jury took two hours and thirty-five minutes to decide that this had been an accidental homicide, although two members of the jury reported they could not determine whether it was accidental or excusable homicide and one person felt that it was an excusable homicide.

A city councilman praised the results of the open hearing, explaining, "My opinion is that both Deadwyler and the police officer were wrong . . ." But only Leonard Deadwyler was dead.

The African-American community accepted the verdict calmly. The hearing had provided evidence that this was not a cold-blooded murder but rather police negligence. The outbreak of riots that was feared never happened.

We filed a civil suit against the city of Los Angeles, asking for

$3 million in damages. I could not represent the family at that trial because I was in the midst of an eight-month conspiracy trial, defending Black Panthers. Mrs. Deadwyler's case was handled by my new partner. Had we been able to try this case under the law as it exists currently we would have been awarded many millions of dollars, but not in Los Angeles in 1971. We lost that case 9 to 3. White jurors at that time just refused to believe—in any trial—that a police officer would raise his right hand and swear to tell the truth, then get on the witness stand and lie.

It wasn't slavery, it wasn't a lynching; it was another form of destruction. The system had not been set up to allow Leonard and Barbara Deadwyler a fair hearing. We never claimed the police officer shot Deadwyler on purpose. We claimed he was negligent, he was stupid for approaching that car with a cocked weapon. The officer stuck a loaded weapon into a car, which violated every gun safety rule he had ever been taught. I didn't know all the details of what happened that day, but I knew that Leonard Deadwyler had been shot and killed and nobody was punished for it.

There have been many victories, as well as a lot of losses in my career, but no case affected me more than the shooting of Leonard Deadwyler. I was just overwhelmed by the injustice of it, which was then compounded by having to watch the system desperately try to protect itself. And succeed. I felt terrible that I was not able to help Barbara Deadwyler. Her baby was born and named Michael. He grew up to become a minister in Southern California. She never remarried. But Barbara Deadwyler and I were bound together by this event. We've stayed in touch through the years, as I have done with many of my former clients, and I have seen her on occasion.

If during my childhood I had learned how to quit, this might have been my time. I'd spent years in law school learning the rules, then I'd worked within the system as a prosecutor and defense attorney to apply them. Any last illusions I still harbored about the existence of equal justice for all and Lady Justice being blind disap-

peared forever with the death of Leonard Deadwyler and the subsequent proceedings. But rather than see it as a personal failure,
instead I decided it was going to be a beginning. It just made me
want to work that much harder to extend the protections of the system to the people of my community.

The Deadwyler case gave me tremendous visibility. On the
street, in restaurants, people recognized me. The phrase *Mr.
Cochran wants to know*... was repeated often and proudly within
the African-American community. And clients decided they wanted
me to represent them. This early in my career the system had
beaten me, but I believed as completely as I have ever believed anything in life that my fight had just begun.

TWO

Following the acquittal of O. J. Simpson I was accused by many, many people of helping a killer go free. Those people just chose to ignore the fact that the members of the jury had willingly surrendered almost a year of their lives to judge this case on the facts presented in the courtroom—and that the jury had decided overwhelmingly that the evidence presented by the prosecution was not sufficient to allow them to find Simpson guilty "beyond a reasonable doubt." That reasonable doubt clause was not just an afterthought; it was the core of the criminal justice system. A juror can't think someone might be guilty, the juror isn't supposed to judge a case on his or her emotions—the evidence has to be strong enough to remove resonable doubt from the juror's mind. We proved that the most important evidence against O. J. Simpson had supposedly been found in unusual places by a thoroughly racist LAPD detective—a detective who had been caught on audiotapes made years earlier admitting the LAPD planted evidence—a detective who for some unknown reason had been present in places he had no legitimate reason to be.

But the fact is that I have defended a client in a murder case who I learned during the trial was guilty of that murder—but it wasn't Simpson. I know what it feels like to defend a confessed murderer. It is a dreadful feeling. And it is not something I ever want to do again.

There is one question I never ask a potential client: Did you do it? It's a ridiculous question. And the answer has very little meaning. Usually what happens is an individual comes into my office, or

31

his mother or other relative comes in because the accused person is in prison, and tells me, "I'm charged with..." or "My son is charged with ..." whatever the crime.

The first and most important questions I'll ask my client are, "What do you want to see happen in this case?" "What are you looking for?" "Tell me your wish list."

The answers to those questions are often the answer to the unasked question. Some clients look right at me and state flatly, "I didn't do it. I want to get out of this." That's a pretty straight answer. It doesn't mean the person actually is innocent, of course, just that he or she intends to fight the charge all the way.

But some clients understand the system. It's a pretty strong indication that they were involved in the crime when they tell me, "I want to get probation," "I want you to keep me out of state prison," or "I don't want to go to prison for too long." Con-wise clients have told me, "I can't plead to that."

And there is little doubt left when a client facing a death penalty charge tells me, "Save my life. I don't want to get dead early."

Simpson stated flatly and consistently, "I didn't do it."

I've never told a client, "Look, I know you did this ..." Usually I'll ask for the general details, tell me the charges, tell me where you were and what you were doing. Tell me everything that you know about the case. Tell me your involvement. Then I'll explain, "We're going to investigate what you say and see what we come back with. Then we'll talk about your defense."

Then I do exactly that, I check the alibi. I check the story. When I was a young lawyer I would do a lot of this checking myself. Eventually I began using investigators. If the story didn't hold up—and that has happened many, many times—I never confronted the client and told him, "You're a lying so-and-so. You lied and I know you're guilty." Instead after two or three interviews I would explain, "Listen, that story you told me doesn't check out. It looks to me like you've got some problems here and maybe you'd better let me talk to the DA for you."

A lot of the stories told to me by suspects admittedly stretched credibility. That didn't mean they weren't true, but rather that it would be difficult to convince a jury that it was true. And on occasion the suspects just destroy their own alibi. I remember being in a prison discussing a murder charge with a suspect. The man insisted he had never been in the house where the murder took place. Never. But during our conversation he happened to mention, ". . . when I was in the kitchen . . ."

"Wait a second," I interrupted him, "you just told me you weren't in the house. There's no way you're ever going to survive a cross-examination. We'd better talk to the DA and see what we can work out."

Everything that O. J. Simpson told us, everything, that we were able to investigate turned out to be true. If he told us that there was a letter in a safe deposit box in a specific bank, that letter was there.

None of this means that the accused person isn't lying to me. People do lie to their lawyers. A client of mine was accused of a particularly brutal murder. While by law I'm not permitted to reveal this person's identity, very generally the murder was committed with an unusual gun and when he was arrested the police found the gun in his home. From the day I met him he insisted he had found the gun in a Dumpster and thought it might be valuable. There was quite of bit of additional circumstantial evidence, but there were no witnesses and even the circumstantial evidence could be challenged. Nothing I asked him, or the little investigation we were able to do, shook his story. But generally it was his word against the circumstantial evidence. "I didn't do this," he told me over and over, "I really am innocent." His insistence that he did not commit the crime combined with his determination to get on the witness stand and testify convinced me he was probably innocent. So we went to trial.

The trial went very well. The district attorney was a man with a large ego, who liked to brag that it had been many number of years since he'd lost a case. The road to state prison is paved with people who flunked cross-examination. Cross-examinations are a great arbiter of truth. But my client got on the witness stand and he was superb. Unshakeable. The DA tried every tactic, but my client stuck to his story and insisted he was innocent.

When he concluded his testimony the court adjourned. The only thing left was closing arguments. I was with my client back in the lockup and he said to me, "You know, you've really done a great job for me and I really trust you. Let me just ask you, it's true that if I tell you something you can never reveal it, right?"

"That is absolutely correct," I replied, "an attorney-client relationship is inviolate."

"Okay." He took a deep breath, and told me, "I don't know what happened that night. I don't know if maybe I smoked too much weed or what happened, I can't remember too much. But I shot him. I don't know why, I just shot him."

I didn't know what to say. "Wait a minute," I said, "now you're telling me this? You just got through testifying and you tell me this now? All right, here's what I'll do. I'll go see the DA and see if we can still make a deal. I can still probably get you second-degree murder."

"No," he said, "no f——g way. You can't do that. I don't want you telling nobody nothing. You just gotta continue with the case. You're my lawyer and I want to walk."

I got sick to my stomach. I was in a box. There was nothing I could do. I was bound by law to keep my silence. I probably could have asked the judge to relieve me, but there was no way the judge would have agreed to that. Jeopardy had attached. If the judge had dismissed the case the defendant could not be retried on the murder charge. I certainly didn't want to endorse his crime. There were no more witnesses to be called, but I know for certain I would not have called another witness. I wouldn't have participated in perjury.

I was a young lawyer, I certainly had never experienced anything close to this, and I didn't know what to do. I was in the horrible situation in which I had to argue the case to the jury and hope,
and pray, that justice would be done. In this case justice would be
that my client would be convicted. It was one of the most difficult
days of my entire life.

So I crafted a closing argument in which I walked a tightrope. I
simply laid out the facts of the case and then reminded the jury, you
have to decide who you believe. If you believe the prosecution witnesses you have to find him guilty. You saw the cross-examination;
did you find the defendant's testimony reasonable?

It took the jury more than a day to reach a decision. As I later
learned initially it had been 9 to 3 guilty, but eventually several of
the jurors admitted they had reasonable doubts. He was acquitted
of the murder. A murderer walked out of the courtroom that day.

I went to church that night and prayed.

He came to my office the next day. I don't remember much of
the conversation. I told him that I would protect the information in
every way possible. I'm sure I told him how fortunate he had been
and reminded him that few people ever got a true second chance at
life. I suggested he not waste it.

I was just aghast. A killer walked out of my office that day. I
never saw him again or heard his name again. I have absolutely no
idea what happened to him. But that situation was as morally complicated as anything I experienced in my career. Through the years
I've thought about it a lot. And I've come to believe that the only
thing worse than having a guilty man walk free was having an
innocent man convicted, which was what happened to Black Panther Geronimo Pratt.

After the Deadwyler case I never again lacked for clients. There
never has been a shortage of black people arrested by the police.
And in addition to those clients who approached me, I also accepted
cases as a court-appointed defense attorney, for which I believe I

was paid $35 an hour. It might not have even been that much. Much later in my career I was able to choose among many cases offered to me, those in which I wanted to be involved, but at this time with rent to worry about, I took pretty much anything and everything that came along. That included hundreds of criminal cases covering all types of serious crimes. And during that period I sometimes think I saw or heard just about anything and everything it's possible to see or hear in the criminal justice system.

I was so busy that at one time I was actually involved in two trials simultaneously; a civil trial in the afternoon in which the plaintiff suffered brain damage when hit in the head with a police baton, and in the evening I went across the street to defend a woman who'd shot and killed her husband as he was jumping out of the second-story window of their home. I was literally in a courtroom from early in the morning to late at night. Within a day of each other we settled the civil case with the county of Los Angeles for a substantial amount and the jury acquitted my client in the murder case.

I was crazy to do it, but it became part of the lore of the legal system in L.A. For years judges there would tell lawyers requesting delays because they were too busy, "Look, Mr. Cochran tried two cases at once . . ."

The fact is that I won most of my cases. Not all of them, but most of them. At one point, for example, I won ten consecutive murder cases. Almost without exception my clients were African-Americans. And as I discovered, the reality was that I was better able to defend them than white attorneys. Not because my skin was the same color, but much more importantly, because I was able to bring my cultural experience into a legal system tailored to white people. The courts were almost all white; the judges, the lawyers, and most if not all of the jurors. Too often the only black person in the courtroom was the defendant. It did not take me long to realize that black defendants were being misunderstood in white courtrooms. Not sociologically, but literally.

At the beginning of my career I sometimes felt like a cultural translator. When I was working for the city I was trying a battery case in front of a fine, fair judge named Bernard Selber. A husband was accused of assaulting his wife. The wife got on the stand and said angrily, "He came over and he was raisin' sand."

Judge Selber looked at her quizzically. Nobody in that courtroom except this woman, the defendant, and me knew that *raising sand* is a Southern expression meaning "causing a ruckus." It means raising all kinds of hell.

It wasn't just cultural slang that caused difficulty, it was the entire difference between cultures. In an early case as a defense attorney I put my client on the stand and the prosecutor asked him, "And where were you when this robbery was committed?"

My client responded, "Standin' on the corner."

"And what were you doing 'standing on the corner'?" the prosecutor asked derisively.

My client shrugged, "Just standin'." The fact is that he probably was standing on the corner, but there was absolutely no way the white people on that jury would understand that. In the black neighborhoods people congregate on the street corners. There is nothing else to do, no place else to go. There were no beautiful parks in black communities so the corner became the meeting place. The men didn't have jobs, they were done with school, they had no place else to go. It wasn't far-fetched at all—but unless there was someone in the courtroom who knew from life experiences that some people do stand on the corner, it was worthless as an alibi.

In a case that became known in Los Angeles as the "Good Samaritan Murder" two men gained entry to a house on the pretext that they needed to use the telephone to inform the gas company about a leaking gas pipe, then killed the wife and bludgeoned the husband. My client was positively identified by a neighbor who claimed that he had known him previously, recognized him that night, and even had a brief conversation with him. This witness described the man he had seen leaving the house in great detail, including his height, weight, and hairstyle. He told police that the killer had a Quo Vadis, a short, sharp cut. But in a photograph taken by police only hours after the crime my client's hair was several inches long, in a style known as Superfly. Either the identification was inaccurate or somehow my client had managed to grow several inches of hair in a few hours.

But there wasn't a single white person in that courtroom who knew the difference between a Quo Vadis and a Superfly. I pointed out the difference, but fortunately there was a black man on the jury. He explained the difference to the rest of the jury and, within two hours, they returned with a verdict of not guilty.

Truthfully, as a defense lawyer I wasn't adverse to taking advantage of this situation when I believed it could help my client. I had a robbery case in which the white victim positively identified my black client as the perp. My client swore it was a case of mistaken identity. When the victim took the stand I asked her to identify the man who had robbed her. Without hesitating she pointed right at the man sitting at the defense table and said firmly, "That's him, sitting at the table."

But knowing that I was going to ask that question, I'd seated my client among the spectators and had a man of about the same build sitting at the table. The victim had identified the wrong person. She couldn't identify the person who'd robbed her. But she knew it was an African-American, the police had arrested an African-American, it must have been the right person, otherwise the police wouldn't have arrested him. My client was acquitted. That was about as close to pulling a Perry Mason defense as I've ever done in my career. In those days the courts gave lawyers a bit more license to be creative in their defense; they do tend to frown on it now.

But I felt it was a legitimate defense tactic, as I had never seen a white witness look at a black suspect and decide it wasn't the person they had seen at the crime scene. It never happened. Apparently the police have an amazing ability to arrest only guilty people, they never make a mistake. There was a bedrock belief in the white community that if the police arrested and charged a black man with a crime he was guilty of that crime. If a witness had to be a bit more positive in the identification than they really felt comfortable, well, they always went back to that core concept—the suspect had to be guilty or the police wouldn't have arrested him.

A lot of people don't remember that the legal system, in addition to the educational system, first opened to African-Americans in great numbers in the 1960s. A lot of young blacks had absolutely no idea how the system actually worked. A client I will never forget was a seventeen-year-old man named Stanley "Tookie" Williams. He had been arrested for robbery and his mother had come to my office to hire me to represent her son. This was a street crime. In the courtroom the victim identified my client as the robber, but told the jury that during the robbery he had said, "Is that you, Tookie, man?"

That was all I needed. During my closing argument I pointed out that the victim hadn't said, "Why are you doing this, Tookie?" Obviously he didn't know for certain whether or not it was my client. He couldn't positively identify the thief. "Is that you, Tookie, man?" is a question, not a statement.

The jury deliberated for seven minutes before acquitting Williams. Seven minutes. It set a record for that particular courthouse. When the jury foreman read the not guilty verdict, Williams leaned over and asked me, "What's that mean, cuz?"

He did not even understand that he had won back his freedom. I explained, "That means you can go home."

Tookie Williams eventually founded the gang known as the Crips and was convicted of committing several murders. I did not defend him in his murder cases. He's lived on death row for many years. But during that time he's also become a prolific writer, writing several acclaimed books about his life in the gang world and in prison. On occasion I have wondered how different his life might have been if he had been convicted of this first charge. Maybe not at all, or maybe a few years in prison would have made an impact on him.

So many of the cases I tried in those early years taught me lessons I would later put to good use. I did have one client, for example, who voluntarily confessed to a brutal murder, admitting to police that he had slashed the victim's throat. When someone's throat is cut there is a great amount of blood, and the investigating police officers testified that they had "observed a shoe print in that blood." When my client was arrested police found a pair of his shoes that very generally matched the shoe print—but there was nothing unique about these shoes; no wear, cuts, or other marks that could prove that these shoes and only these shoes made the print.

My client spent eighteen months in prison. The police considered the murder solved. It took me only a few brief times with my client to realize that this man was incapable of confessing to any crime. I had him examined by several psychiatrists, a psychologist, and a neurosurgeon. These experts established that my client had an IQ of 59; he was mentally retarded, illiterate, and suffered from organic brain damage. And he was in prison because he had confessed.

I was also able to demonstrate that the murder had taken place between eight and ten hours earlier than the time cited by my client in his confession. This man wasn't guilty of anything except being retarded. To please the police he probably would have happily confessed to every crime they asked him about. He never should have been in prison.

But he wasn't the only mentally deficient client I represented. I represented a man who beat a carpenter to death with a dowel. He knocked out the victim's dentures; I don't know why I remember that detail but I do. Knocked his dentures right out of his mouth. My client was legitimately crazy. While I was busy picking the jury that would ultimately decide his fate I looked over at the defense table—and he had fallen asleep. I don't think he had any real understanding of what he had done or the consequences of his actions. In prison he would suddenly start singing "America the Beautiful" at odd hours. Or when I tried to explain to him that his life was at stake he would start whistling. It wasn't an act, jail officials observed him for a long time. This man was clearly too dangerous to be out on the street, he was crazy and he was violent, but he didn't deserve to die either.

Winning comes in all forms. For some clients winning isn't being acquitted, it's making a deal with the prosecutor that he will serve time in a county jail as opposed to a state prison. My client was being tried for first-degree murder, a killing during the commission of a felony, a burglary. There was no way to get around that, and I certainly couldn't put him on the stand. He was the first client I had who was convicted of first-degree murder. After his conviction I had to fight for his life in what is known as the penalty phase.

I am against the death penalty. Unequivocally. Without exception I am against the death penalty. Even if it was applied fairly and uniformly—which it is not—I would be against it. Even if it could be guaranteed that no person innocent of the crime for which they were being executed would ever be killed by the state—which they cannot guarantee—I would be against it. It's wrong; the state shouldn't be in the business of killing people. And I say this from both the point of view of a defense attorney who has defended clients in death penalty cases and as a family member of a man who was murdered in the street.

In 1998 this belief of mine was tested about as mightily as possible. My much younger brother, Ralonzo Phelectron Cochran, was murdered. He had a problem with drugs and he was probably where he should not have been, but we all loved him very much. Someone pulled a gun on him, my brother grabbed it from him and just threw it away down the street. Then my brother turned around and started walking away. He was walking away. This person pulled a second gun and shot him. Basically, he executed him. He stood over my brother and killed him. It was cold-blooded murder.

My brother wasn't a criminal. He wasn't a bad person, but the drugs prevented him from ever fulfilling his potential. My father was just devastated. My brother's killer was arrested and charged with first-degree murder, a death penalty offense. But before the trial began my family met with the district attorney and told him we did not want to see the death penalty imposed because we didn't believe in it. Truthfully, that was not a unanimous family decision, as at least one of my sisters felt differently. And my wife, Dale, is not opposed to the death penalty. I understand their thinking, I just don't agree with it. My father and I knew we were being tested, and had to remain faithful to our belief.

I went to court at the end of the trial, not wanting to cause a stir by showing up every day. It was tough sitting there in that courtroom, very tough. It was an odd feeling to be sitting in the back after spending much of my life on the other side of the bar. It was hard to look at my brother's killer with any sense of compassion. That man had brought so much pain to our family. Ultimately he was convicted of first-degree murder and sentenced to seventy-five years to life.

So I remember standing up next to my crazy client as the jury foreman read the life or death decision. I was shaking. He was distracted. "On the issue of life or death," read the foreman, "we find life is the appropriate penalty." And for some people, life in a cage is the appropriate penalty. And as far as I know, he spent the rest of his life behind bars.

One of the most important elements in the Simpson case, according to Marcia Clark and Chris Darden, was Simpson's history of domestic abuse. This was supposedly further proof of his guilt. I brought a lot of experience in this area to the Simpson case. This is an issue on which I've really been on all sides; I prosecuted men who battered their wives, I defended people accused of spousal abuse, and during the Simpson trial my former wife claimed that while we were married I struck her—which is absolutely false. I was furious. That claim truly upset me because domestic abuse is an issue I know a lot about and take very seriously. In addition to being involved in many cases, I served for three years as the first chairperson of the Domestic Violence Council of Los Angeles.

For many years police throughout the country failed to take the proper action to prevent domestic abuse. The local police would be called in the middle of the night to break up a fight between a husband and wife. The husband might have been battering his wife half to death but the police would report it as a "domestic dispute" and leave. That wasn't completely the fault of the police; most people did not want the police interfering in what were considered household arguments. People didn't want to talk about it. It was a private matter. Nobody had ever even heard the phrase *battered women*.

While I was on the Domestic Violence Council we emphasized the importance of establishing shelters for abused women and we were the first city to have police give cards to women informing them of their rights, the location of those shelters, and how to get help. We tried to empower women. At one point an exceptional attorney named Syd Irmas and I settled a case in which schoolchildren had been molested by their teacher—who was known by district authorities to be a pedophile—for almost $6 million. We took some of the money we received and set up a shelter, a safe place, for homeless families. So I know about domestic abuse—and in fact, among my early cases were women who killed abusive men and claimed they did it in self-defense.

It's difficult to make a claim of self-defense in a murder case when the victim has been shot in the back. Or while sleeping. I represented a woman named Ruby Chedaka, who was accused of killing her husband, Billy, by stabbing him when he was asleep. It made headlines in Los Angeles as the "Hot Chitlin' Case." The Chedakas were black Seminole Indians. Chitterlings are hog intestines; black people traditionally eat them on January 1st to celebrate the new year. They're considered good luck, although I can report from personal experience that they smell awful, just awful.

Billy Chedaka abused Ruby terribly. One night in a drunken stupor he threw a pot of hot chitterlings at her. She was scalded and had the scars to prove it. Then he fell asleep. While he was sleeping Ruby stabbed him to death. This was at a time when jurors believed that a woman who was being beaten by her husband should simply walk out the door. It had not yet been established that women could be abused into submission, that the fear of being beaten would be strong enough to prevent her from fleeing to safety.

Ruby Chedaka pleaded self-defense. She did not deny she killed her husband, but testified that she believed if she didn't kill him, when he woke up later that night he would have killed her. He'd threatened her before. When I tried this case I knew it was essential to have as many women as possible on the jury. We ended up with a six-man, six-woman jury. The prosecution argued—just as I would have done—that she could had fled when he was asleep. We responded that she had been physically beaten and emotionally intimidated for so long that she was not thinking rationally. She acted to save her own life.

The jury liked Ruby Chedaka. They believed her; maybe they sensed her fear. And they acquitted her.

I had a more difficult time proving that another client had shot her husband in the back in self-defense as he was going out the window. Normally when someone shoots a victim while that victim is running away from them, they are going to be convicted of murder. When I first heard the facts of the shooting I believed my client completely, but I wasn't confident I could convince a jury to believe her. This was a classic case of spousal abuse syndrome; unfortunately it was long, long before psychiatrists had defined that. It was even long before the networks made movies for television about battered women fighting back. There had been few, if any, cases in which a woman afforded the opportunity to leave had instead killed her

husband and pleaded self-defense. Our strategy was pretty basic—
we intended to convince the jury that if this man had left their
home alive, she wouldn't have survived.

Self-defense in these cases is a lot easier to prove when the husband is moving toward his wife with a weapon. Then it is clear the
woman is just reacting to the situation. What is known as "detached
reflection," an opportunity to consider the consequences of the act,
is not expected in the presence of an uplifted knife. But in this
instance we had to try to demonstrate to the jury that my client had
reason to believe that her life was in danger. The night of the
killing he had been beating her. We were able to show that this was
a pattern. Finally she couldn't take it anymore, she pulled away
from him, and grabbed his gun. I think she took it out of a drawer.
When she pointed the gun at him he turned and tried to get away.
At that moment, at that second, my client believed without any
doubt that if he got away he would return with a gun and kill her.
She had no time for detached reflection, we argued; she believed
that if he got away her life was in jeopardy—which is pretty much
the foundation of a claim of self-defense. So she fired the gun at
him, two times, three times, striking him in the back, killing him.

I think we were able to describe that night in sufficient detail for
the jury. Later in my career I probably would have tried to take the
jurors to the house so they could see the scene; they could see the broken walls that he had slammed her into, they could see the disheveled
bedroom where he'd beaten her. Whenever possible in my career I've
tried to take the jury to an important location in the defense case; in
Simpson, for example, we took the jury to his home, so the jury could
see how unlikely it was that Detective Mark Fuhrman had just sort of
wandered round back and found a bloody glove. In the self-defense
murder case they got it, they understood. Whatever their own beliefs,
they accepted my argument that my client believed her life was in
jeopardy and had acted in self-defense. And acquitted her.

One of the most important lessons I learned early in my career is to expect the unexpected. I handled a lot of rape cases, but two of them I remember very well. The first one was known in the media as the "Case of the Phantom Rapist." It took place in an area of L.A. known as the Jungle. It's called that because it's almost all black, although the apartments were very nice. One night a very attractive white woman was in her apartment when a black man wearing a ski mask climbed in through a broken rear window and started to assault her. Right in the middle of the assault he stopped and performed oral sex on her. He didn't hit her, and when he was leaving he said to her, "Be sure to get that window fixed. I want to make sure nobody ever does this to you again." The moment he left she reported it to the police.

The next day the victim found a note under her door. "I've never done anything like that before," it read, "I'm so sorry. Please forgive me." He signed it the Phantom, and included his telephone number. Several days later he hired me to defend him.

The Phantom was actually a handsome, relatively decent man. He had never committed any crime before in his life, but that night . . . that night he committed a heinous crime. He was released on bail—and started dating the victim. They fell in love and she asked permission to testify on his behalf in his trial. Maybe I hadn't been practicing that long, but it was the first time I had ever heard of the victim offering to be a character witness for the rapist.

The DA was very politically astute but he was willing to work out a deal. The Phantom Rapist walked into the sentencing arm-in-arm with the victim. He served a couple of years and they ended up together.

The second rape case was much more difficult, as my black client was positively identified by the young white female victim. The victim claimed that her husband had become ill while driving home from a party and he had pulled their car to the side of the road and both of them fell asleep. She was awakened, she testified, by my client, who kidnapped her, took her to his own home in Compton, and raped her. Eventually she escaped and went home, then returned to lead police to my client's home.

My client was facing forty years in prison. This took place in 1968, only a few years after the publication of the Pulitzer Prize–winning novel *To Kill a Mockingbird*; the story of a black man falsely accused of rape by a white woman with whom he'd had consensual sexual relations. In author Harper Lee's story, as well as the subsequent Oscar-winning film starring Gregory Peck as the black defendant's white defense attorney, the jury had ignored the evidence and voted for conviction.

I was playing the real-life role of Gregory Peck. And while *To Kill a Mockingbird* took place in the South, the situation wasn't very different in Southern California. The thought that a white woman—the young mother of two small children—would voluntarily have sex with a black man greatly upset a lot of people. In cases like this sometimes the jury just couldn't see beyond the race of the victim and the defendant.

But the victim's description of the crime made no sense to me. According to her testimony, after being raped she went home, got undressed, and went to bed. She didn't call the police. Only after her husband came home and confronted her did she tell him about the kidnapping and rape—and he insisted they report the crime to the police. And in the middle of the night she was able to take police straight to my client's house. Obviously she knew where he lived. He certainly didn't act like a guilty man. He didn't run, he didn't hide.

In those early years I did most of my investigating myself. I was a street lawyer, I like to say, not a suite lawyer. My client was a responsible citizen. He was a longshoreman, he worked hard, he had no criminal record. I started knocking on his neighbors' doors. Almost immediately I found several people who were willing to testify that they had seen the victim at my client's house on several occasions. So it was pretty obvious what had happened that night. To save her marriage, to protect herself, she was willing to send my client to prison for forty years.

I still didn't want to risk putting my client's fate in the hands of a jury. Instead I agreed to a submission of the case on the preliminary hearing transcripts. It was a way of saving time by enabling judges to make certain rulings based on testimony given during preliminary hearings in felony cases, rather than having to call the same witnesses to make the same statements in the courtroom. The judge dismissed all the serious charges—and found my client guilty of simple assault, a misdemeanor. I wasn't about to appeal that decision.

Most people believe that the testimony of eyewitnesses is the best possible evidence; in fact, it can be refuted. When Sean "Puffy" Combs was accused of firing a gun in a nightclub, for example, we were able to show the jury that every one of the supposed eyewitnesses had filed a civil suit for damages against Sean Combs—and they would have a much easier time collecting if he was found guilty at the criminal trial.

But the most difficult eyewitness testimony I had to refute involved not one—but four—eyewitnesses who identified my client as the assailant. This was arguably the most difficult criminal case of my career. Actor Todd Bridges had become famous playing Gary Coleman's older brother, Willis, on the popular television sitcom *Diff'rent Strokes*. When that show went off the air Todd Bridges descended deep into the drug world. If he hadn't yet hit bottom, he was going fast in that direction. My involvement with him began when his mother came to my office to ask me to represent him. The mother, again; it seems like it's always the mother. The facts of the case were horrendous for a defense lawyer; Bridges had been indicted for attempted murder, attempted involuntary manslaughter, and assault with a deadly weapon. Four eyewitnesses, including the victim, positively identified Todd Bridges as the man who fired eight shots into the body of a drug dealer—including one shot at point-blank range right into the victim's mouth.

Apparently this was a drug deal gone bad. The dealer had been shot eight times. When the paramedics arrived he didn't have a pulse; they didn't think they could save his life. They got out a body bag and started to slip him into it. Generally the law does not allow hearsay evidence to be presented at a trial; you can't put someone on the stand to repeat what another person said. One of the few exceptions to that rule is what is known as a "dying declaration." The theory is that when someone is going to meet his or her maker he or she will tell the truth. It is a fundamental human belief that dying people, people who no longer have anything to lose, will tell the truth. So as they were putting this drug dealer into a body bag they asked him his name. That's all, his name.

In response he gave them a phony name. The man was knocking on death's door and yet he lied about his identity—because he knew if he gave his real name and survived he would be arrested. He did survive—eight bullets—and told police that Todd Bridges had shot him. Three other people who had been inside the crack house doing drugs at the time also identified Todd Bridges as the shooter.

Just like in the Simpson case, the police rushed to judgment, although admittedly in this case they certainly had a lot more reason to do so. They had four witnesses positively identifying the shooter. As far as they were concerned this case was closed, so they didn't even bother to do any further investigating. Bridges was arrested. A judge set his bail at more than $1 million. There was a strong case against him. In addition to the victim, Bridges's co-defendant testified he gave the gun to him. And Todd Bridges was no help in preparing his defense, as he had been so strung out he couldn't remember what had happened. He could not deny with any certainty that he had not been the shooter—although he had absolutely no memory of the shooting. He had become suicidal; he stopped eating.

When his mother came to see me it was almost as a last resort. She had lost control of him long ago. For the prosecutor this case was a dream; it was going to make headlines and he would get a conviction. The perception would be that the criminal justice system worked, people would feel safe, and the prosecutor would get the credit. This was as close to an unwinnable case as I had ever seen.

It was also a classic example of the best advice I can give to young lawyers. As I've said, there are three extremely important aspects to presenting a case: preparation, preparation, and then additional preparation. You have to know more than your opponent. The police wrapped up the case immediately. They didn't even bother to walk right next door and interview the neighbors. That was our job. We started to canvas the entire area just in case someone had seen something that might be helpful. Truthfully we didn't have a lot of hope, but we also did not have any options. This was a high-profile case, there was the opportunity for a lot of publicity, so there was no way the prosecutor would even discuss some sort of plea bargain.

My investigator called me in my office one afternoon and told me, "You're not gonna believe who I found." The next-door neighbor, he said, "The only guy in the whole case who's credible. He told me that he saw Willis—that's what he called him, Willis, the character Bridges played on TV—walk out of the house before the shooting and then go back in afterward. He wasn't even inside when the guy got shot."

We had a credible witness who would testify that Todd Bridges wasn't in the crack house when the shooting took place. It was a foundation on which to build a solid defense. But while that witness was vitally important, he was still only one witness. Then we found out that this witness wasn't alone, his girlfriend was with him and she saw—and would testify that she saw—Todd Bridges leave the house and return. "I saw Willis after all the shooting had taken place," she said, "I know it, he wasn't even over there. He was wandering down the street."

We had witnesses for the defense, we could make a case, but it wasn't enough; we also had to destroy the credibility of the prosecutor's witnesses. During the trial I emphasized to the jury that the shooting took place inside a crack house—and everybody there was using crack cocaine. These were drug addicts testifying against another drug addict. Their drug use made their testimony suspect. The victim had made a deal with the prosecution that in exchange for his truthful testimony against Bridges his own legal problems would go away. The prosecution had made a deal with the devil. That's always a risky proposition for the prosecution, because jurors understand few people would ever turn down a deal that good. It didn't make any difference to the victim who went to jail as long as it wasn't him. The victim was a drug dealer, the victim lied with what might have been his final breaths—is he going to have any moral qualms about lying in a courtroom to stay out of jail?

I wanted to make each juror answer that question. Some of them, I knew, would understand that his testimony was purchased in exchange for his freedom. But even if the jurors discounted his testimony, there still were three other supposed eyewitnesses.

One of those people was a woman. On direct testimony, answering the prosecutor's questions, she did very well. Then I began my cross-examination. Every witness reacts differently to cross-examination. A lot of cross is done by feel; you have to have control of the facts of the case, you have to know what answers you want to your questions before you ask them, but getting those answers can be difficult. Sometimes you have to be very gentle with the witness and other times very tough, even bullying—and you have to remember the jury is watching you and, ultimately, much of their verdict will be based on their feelings about the competing lawyers. Initially I'm usually very nice to witnesses, almost deferential, and then as I go along I move with the emotional breezes to get where I need to get.

But as I was questioning this witness I noticed that she was having difficulty focusing. She seemed to be having difficulty staying awake. I don't know when it occurred to me that she was on drugs.

Suddenly she turned to the judge, Judge Florence Cooper, and told her that she was about to have a seizure. Judge Cooper dismissed the jurors and got her medical assistance. They struck her testimony, meaning jurors were instructed to proceed as if it had never taken place and anything she said could not be used in deliberations, and she was unable to return to testify. But the damage to the prosecution's case had been done. The jury lost confidence in the testimony of the eyewitnesses.

In the first trial the jury acquitted Todd Bridges of attempted murder, eight of the twelve jurors voting not guilty on the lesser charge of assault with a deadly weapon. But they couldn't reach a unanimous verdict on the lesser charges, so there was a second trial. And he was acquitted of all charges.

In another world Todd Bridges, all my clients, would learn a lesson from their acquittal, turn their lives around, and become trustworthy and productive citizens. But in this world it doesn't always happen that way. In many cases people are accused of crimes because they're known to the police, they've been there before. Sometimes being acquitted of a crime even serves to reinforce the belief of some of these people that they can beat the system. Todd Bridges's struggle with drugs didn't end with his acquittal—although by 2002 he was once again working successfully on television. Unfortunately, some of the clients that I successfully represented later committed other crimes. But the job of a criminal defense lawyer isn't to decide who deserves the best possible defense and who needs to spend time in prison. Lawyers have done a very poor job educating the public as to the function in a free society of a criminal lawyer.

Sometimes my wife, Dale, who is as intelligent and loving as any person I have ever known, doesn't even understand this. When I'm approached about taking a criminal case, she'll tell me, "Well, you've got to figure he pretty much did it, you have to know that."

To which I'll respond, "I don't know that at all . . ." and add for maybe the millionth time, "Everybody deserves a defense."

Part of the problem criminal lawyers encounter is that criminal trials are covered so extensively by the media that they have become a form of entertainment. Crime sells. Criminal trials often include tales of sex, drugs, violence, ambition, betrayal, good guys and bad guys, all of it filtered through heightened emotions and an overtaxed system of law. The Simpson trial was only the most extreme example of this. The Puffy Combs trial was another example of this. People react to these trials as if they were soap operas; they pick favorite characters, they try to predict the action, they plot strategy with the attorneys, they debate the decision with the jurors. And their emotional involvement causes them to take the result of the trial personally. When Simpson was acquitted so many people believed I had pulled some sort of magical trick, I had entranced the jury, the jury was all black so the jurors didn't know any better. None of that was true.

The job of the defense lawyers, the "dream team," was to give to O. J. Simpson the best possible defense he could afford. And he was fortunate enough to be able to afford the best possible defense. Most defendants can't. We did not have the almost unlimited economic support of the state to build our case. But we had the resources we needed. As a result, the jury had reasonable doubt.

But at some point in the history of our criminal justice system people began confusing the criminal attorney with the crimes his client was accused of committing. I can represent a client charged with a particular crime without condoning that crime. I have represented many people charged with committing murder, some of them probably did commit these crimes, but that doesn't mean I condone murder. My family has been a victim of murder; I've seen what it did to my father. But I believe that for the legal system to continue functioning, even in its clunky, broken fashion, prosecutors and defense lawyers have to do their jobs—even in unpopular cases—to the best of their ability. They have to prosecute to the full extent of the law and they have to offer the best possible defense.

There is one thing that remains as true today as it was when this country was founded: If one man cannot get a fair trial, no matter how hideous his crime or evil the man, none of us can be certain of getting a fair trial. As Robert Bolt wrote in his great play about Sir Thomas More, *A Man for All Seasons,* "I'd give the devil benefit of law, for my own safety's sake."

There is, however, one type of criminal case I decided long ago I did not want to take. At one time I represented a man who had been charged with a number of different crimes. Including a murder. After a trial he was acquitted of murder, and I was able to work out a deal for him to get a substantially reduced sentence. But while he was in jail he was indicted for several very serious drug-related crimes. He was facing major time in jail and he wanted me to represent him.

I had defended clients in several minor drug cases, but I just hadn't gotten involved with major drug cases. While I was deciding whether or not to represent him somebody came to my office with suitcases stuffed with money—more cash than I had ever seen in my life. It took us more than a day just to count it, it seemed like we were counting forever. Our hands got dirty from that money. And when we were finished the total was more than $600,000. In cash. Mostly in small bills. In my office.

Clients paid me in cash all the time. Clients in criminal cases like to pay in cash. I would accept cash, but I knew I had to be accountable for all of it. I was aware that my cases against the LAPD made me less than popular with certain segments of the community, and that if there was any legal way I could be eliminated, it would happen. Taking cash, putting it in my pocket, and not paying my taxes could cost me my career. So when I was paid in cash I always wrote down a receipt for the money. I wasn't going to hide it, I always paid my taxes.

But usually we received a few hundred dollars, a couple of thousand at most; $600,000 in cash was the most money I had ever seen in one place in one time. It remains the most I've ever seen. My immediate reaction was pretty much complete paranoia. I didn't have any idea what to do with this money. I didn't know where to put it. It was much too big for a safety deposit box. That's when I began thinking that maybe I was being set up. Maybe somebody was going to come into my office and rip us off—not just for the cash, but to force me to represent him. I hadn't agreed to take the case, but if the money was stolen from me I would have no choice. "I paid you the money," he'd say, "either give it back to me or represent me."

There was no possible way at that time of my life I could have paid him back. Basically, I would have been bought. The next morning I made sure he got every penny back and told him I would not represent him. More than that, I made the decision that I would never represent anybody charged with a major drug offense. That cash was in small bills. I didn't know where that money came from, but I assumed it was drug money. I decided I didn't want to have anything to do with the drugs that were poisoning our community. Now, there have been a few times when a first-time offender was charged with simple possession of a small amount of marijuana and I could advise them how to get it diverted out of the system, but I never defended anybody dealing a significant amount of hard drugs. And I've never regretted giving back that money, and I never regretted that decision.

At that time the money would have made a significant difference in my life. And, admittedly, while my career has never been based on money, like everybody else I like to get paid for what I do; I like to get paid well and I like to enjoy the rewards of my work. That's never been a big secret. I drive a Rolls-Royce in Los Angeles, I eat at very nice restaurants, I wear . . . I wear very nice clothes. My work as a lawyer has made me a relatively wealthy man. But defending wealthy clients also made it possible for me to defend "the No Js," as I refer to those cases I've taken in which the chances of getting paid for my work are actually pretty slim.

Money plays the most important role in the criminal justice system of the United States of America. I don't believe anyone familiar with this system would argue that it works equally for all defendants. It is deeply flawed. There is no question that minorities are treated differently by the system than white people. There is racism in the system, there is tremendous unfairness. No question about it. But I have always believed that the breakdown in the system is not primarily racial; rather, it is economic. The phrase I like to use is that a person is innocent until proven broke. And when you're broke, that's it. You're done. It's not so much black and white, it's rich and poor. Although it turns out the poor are mostly black and brown.

This was the primary lesson for me in the Simpson trial. He had the resources necessary to battle the state with its seemingly endless resources. When I needed to fly to Winston-Salem, North Carolina, to listen to the audiotapes made by Mark Fuhrman revealing what I had known to be true for a long, long time—that some L.A. police officers framed people, set up people, and brutalized innocent people—my client had the resources to make that possible. When we needed to hire the best legal experts on DNA, Peter Neufeld and Barry Scheck, we didn't hesitate. O. J. Simpson got the best defense his money could buy.

The way our system works is that if you have the resources you just might be able to get a fair trial, but if you can't afford it, it is very difficult to present a reasonable case. That's the way it is, not the way it is supposed to be.

Admittedly, I have benefited from this reality. A lot of people have. But I can't help thinking about all the people who have suffered because of it.

Many of my complaints about the system came together in the case of Ray Newman, a black Los Angeles attorney. Ray Newman accepted a lot of court appointments, for which he was paid an hourly rate. He had represented several indigent people in death penalty cases. And he was an excellent trial lawyer. The state was getting what it was paying for—a good defense for people who could not afford it. But when the state decided it was spending too much money providing legal counsel—as required by law—to poor people whose lives were at stake, they began investigating billing records. And right at the top of the list was Ray Newman. After examining his records the state accused him of grand theft, of fraudulently billing for hours he did not spend working on cases. According to Newman's records he had billed the state for fifteen hours a day, every day of the year, including holidays. On Christmas Day he billed about twelve hours. The state charged that he had billed for work supposedly done while he was vacationing with his family, coaching Little League baseball, or even while spending romantic time with his girlfriend. The prosecution's key witness was the married Newman's former girlfriend, a woman who kept detailed records of the date and time the two of them had spent together—and those records included times he supposedly was working on cases.

The state built a very strong case against him. Prosecutors had a small mountain of evidence. Ironically, the money he'd made representing indigent defendants, the money that was the source of this criminal indictment, permitted him to mount a strong defense. But even though he could afford it, several lawyers refused to represent him.

I believed Ray Newman was doing a good job. But more importantly, having defended several clients in death penalty cases, I knew what it felt like. The basic position we took was that district attorneys—who punch in and out every day—could not possibly understand how much time, mentally as well as physically, it takes to represent a defendant in a death penalty case. As I pointed out, prosecutors who have never defended a client whose life is at stake just couldn't imagine the continuous pressure. "If you mess up," I explained in court, "your defendant is going to die. He's going to *die*." I knew from experience the weight I carried all day every day when my client's life was at stake. I remembered the nights I got two or three hours of sleep, I remember that I was never free of the case; while I was in my car, while I was eating, never. The pressure never goes away—if you care. And I believed Ray Newman cared. He had started out in life picking cotton in Louisiana and by incredibly hard work had become a fine lawyer. He is still a fine lawyer. He didn't take a gun and steal money. The judges had signed off on every bill he'd submitted. We weren't claiming that every hour for which he'd billed the state he'd been in his office or with a client, but rather that records on paper could not possibly reflect the amount of work that went into a case, and most importantly, that there hadn't been an intentional effort to defraud the state.

Ray Newman obviously hadn't been as careful in his billing as he should have been. And that was probably an understatement. But I knew that in addition to the specific charges, we were fighting the image of the corrupt attorney ripping off the state. This was another case in which the accused was convicted in the media before his trial started.

The key moment of the trial occurred when Newman's former girlfriend testified that she had not known he was married while they were having an affair. I was able to put the person who had told her that he was married on the stand, which destroyed her credibility. I was also able to establish the fact that she was still angry that he hadn't left his wife for her—and she had allegedly said she would do anything to get Ray. Her own testimony demonstrated she was an unreliable witness—and was the key to Ray Newman's acquittal.

The county of Los Angeles responded to this case by changing the billing system for court-appointed counsel, setting a flat fee rate for death penalty cases. Obviously, the county believed it was investing too much money to make sure poor people accused of a capital crime got the best available defense.

THREE

While swimming in the Bahamas in the summer of 2001 a young man named Krishna Thompson was attacked by a shark and lost his leg. He saved his life by swimming to shore and before losing consciousness writing his hotel room number in the sand. His wife, Ava Maria Thompson, a DA in Queens, New York, was friendly with a young member of our firm, an excellent attorney named Derek Sells, and through him asked our firm to represent her husband in a negligence action against the hotel. When it was announced that I had taken the case Jay Leno said in his nightly monologue, "It's not bad enough that he already lost a leg. Now that Johnnie Cochran is representing him he's going to lose his arm, too!"

Ba-dum-dum! While I didn't think it was particularly funny, I realized that long ago I'd set myself up for it by speaking out on issues I care about. I don't mind being the punch line of jokes. Unfortunately, the basis of that particular joke is the public perception that lawyers are ambulance chasers, perpetually looking for someone to sue to enrich themselves—which is one of the things I've been speaking out against. Obviously, there is that element among lawyers. There are bad lawyers, greedy lawyers just like there are greedy plumbers and bad everything else. I've been involved in several cases in which I was literally embarrassed for my profession by actions taken by other lawyers.

Contrary to all the jokes, though, I did not become a lawyer to sue sharks. Here's what made me want to be a lawyer, here's what the law can be to people: In 1857 the Supreme Court ruled in the case of a slave named Dred Scott, who was suing for his freedom after having lived for seven years in a free territory. The court argued, "When the Constitution was adopted, they [slaves] were not regarded in any of the States as members of the community which constitute the State, and were not numbered among its 'people or citizens.' Consequently, the special rights and immunities guaranteed to citizens does not apply to them. And not being 'citizens' within the meaning of the Constitution, they are not entitled to sue in that character in a court of the United States."

In a ruling three decades later in the case of *Plessy v. Ferguson,* the court found segregation of the races perfectly legal so long as separate but equal facilities were provided. In the world into which I was born, the facilities were often separate but rarely equal. But that was the law of the land. It was perfectly legal.

Almost a century after the Dred Scott decision, Chief Justice of the Supreme Court Earl Warren wrote for the majority in the case *Brown v. the Board of Education of Topeka, Kansas,* "Segregation of white and colored children in public schools has a detrimental effect upon colored children. The impact is greater when it has the sanction of law, for the policy of separating the races is usually interpreted as denoting the inferiority of the Negro group.... We have now announced that such segregation is a denial of the equal protection of the laws..."

It is impossible for any white person to truly appreciate the impact of this decision on a young black man. It changed my life. It changed the lives of millions of Americans. It changed this nation forever. While perhaps a majority of white people did not want to integrate the schools and restaurants and public transportation, most of them accepted it peacefully—because it was the law. The Supreme Court of the United States had ruled and the citizens accepted it. It made me appreciate the power of the law to change society, to change people's lives. And I wanted to be part of it. I wanted to be a lawyer.

I used to believe that the law was "an attempt to introduce a modicum of rationality into the disproportionate bestiality of human nature." I don't remember where I read that quote, but long ago I came to understand it's actually a lot simpler than that. The law is a sometimes messy attempt to resolve society's most vexing problems. It's a tool to be used to insure that the promises of our democracy are available to all of us equally. At least, at its most eloquent, that is what it is supposed to be.

Reality is often quite different, however. There have been people who have misused the law, no one would argue that. There have been abuses. There have been too many ridiculous lawsuits filed. The system doesn't work any better for civil litigation than it does in criminal law. I know the joke about the shark who wouldn't eat the lawyer because he extended him professional courtesy. But . . .

Does anyone really believe that Firestone would have recalled its defective tires if it didn't cost them millions of dollars to keep them on the road? Does anyone believe chemical companies would volunteer to clean up the land and water supply that they have polluted if they weren't liable for millions of dollars? The threat of civil litigation has moved companies to improve the safety of its products in just about every field of manufacturing, production, and service. I represented a lovely lady named Jackie Newbon who was standing behind a truck when it began backing up. Her leg was crushed between that truck and a car. Had the truck been equipped with a warning device, a simple beeper costing about twenty dollars, that woman would still be able to walk without pain. Failure to spend that twenty dollars cost the trucking company—or its insurance company—$1,300,000. But the message that went out to the entire trucking industry by that decision was clear. I guarantee a lot of truck owners reading about that decision made sure their vehicles were equipped with this simple twenty-dollar safety device. When used for the public good, the law really does level the playing field. It allows poor people to take great actions against mammoth companies. It can change society for the better.

I originally began doing civil litigation when I left the Los Angeles City Attorney's Office. At least I intended to. But it was hard to get cases. At one time I represented a young African-American named Joe Louis Dickerson charged with robbery in Torrance. It was not an easy trial, most of the jurors were white, but I managed to get him acquitted. His mother was particularly grateful. She was so grateful that about eight months after the trial she came to see me again. She had some legal papers she wanted me to look over. Her husband, I learned, was a longshoreman who had been injured in a work-related accident. According to these papers, he was receiving almost a million dollars. Mrs. Dickerson had come to me because she didn't trust the white lawyer who'd arranged this settlement. I asked her, "Mrs. Dickerson, I don't understand. Why didn't you bring this to me in the first place?"

She replied, "I didn't think you could handle that kind of money. They say those white boys can get more money." I had saved her son, she trusted me enough to make certain that another lawyer wasn't cheating her, yet she wouldn't bring a personal injury case to me. That's just the way it was. I couldn't get cases like that. No black lawyer could. The profession still hadn't been de-Calhounized—but it was starting to happen. It was very frustrating; I had won ten murder cases in a row. It was unprecedented. In those days criminal law was the glamorous part of the profession, everybody wanted to be Clarence Darrow, so it was a big deal. But I couldn't get clients to come to me to handle a fender bender. The belief was that a white lawyer would get more money.

Everybody knew it. In Los Angeles we had two courthouses, the civil courthouse where the civil cases were tried, and the Criminal

Courts Building. I spent almost all my time in the Criminal Courts Building. But when the criminal calendar got too full, by law they had to send cases over to the Civil Courts Building. More than once, as I walked through the halls of that Civil Courts Building, someone would greet me, "Hi, Mr. Cochran, what are you doing over here?" I understood it was meant to be a friendly greeting, but it was terribly insulting. What was a black lawyer doing in that part of the law? That's where the money was, that was the exclusive domain of white lawyers. I took umbrage at that. What was I doing over there? I was a big-time lawyer; I just didn't have the cases to prove it yet. That's when I decided I was going to become the only lawyer in Los Angeles who could both try a death penalty murder case and get a million-dollar verdict in a civil case. I didn't tell that to anybody, but I knew without reservation that I could do it, and I would do it.

At that time pretty much the only civil cases I could get concerned police abuse. White attorneys didn't care too much about those cases as almost always they ended up with police procedure, whatever it was, being upheld. But as a black man I knew too well that there was practically a war going on between the African-American community and the Los Angeles Police Department. Mothers there were more afraid of the police injuring or killing their children than they were of muggers or gangs. And the courts permitted it. Cops would routinely come into court and lie. It was known as "testalying"; they would say whatever was necessary to make the case. But if I dared stand up in court and accuse a police officer of lying they would have locked me up. That was not permitted.

Times have changed in the courtroom. Now it is unusual not to accuse the police of lying.

Most of the civil litigation I did fell into two categories: civil rights law and personal injury law. Often, though, separating the two got a little confusing. When a police officer attacked a citizen who hadn't done a thing wrong, not only was he committing a criminal act, he also was violating that person's civil rights and, unfortunately, too often he was causing personal injury.

Sometimes it seemed like it was actually easier for an African-American to get justice in the criminal court than in civil litigation. The civil courts in Los Angeles just didn't seem to think there was anything wrong with police officers shooting and choking black kids. There seemed to be an unspoken acceptance that the police were permitted to kill or maim a few innocent black kids if it made the streets safer for everybody else. One of the most outrageous cases of my career was the killing by two policemen of twenty-three-year-old Phillip Eric Johns. Phillip Johns was asleep in his own bed in his own apartment in Inglewood. He was a hardworking African-American; he wasn't bothering anyone. He was sleeping and they broke into his apartment and shot him. They killed him.

A fundamental right guaranteed by the Constitution of the United States is that the citizens of this country should be secure in their own homes. But two plainclothes policemen got a tip that a man accused of committing several robberies was hiding out in that apartment. It is so reminiscent of the killing of Amadou Diallo decades later. These cops quietly broke into the apartment—with their guns drawn—and stood over Phillip Johns. Guns drawn. This young man was asleep, one hand tucked under his pillow. To these policemen a young black man sleeping with his hand beneath a pillow seemed very suspicious; they claimed he appeared to be feigning sleep and hiding a weapon. The fact that the sleeping man might be innocent, might not have had anything to do with the robberies, apparently never occurred to these police officers.

Just put yourself inside the mind of Phillip Johns. You're asleep in your own bed, knowing you've done absolutely nothing wrong, not feeling guilty about anything. Maybe you're even dreaming. Suddenly someone shakes you awake. The police claim they identified themselves, but there is no credible evidence to verify that. So you wake up and it's the middle of the night and you're groggy and the first thing you see is some guy wearing a regular shirt and pants standing over you, holding a gun inches from your face. What the . . .

Of course you react, just like Phillip Johns did. He probably grabbed the intruder's gun and tried to pull it away. The police officer fired. Phillip Johns continued to struggle, fighting for his life. The cop fired again. Again. The second cop, standing at the end of the bed, opened up. He shot him once. Twice. Bullets hit Phillip Johns in his temple, in the middle of his back, the back of his upper right arm—and in his heart.

He died on his own bed, never knowing he had been killed because two cops had broken into the wrong apartment.

After a brief investigation, the LAPD decided it was a tragic accident, blaming it on the informant—an Inglewood police officer—who supposedly gave them the wrong address. According to Police Chief Parker's successor, Police Chief Ed Davis, there wasn't enough evidence to take any disciplinary or criminal actions against the police officers.

The whole African-American community was furious. Things had changed since the Watts riots. People just weren't going to accept the same silly excuses that had once been forced on them. This time a grand jury indicted both detectives, charging them with manslaughter. L.A. mayor Sam Yorty expressed regret for what happened, but suggested that the officers should be acquitted because they were simply responding to a rapidly developing situation while trying to do their duty.

As I had become known as the lawyer standing between the community and the police department I was retained by Phillip Johns's mother, Mrs. Johnie Choyce, and we filed a wrongful death action against the city for $5 million. Once again I was in the middle of the action.

Not surprisingly, the police commission recommended to the city council that the city hire and pay for private attorneys to defend the police officers. The city council had to approve that expenditure. Like the coroner's hearing in the Deadwyler case, the attention of the whole city was focused on this city council meeting. At this meeting, Phillip Johns's cousin, Sharon Tucker, said tearfully, "I can't believe that you can vote to give money to defend those two officers. It makes me sick . . . I wonder, if it had been your son, would you have given a hundred thousand dollars to defend these officers?"

His stepbrother, Robert Hampton, said, "What I'm asking is that people in the black community can go to sleep at night without being afraid of being shot in their sleep . . ."

By an 8 to 6 vote, the city council voted to pay for the defense of the officers. It was a disgrace, I thought, and I didn't hesitate to say that. "I think it's a callous act on the part of the city council and majority community," I told reporters. ". . . It also shows the complete insensitivity of the majority community in the shooting of a black man."

While I have always believed a defendant should have the best lawyer possible, what I objected to here was the fact that taxpayers would pay to defend actions of a city employee far beyond the scope of his job. If a city parks employee had negligently shot somebody, the city wouldn't have paid for his defense. By paying these legal fees the city in fact was accepting its own responsibility for the killing, as well as sending a message to all police officers that the city will defend them no matter how egregious their actions. I didn't like it one bit.

But it didn't surprise me. It did not surprise me at all to find that racism had been institutionalized. To absolutely no one's surprise, the detectives were tried and acquitted of the criminal charges.

My co-counsel representing Mrs. Choyce in the civil lawsuit was Syd Irmas, a friend and attorney from whom I learned so much—and from whom years later I would buy my first Rolls-Royce. We sued both the cities of Inglewood and Los Angeles. L.A. handled the case very well; they let it move slowly, very, very slowly, through the system, so by the time it reached a courtroom much of the passion from the community had dissipated. There are a lot of strategies cities use to defuse potentially divisive legal situations. Several years ago, for example, Denver had a trial in which white kids had chased a group of African-American kids into traffic where one of the black kids was hit by a car and killed. Denver's African-American community was ready to march—but as an assistant district attorney explained, to make certain that didn't happen, "We held the trial in February, because it's much too cold then for anybody to hold a rally outdoors." L.A. just let it simmer.

It took almost four years before the Phillip Johns trial for damages was held in Torrance, California. During that time we had settled with the city of Inglewood for $500,000, the biggest victory I'd had up to that moment, and used our fees to finance the case against L.A. The court decided to try this case in the all-white suburb of Torrance. It was a terrible injustice. Going from downtown L.A. to Torrance was like moving the case to Alabama. The jury consisted of eleven whites and one black. My complaint about this had nothing to do with "playing a race card," just that the members of this jury could not possibly understand the case from Mrs. Choyce's point of view. We lost in Torrance the same case we had settled with the city of Inglewood. We found out later that we really had no chance with this jury—the one black member signed an affidavit attesting to the fact that during deliberations at least one white member of the jury referred to the black court reporter as "Burrhead."

We did have an African-American judge in the case, who was so disgusted by the verdict that he threw it out—but the appellate court reversed his action and reinstated the verdict for the city. It was another devastating loss for me. I do take these losses very personally; not because I don't get paid, but because I am an African-American and these verdicts proved to me that a black American could not get justice in an American courtroom. That hurt.

I learned two lessons from that case. We had two defendants and I settled with one at a time. That was a dreadful mistake I should not have made. That allowed the city of Los Angeles to place all the blame on Inglewood. I should have gotten all the parties involved in the trial together in one room and let them point fingers at each other. But when Inglewood offered $500,000 it was difficult not to accept it. To this day, though, I don't believe I did the best thing for my client.

And Syd and I should have fought much harder to keep the trial in Los Angeles. The city liked to send cases from South Central or Inglewood to Torrance for obvious reasons. The values, the trust in the government, of the people likely to form the jury in Torrance were completely different from that of the people who would comprise a jury in Los Angeles. The people in Torrance loved these two white officers. It's a technique still in use today. Although I was no longer representing the mother of Amadou Diallo when the trial of the four white NYPD officers who fired forty-one shots at an unarmed man was moved from the Bronx—where it had been assigned to a female African-American judge—to upstate Albany, New York, supposedly because the enormous amount of pretrial publicity would prevent the officers from receiving a fair trial, I knew from experience that it would be almost impossible to get a conviction. The Bronx is 80 percent black and Latino; Albany is 89 percent white. The people in the Bronx know how the police work. They know the difference between a "good shooting" and a "bad shooting," they know it from their everyday experience. I suspect there were other venues in New York State where the makeup of the population might more closely resemble the Bronx, but finding that place was not the objective.

As in Torrance, in Albany the four police officers were acquitted of all charges.

Mrs. Choyce had asked me to find justice for her son and I had failed to do so. I had to look into her eyes and tell her that I'd failed and there was nothing more I could do about it. Once again I was angry, terribly bitter. But it didn't weaken me, it made me stronger, it made me resolve to move forward, to keep going no matter what.

Unfortunately, there were several more no-matter-whats to come. In *Playboy*'s 1981 college football preview it was predicted that Cal State Long Beach star "Ron Settles will be one of the best runners on the West Coast if he can stay healthy." But before the magazine even hit the newsstand twenty-one-year-old Ron Settles was dead. He'd made the fatal mistake of driving a sports car through the town of Signal Hill, California. Signal Hill was as close to a police fiefdom as existed in Southern California, and most African-Americans stayed out of the town if at all possible. Settles was late for an appointment and took the short route through Signal Hill. According to the arresting officers, when Settles was stopped for speeding he refused to cooperate; rather than handing over his driver's license he began fighting with the police officer. Supposedly, he grabbed one of the officers in the crotch. It was never possible to verify the officer's statements; all the tapes of radio calls and written records of the incident were destroyed a month after Settles's death. Standard procedure, it was explained.

But whatever happened, he was arrested. Police officers searched his car and announced that they had found drug paraphernalia and a nine-inch knife. He was taken to police headquarters and put into a cell. Three hours later he was found hanging from the bars, a mattress cover wrapped around his neck. After an examination, the coroner ruled that his injuries and the bruises on his body were consistent with suicide. That was the official verdict, Ron Settles had committed suicide by hanging himself.

His parents refused to believe that. They asked me to fight for their son's reputation. I had recently returned to private practice after spending three years working as the number-three man in the Los Angeles District Attorney's Office. With the complete support of District Attorney John Van de Kamp, we had instituted several important changes in accepted police procedure. But among those things I failed to do was outlaw a dangerous choke hold commonly used by police to subdue combatants. This hold required the officer to apply tremendous pressure with his forearm across the windpipe; it worked by preventing the person from breathing. The problem with it was that too often it resulted in death.

I didn't want to take the Settles case. This was not a good financial time for me. I'd taken a major cut in salary to return to the DA's office; my daughter Melodie was in college and I had just gotten divorced. I needed to earn some money and based on my past experiences, this was going to be an extremely time-consuming and expensive case to fight—with little chance of victory.

But none of that mattered. I looked into Mrs. Settles's eyes and I was convinced. I had to take this case. It really wasn't even a case, it was a mission. I fought it with a Harvard-educated white civil rights lawyer named Michael Mitchell, who had successfully obtained an injunction in federal court to prevent the LAPD from using choke holds unless the officer's life or safety was threatened.

As we predicted, it was expensive, and time-consuming. And frustrating. Once again we began with a coroner's inquest—but this time I was permitted to ask my own questions. This time the inquest was being held under new laws I had helped promulgate. At first few people took the inquest seriously. When questioned, all but one of the officers present in the jail that night claimed their Fifth Amendment right against self-incrimination. Their attorney noted the inquest had "no legal significance," and was "a three-ring circus. . . . No matter what occurs in the way of a verdict everybody is going to walk away, and the only thing that has happened is the public has had some entertainment." Entertainment? This attorney also suggested that Ron Settles, running toward a bright future, had gotten so depressed when he was arrested for assault and cocaine possession that he committed suicide.

That was absurd; it was a disgraceful accusation, and we proved it. The police officers claimed that the knot forming the noose was found on the right side of Settles's neck, but the coroner found bruises on the left side of his neck. The police were never able to explain that. Several witnesses, including a prisoner who had been in this particular cell prior to Settles, testified there was no mattress cover on the bed. The police were never able to explain that. The coroner's office staged a re-creation of the event to prove it was physically possible for Settles to hang himself; incredibly, when police "cut down" the volunteer, they found that they had cut the cover used in the re-creation in precisely the same place as was the cover Settles supposedly used to hang himself. Incredibly, because the volunteer used in the recreation was six feet, six inches tall and weighed 170 pounds while Settles was five feet, ten inches and weighed 210. The police were never able to explain that. And coincidently, just a week before Settles's death, another man had supposedly hanged himself in the Signal Hill jail.

Mike Mitchell and I strongly believed we knew what had happened in that cell. Just as in the Diallo case, the police officers were angry at Settles for fighting back when arrested. In Signal Hill they had a way of handling troublemakers like that. Usually it was a beating, with the bruises explained as having been incurred while resisting arrest. That's when the victim's face "made contact with the concrete," as reports read. But in this case the beating went too far. To prevent Settles from fighting back, they held him in a choke hold—and they had killed him. During the inquest Mike Mitchell and I wanted to demonstrate our theory to the jury. This was perhaps the first time in my career that I put on this sort of demonstration, but it later became a hallmark of my courtroom strategy.

I wanted the jury to feel what had happened that night. Mitchell wrapped his forearm around my neck and applied pressure to my windpipe. I was having trouble breathing. There wasn't a sound in that courtroom. When he finally released me it took me several minutes to catch my breath.

The jury consisted of four African-Americans and five whites. After five hours of deliberation the jury ruled 5 to 4 that Ron Settles had died "at the hands of another and other than by accident." It was not a suicide, it was a homicide.

The five-person majority consisted of all four blacks and a white minister. The other white jurors accepted the official version. Many people claimed that the verdict was based on race. That might be true, though personally I did not see how those four white jurors could have found it to be suicide. But interestingly, the five members of the majority ruling were all college graduates, while none of the minority had graduated from college.

The day after the verdict was reached I filed a $50 million suit against the city of Signal Hill. Making the city pay for this crime was one way to insure the brutality would end.

A few days later I received an extraordinary letter. "Dear Mr. Cochran," wrote Jewell White, whom I had never met, "I listened a few minutes ago to the jury verdict of the Settles coroner's inquiry. I'm sure that I felt as many other black mothers in this nation feel, that it takes a mightily whole lot of fighting racism to get a decision on something that had stared us in the face for generations . . .

"Beyond that, however, the second thought that came to me was that we have got to let attorney Cochran know that in soul and spirit we support and love and recognize respectfully the dedication and competence he is showing daily. . . . The fact as I see it is that we *do* have, truly we do, competent young black men and women who will dare to use their eloquent intellectual abilities to defend our people in these never-ending struggles against injustice and brutality ...

"I will continue to soulfully and spiritually support you as this madness plods on."

Progress, we were making progress. "Fifteen years ago," I told reporters, "this would have been a situation where people would just wipe it off and go about their business." We were standing up tall and proud. The Calhoun image, the black buffoon, was long gone. It had been replaced by a growing number of young black professionals who were not afraid to speak out loudly. I knew without a doubt that only a few years earlier this verdict would have been impossible. The times were changing indeed.

The L.A. Sheriff's Department initiated an investigation of Settles's death. Although four Signal Hill officers would eventually be charged with assaulting other prisoners, it proved impossible to find enough evidence to bring charges against anyone in the Settles case. His killer, probably killers, walked away free.

In preparation for the civil suit the defense tried to dirty up the victim. Destroying the victim's reputation is a tactic that is often attempted because—admittedly—it sometimes works. This time they claimed a trace amount of PCP, angel dust, specifically 6/1,000,000,000 of a gram was found in his system. It was an amount small enough to show up in toxicology tests if he simply had been in a room where PCP was being smoked. But the obvious inference was that rather than being an innocent football star, Settles was a jacked-up crackhead who forced the police to protect themselves. Mrs. Settles particularly was irate at that charge. "We taught him to live within the system. We had a clean kid. He was a health nut. We didn't even allow people to smoke cigarettes in our house. And yet they tried to assassinate his character with that drug stuff."

Unfortunately, the only possible way to refute this allegation was the stuff of nightmares. We would have to exhume Ron Settles's body from his resting place in a family plot in Memphis, Tennessee, and conduct a complete autopsy.

The cases in which I've been involved have taken me to many places, but none so terrible as the basement of the Suffolk County Coroner's Office on Long Island, where four forensic pathologists conducted the autopsy. It was a gruesome scene I'll never forget. X rays of the body revealed broken bones that no one knew about. The two pathologists we retained found strong evidence that Ron Settles had been choked to death. Michael Baden, regarded by many people as the finest forensic pathologist in the nation, stated emphatically that only a choke hold could produce the damage to the windpipe that was present.

The pathologist hired by Signal Hill did not agree. And Los Angeles coroner Dr. Thomas Noguchi, who would soon be demoted to physician/specialist at least partially because of his work in this case, continued to support his original conclusion, death by hanging.

But all four men agreed that there was absolutely no trace of any type of drug in Settles's body. It was a substantial victory for the Settles family. It gave them back their son's reputation.

Mike Mitchell and I wanted very much to go forward with the lawsuit against Signal Hill, but when that city offered $760,000 to settle the case the family decided to accept it. "This was not a case about money," Helen Settles explained, "this was a case about human dignity. No amount of money could ever bring our son back . . ." The payment was by hundreds of thousands of dollars the most that had ever been paid in California in a police abuse case. And the money talked loudly; to make sure that city would never again be faced with that kind of situation, the people of Signal Hill voted a reform government into city hall, the police chief was replaced, and the police department was reorganized.

The legal climate was changing in L.A. Black men were still being killed by policemen, but finally police departments were being held responsible for their actions. And they were going to have to pay for them. This change was a long time coming. While this was the first substantial settlement I had made, obviously it was not a time for celebration. Personal injury law can cause an assault of the emotions; this was payment for the death of an innocent young man. It was not possible to separate the satisfaction derived from making them pay for their brutality from the result of it. That probably is the most difficult aspect of personal injury law; it's payment for human suffering. And the amount of payment is based, at least partially, on the degree of suffering. Many times I've stood in front of a jury and urged them to determine the cost of pain. That's the harsh reality of personal injury law, and the fact that there are lawyers who take advantage of hurt and injured people has severely damaged the professional image of the personal injury lawyer.

Admittedly, I've earned a great deal of money as an attorney. More money than the great-grandson of a slave ever thought possible. I have received the largest verdicts or settlements in personal injury cases in four different states. I've also been successful in several civil cases; in Florida, for example, a fantastic attorney, and friend, named Willie Gary and I won a $240 million jury verdict against Disney in a theft of intellectual property decision—although it may be a long time and several appeals before that settlement is finally concluded. The accruing interest alone on that judgment is more money than I ever imagined earning.

I like to believe that I have never walked out of a room and left money on the table, although I suspect every lawyer likes to believe that. It was easy for critics—and few people have been criticized more for doing a good job than I was after the Simpson verdict—to point to my expensive cars and my nice houses on both coasts and my very nice custom-made suits and, my oh my, all those colorful ties, and declare that I'm just another one of those slick money-grubbing lawyers taking advantage of people who have been hurt to squeeze millions of dollars out of insurance companies. I suspect that there are times people can't decide who they like less, negligence attorneys or insurance companies.

People who think that about me are wrong. Money is always the five-hundred-pound gorilla looking over your shoulder in a lawsuit. Whether it is discussed or not, every participant in the case knows it's there. But the fact is that long ago I made enough money to make Dale and I very happy for the rest of our lives. I made a firm decision that I would retire in 1999. Then it became an absolute decision that I would retire in 2000. Then I guaranteed I would retire in 2001. And I did, at least partially. I retired from criminal law—but I would not give up civil law. I'm finally in a position to influence social change in this country. By picking carefully the cases on which I work I'm able to accomplish things that once I thought were impossible.

In the Abner Louima case in New York, for example, Peter, Barry, and I helped break down the famous "blue wall of silence." In the case of the New Jersey Four, four black teenagers, we proved for the first time the existence of racial profiling—and then helped institute concrete steps to end it. In Montgomery County, Maryland, and Chicago we've caused them to make fundamental changes in law enforcement methods.

I do collect a fee. Sometimes it's a very good fee. There is absolutely nothing wrong with that. Like other personal injury lawyers I work on contingency, meaning I take a percentage of the final settlement. If I fail to get a settlement for my client, I get nothing. Contingency fees are known in the legal profession as "the keys to the courthouse," and there are lawyers who take advantage of clients. But without these contingency fees lawyers wouldn't be able to afford to do the work necessary to properly prepare a case. Making a case for your client requires a substantial investment with no guarantee that you'll ever see a penny in return. We hire experts and buy transcripts, sometimes we travel to gather evidence, we certainly pay investigators. Just to do an initial investigation to determine if a case exists costs a minimum of $5,000. If we have to hire an expert it will cost considerably more. In a Washington, D.C., shooting, for example, we weren't satisfied with the public coroner's investigation, so we hired our own forensic coroner who charged $5,000 plus an hourly rate. Developing the necessary background research to bring a class action lawsuit against Lockheed Martin cost my firm $220,000—and we paid every penny of that—only to have the judge refuse to recognize that there was discrimination against a class of people. If clients were paying us by the hour, few of them could afford that proverbial free day in court.

So money is the necessary component. It's the fuel that keeps the engine running. But it's not a reason to celebrate when we make a substantial settlement. What is worth celebrating are those changes for the public welfare that otherwise would not be made. When it makes the world a safer or better place. Several years ago I began making sure that in every settlement I would get something extra, something that benefited the community. I forced change. When I came to New York Peter and Barry invited me to work with them, and we agreed the only cases we would accept were those in which we felt there was a larger issue at stake. Cases in which we could send a message. Cases that could make a difference in the lives of a lot of people. As Peter said, we believed we could use our collective talents to seek out particular cases where there were very significant social, political, or legal issues at stake. We wanted to look beyond the interests of one client and find cases that could be used to generate social, political, and legal reform. Our objective was to expand the rights of people who have been deprived of their civil rights. From the very beginning we knew that to accomplish that we were going to have to be creative when fashioning settlement proposals—in addition to money.

Although, admittedly, one of the very first cases we fought did not fall into that category. It concerned a lovely older woman living in Queens, who worked at a hospital. Just a good person. The police were looking for a drug dealer and someone gave them the wrong address—her address. Does this begin to sound familiar? The police broke down her door and stormed into her apartment. Fortunately, she wasn't home. But before they left they ransacked the place. Eventually this woman submitted an application to the NYPD, asking that the damage be repaired. She needed a new door and a couple of broken items rebuilt. The cost was practically nothing. But the police department didn't even respond to her request. I don't remember how we got involved; a friend of a friend of a friend. This was not exactly the type of envelope-pushing case we had anticipated, but this was a person who needed help and we could help.

Just imagine a city clerk sitting at a desk piled high with paperwork. Somewhere buried in that pile is this woman's request. It was going to get taken care of when this clerk was good and ready to deal with it. To this clerk it's a minor problem—and then the phone rang informing him that Peter Neufeld, Barry Scheck, and Johnnie Cochran have taken her case.

Within two days, crews were at this woman's house making all the requested repairs.

The authorities responded to this so quickly not because it was the right thing to do, not because Neufeld, Scheck, and I are such wonderful human beings—although we like to believe we are—but because otherwise it might have cost them a lot of money. Money motivates. The fear of having to pay causes people to take actions much more rapidly than they might otherwise. And the more they believe they will have to pay, the faster the response.

In addition to my association with Peter and Barry, my base in New York is The Cochran Firm/Schneider Kleinick Weitz Damashek & Shoot, which prior to my association had already established itself as one of the finest plaintiff firms in America. I get personally involved in only a small number of our cases. And even in some of the cases in which I do participate, other members of the firm throughout the country do the work in the trenches, building a case, preparing for trial. Although I might not be present for the preparation and pretrial motions, I am kept aware of everything that takes place. I'll also participate in the most important depositions. When the trial is about to begin, I'll come into town fully prepared to represent our client.

Decades of experience have taught me what I need to know. I will have read all the correspondence, all the depositions, I will have had long strategy discussions with my co-counsel; we will be ready to try the case. On several occasions, we've found, my presence alone is enough to cause the other side to initiate settlement discussions. I'm sort of the legal gunslinger, the celebrity lawyer. Money does motivate.

That isn't because of my work in the Simpson trial. The stakes are very different in a criminal trial and a civil trial. The difference between criminal law and civil law are sort of like the difference between baseball and football. While you can play them both with a ball in the same ballpark, the rules have absolutely nothing in common. At the conclusion of a civil trial nobody goes to prison. So my reputation as a criminal lawyer doesn't really have much of an impact in civil law. In one case, for example, I participated in a settlement conference. Our adversaries were very good lawyers and they didn't concede a single point. They certainly were not intimidated by my presence. At times they were pretty cutting. And yet, at the end of this sometimes rancorous meeting, when about the only thing on which we had agreed was that we would meet again, these lawyers paused to ask for my autograph—for their wives.

But that was the autograph of O. J. Simpson's controversial lawyer, not Leonard Deadwyler's or Ron Settles's or Cynthia Wiggins's. I have earned my reputation as a personal injury lawyer by winning or settling cases for substantial sums. In this branch of the law they keep score by dollars. I became known in Los Angeles for representing people who had been abused by the police. Not exclusively, but primarily. Literally, I started by getting nothing for Barbara Deadwyler; in the 1960s nobody beat the LAPD in court. I vowed to myself that someday I was going to win a million-dollar verdict or settlement. That was my goal, one million dollars.

I received a million-dollar verdict for the first time in the case of a neighbor of mine, my friend from UCLA Dr. Herbert Avery, a black man who had become a very successful obstetrician. Ironically, it was Dr. Avery who had sent me the Deadwyler case. One day, while driving down Franklin Avenue, near our homes, he saw his son had been stopped by two policemen, who had him up against a wall and were searching him. He stopped to find out what was happening. When he refused a police order to leave, explaining he wanted to know what was happening to his son, the police kicked him in the groin, put him in a choke hold, hit him with a baton, kneed him in the back, handcuffed him, and took him into custody. And they did it right in front of his son.

This for the crime of trying to help a family member while being black. No criminal charges were filed against Dr. Avery, but he had suffered severe physical and psychological damage. In addition to a continuing pain in his back, his sense of security was broken forever. The message to him was clear; no matter how hard you work, no matter how successful you are, in the eyes of the Los Angeles Police Department a black man had no civil rights at all. It was so terribly dehumanizing.

A jury awarded Dr. Avery $1.3 million, the largest judgment

against the LAPD in a jury trial at that time. A judge later cut it to $750,000, which we accepted reluctantly. Dr. Avery wanted to keep fighting, he wanted to make the system pay for what those officers had done to him, but there really wasn't enough money for that. What the system has done to an entire race, in fact, is the reason many years later I got involved in the debate about whether reparations should be paid—and what form might they take—to African-Americans.

The judgment in the Avery case was the first of many substantial judgments against the police I would win. Winning these large verdicts required a case of police misconduct to which jurors could potentially relate and my ability to make them relate to it. I had to appeal to their sense of justice—and I had to make them angry. Unfortunately, the L.A. Police Department continually provided me with such cases. There was a time when I began to think I might have seen the worst examples of police misconduct possible, but then they would surprise me. Being a police officer is a difficult and dangerous job, many police officers are extraordinarily brave men, but if all police officers were properly trained and supervised many of the terrible injustices I've seen never would have taken place. Murphy Pierson, for example, was a proud black man in his early seventies. He lived with his wife, Katie, in South Los Angeles, a deteriorating neighborhood in which drugs were sold openly on the street and the police didn't seem to be able to stop it. Murphy Pierson wanted to stop it. And one night he decided to do it. . . .

Now just imagine you're a member of the jury. You're sitting in a comfortable wooden chair and I'm standing almost directly in front of you making my opening statement. Murphy and Katie Pierson are sitting with me in the courtroom. He's an old man, bent over, he doesn't hear very well anymore, and he walked into the courtroom leaning heavily on the cane he's been forced to use because of the injuries he's suffered. That's Katie, his wife of almost forty-five years, sitting next to him, holding his hand.

Ladies and gentlemen, this is a brave man who simply wanted to take back his community. One day a bunch of young kids were doing a drug deal right by the bushes in front of his house. That was just too much for him, just like it would be too much for you. But he decided he wasn't going to let these punks push him around. So he went into his house and got his shotgun. He came outside and warned them, "Get off my property."

They ran, oh this time they ran. Then he turned around to go back into his house. He never saw the LAPD squad car, cruising the block on regular patrol. There were two rookie cops in that car, two young men without the guidance of a veteran officer, somebody who really knew the neighborhood. These two young cops saw the shotgun, jumped out of their squad car, and started shouting orders at Mr. Pierson. But he didn't hear them very well, he can't hear them, but he heard screaming. And so he turned around.

And these cops started firing at him. Eleven shots. They fired eleven shots at this old man. The bullets hit him and knocked him down. And those bullets that missed him went through the window of the house. Mrs. Pierson is a devout Roman Catholic. At this moment she is on her knees reciting the rosary as she does every night. Ladies and gentlemen, I'm not making any of this up. Every bit of it happened. I want you to look at these people and just try and imagine the pain and fear.

But it wasn't over. Mrs. Pierson couldn't imagine what was happening. As fast as she could she went to the front of the house. And there was her husband laying on the ground, bleeding. But Mr. Pierson didn't die, he was just lying there bleeding.

The police ran up to that front porch and grabbed her and dragged her over her husband's body and forced her to get down on her knees and handcuffed her, then put her in the back of a squad car and raced to the station. This was the way they

treated Mrs. Pierson, who hadn't done anything at all but find
her husband bleeding on the ground.

They took Murphy Pierson to the hospital. He was very
lucky, he was going to live—but they didn't tell that to his wife.
She was held at the police station for six hours, six hours, with-
out being told that her husband was alive. Just imagine what
was going on in her mind. Think of your mother in that same
situation. Now some of you might have read about me, and
maybe you've read that I can make a very good speech. But
believe me, even I don't know the right words to convey to you
the fear, the pain, and the humiliation suffered by Murphy and
Katie Pierson that day.

And all Mr. Pierson did was try to scare the drug dealers
off his block.

When I finished my opening statement I was certain that the jury
understood my case. After you've stood in front of enough juries
you know whether or not you've made an emotional connection.
And then you have to back up with evidence the statements you've
made. In cases like this, when your clients are elderly people, there
is generally much less of a settlement, based on the fact that
because of their age, the fact that they were living on a limited
income, they had not suffered substantial economic damage. They
already had lived the best years of their life. But I wanted—as
closely as possible—the jury to feel what my clients felt.

I glanced at the city attorney while I was making my opening
statement. From the look on his face I could tell it was effective.
Early in this case we did have one brief conversation about a settlement. He offered $50,000. That didn't surprise me; it is always dif-
ficult to get a large judgment when elderly people are involved. At
the conclusion of the trial the jury awarded Murphy Pierson $1.8
million. Katie Pierson received an additional $430,000 to compen-

sate her for false arrest, but I believe the jury was also making the city pay for the extreme cruelty exhibited by those police officers.

The judgments were getting larger and larger. A man named Leonard Johnson was stopped by a highway patrolman in South Central. Leonard Johnson was a pretty tough guy and he resented the stop. Truthfully, he probably was pretty angry. I don't think that was too unusual, a lot of people get upset when they are stopped in their car by a police officer. The police officer wanted to show Leonard Johnson how tough *he* was and he stuck his baton through the open window and began poking Johnson in the face. That was a complete violation of all departmental rules. A baton is a potentially deadly weapon—it's hardwood, it can crack open a skull—so officers are never supposed to hit people in the head with it. Johnson grabbed the baton and yanked it away. The cop obviously panicked; he took several steps backward, then began firing his weapon. Leonard Johnson died on the spot. For an ordinary traffic violation. We got almost $3 million for his widow.

After Dr. Avery's case million-dollar settlements became almost routine.

Some people claim I was able to consistently receive substantial verdicts because I seduced the jury with my words; others suggest I was able to stack my juries with minorities willing to give large settlements of city dollars to people just like them. But the fact is that I represented clients who had been abused by the system and I was able to tell their stories to juries in a manner that these jurors could understand. The advantage I had was my experience as a criminal lawyer, which enabled me to bring investigative techniques commonly used in criminal law to civil rights cases. In many of these cases my investigation was more thorough than the police department's; often I found witnesses that law enforcement officers didn't even know existed, or I provided information to the prosecutor's office that its own investigators had been unable to develop.

In criminal cases the objective is obvious: to as much as possible discredit the prosecution's evidence and witnesses and develop our own evidence and witnesses to prove our client's innocence. But in civil cases I begin by developing a theme. Then I try to tell a story that the jury can understand, a story with real people; a story with a beginning, a middle, and an end. Good lawyers are storytellers. I try to make my story as graphic as I can. If I am successful the jurors will understand both intellectually and emotionally what happened to my client. They'll be able to relate it to their own lives. I'm always looking for ways of describing justice to my audience, the jury. I might write down some of the things I want to say, but ultimately I will be speaking from my heart.

And to speak honestly from my heart I have to engage my emotions. The case to which I often refer is that of thirteen-year-old Latina Patty Diaz. Patty is a normal young woman, a good student, and what she wanted out of her life were the same things all thirteen-year-old girls want. But she never got it.

Early one morning a uniformed police officer named Stanley Tanabe knocked on the door of her home and told her parents, who did not speak English, that he was looking for a robbery suspect. Apparently he had a drawing of a suspect with him. These were law-abiding people and they let him search the house. Telling the parents to remain in the living room, he went into the room where Patty Diaz was sleeping and put his hand down her pants. He didn't penetrate her, but he molested her. He warned her that if she told anyone he would hurt her family. Then he told her he would be back.

Patty Diaz was a brave little girl. The next day her parents filed a complaint at their local precinct. But the police made no attempt to investigate. They did absolutely nothing about it. The encounter with the officer devastated this little girl. She'd be in school reading a book and suddenly she would see his face on the page. She lived her life in terror that the policeman would return in the night to touch her again and there was no one who could help her.

A month later, like a creature from some horror movie, Tanabe did come back. Patty was alone when he broke into the house, but before he could molest her again her mother returned. Patty Diaz escaped and ran to a neighbor's house. Tanabe tried to get away, but he was arrested in the unmarked police car he was driving. Eventually he was convicted of sexual battery and burglary and served slightly longer than a year. One year, for destroying an innocent young girl's life.

Patty Diaz's life was shattered. Her schoolwork declined drastically. She had hallucinations, nightmares. She tried to slit her wrists three times. And Tanabe served one year and was back on the street. The LAPD had known that Tanabe was not emotionally stable enough to be a police officer and had originally rejected his application. Police officers have extraordinary power over everyone's life, they can take away our freedom—or our life—at any moment, so they need to be held to a high standard. The LAPD had a responsibility to the public to require candidates to meet certain criteria and in the case of this officer, they failed to meet that standard.

The difficulty with this case for a personal injury attorney was that Patricia Diaz's injuries were emotional, not physical. This wasn't a shooting like Murphy Pierson, it wasn't a choke hold like Ron Settles, it wasn't physical abuse like Dr. Herb Avery. Patty Diaz had a broken spirit. This was a case in which an absolutely innocent young person was violated by the people who were supposed to protect her. It destroyed her adolescence; and no one could even speculate on the long-term damage inflicted on her.

I knew that most citizens would be outraged by this. There was a lot of money to be gotten in a courtroom, but I didn't want Patty Diaz to have to relive these events in public. I tried to settle. The city offered $150,000, based on the well-known "Mary M." case. Mary M. had been picked up by a police officer for drunk driving—and then he raped her. A year earlier the city had settled the case for that magic $150,000. A city attorney told me, "We'll never give you more than Mary M. Your client wasn't even raped. And besides, that officer was off-duty, so legally we're not even responsible."

This cop may have been off-duty, I replied, but he used the color of his authority to get into her house and molest her.

It was not an unusually difficult case to prove. The police officer had been convicted of the crime. During the trial I was able to get a police captain to admit that the LAPD had totally botched the investigation after the Diaz family reported Patty had been molested. They even failed to give the investigators the perfect description of Tanabe she had provided.

The real problem I faced was convincing the jurors that Patty Diaz had suffered severe and perhaps permanent injury. A jury can see physical damage; they saw Murphy Pierson hobble in on a cane. They saw my client whose leg had been crushed by a truck. But with Patty the damage was to her psyche. If the jury was going to accept the fact that Tanabe had robbed her of her life, I needed to make them understand what her life had been like. So in my closing argument I painted a verbal picture of a typical Sunday afternoon, how Patty used to take the bus to visit her grandmother and make tortillas. But she was much too frightened to do that ever again. I talked about all the things she did to have fun with her family, but now she had become withdrawn, sometimes sullen, very depressed. I took Patty's hand and led her over to the jury box. I wanted the jurors to see the slashes on her wrist where she had tried to kill herself. I couldn't mark her as an exhibit, but I noticed that several jurors had a difficult time making eye contact with her and two or three others started crying. I told my story. It had a beginning, a happy child at the beginning of her teenage years; a middle, that child molested by an authority figure who used the power of his uniform to destroy her self-esteem; and an end—the slashes across her wrist.

On July 17, 1992, the jury awarded Patty Diaz and her mother $9.4 million, the largest award ever granted by a Los Angeles jury in a police misconduct case. As the jurors walked out of the courtroom, each of them paused to give her a hug.

A verdict of that magnitude is always appealed, and is often reduced by the trial judge. In this case we agreed to accept $4.6 million. That verdict was twenty-five years, a quarter of a century, removed from the Leonard Deadwyler case. But it was a lifetime's worth of change.

FOUR

As I've said often, I became an attorney to try to insure that the law applied equally to people of all races and religions, to guarantee that we are all entitled to the equal protections of the Constitution. But it truly was ironic that in perhaps my most famous civil rights case, I would be defending the rights of a white man.

The fact that I represented African-American clients almost exclusively was by choice—white people just didn't choose to have a black lawyer. Admittedly, that was also true for a lot of black people. In the 1960s and early 1970s the nation just wasn't used to black professionals in any field. White people did not go to black doctors. They didn't use black accountants. And it seemed like a white person had to be in a pretty desperate situation to trust his fate to an African-American attorney. I established my practice in downtown L.A. because I wanted to represent people of all colors—just as it is now my dream to establish a legal practice consisting of attorneys of all races, creeds, and colors. But for the most part white people just didn't seem to need my services.

The first white client I represented was a sailor charged with a street robbery, I believe. It was not a significant case or a significant event in my life. It felt a little unusual, but it certainly wasn't material for a TV movie about changing social values. About all I remember is that I got him off. Through the years on other occasions I did represent white people, although obviously the vast majority of my clients were black.

But by the 1990s it was no longer unusual for an African-American attorney to represent a white client. In fact, when I first agreed to represent truck driver Reginald Denny there was almost no mention in the media that a white man had selected a black lawyer, but the fact that I took the case was very controversial in the African-American community—because Denny had been assaulted and almost beaten to death by four black men.

In 1991 a black man named Rodney King was pursued in his car by the LAPD in a high-speed chase in the San Fernando Valley. When the officers finally caught him a fight began. Rodney King was ferocious. He threw off four officers who tried to subdue him. One of those officers then shot him twice with a taser gun, a stun gun that shoots an electrical charge supposedly strong enough to stop an elephant. It barely slowed down King. The cops believed King was stoned on PCP. More officers showed up. And as at least a dozen other cops watched, the first four cops on the scene began beating King with their batons. They hit him fifty-six times, including several blows to the head, which were against regulations. They beat him, they kicked him in his head and body. When they finally placed him under arrest, one of the officers said on his radio, "I haven't beaten anyone this bad in a long time."

A police dispatcher, who recorded one of the officers asking for medical assistance, taped this admission: "He pissed us off, so I guess he needs an ambulance now . . ."

Under normal circumstances the cops would have gotten away with it. Even if King had filed a complaint nothing would have happened. Statistically, slightly less 2 percent of all complaints against LAPD officers resulted in disciplinary action. But these weren't normal circumstances. A man living nearby the scene of the beating had just gotten a new video camera and was trying it out. He recorded eighty-one seconds of the beating on tape and gave it to a local news station. When it was broadcast, the brutality of the beating horrified the nation. Admittedly, the tape did not show the events preceding the beating, the chase, or the fight, but under any circumstances it was obvious that the police had used excessive force, beating him longer and harder than necessary to subdue him, as a dozen other cops stood by passively.

This time the African-American community was joined in its outrage by millions of Americans who saw the tapes. A newspaper poll reported that 90 percent of the people in Los Angeles who saw the videotape believed the police officers had used excessive force. The cops were brought up on charges. At one point Rodney King came to my office and asked me to represent him in his civil suit against the city. That didn't surprise me; by this time in my career I pretty much anticipated being contacted when an African-American was a principal in a major case. It was obvious that this case was potentially worth millions of dollars—and in fact, he later settled it for more than $3 million. But I knew that Rodney King had already been working with a bright black lawyer from Orange County. Apparently, there had been some problem between the two men, which is why he'd approached me. I called this attorney and told him, "Look, man, your client was over here to see me and he's not happy. He's trying to come to me. I consider you a friend. You need to go make up with your client, you got to work this out."

In fact, I was glad I didn't get the case.

Supposedly because the videotape and ensuing pretrial publicity made it impossible to find an unbiased jury in Los Angeles, the trial of the police officers was moved about thirty miles to the suburb of Simi Valley. Simi Valley is so conservative it was selected as the site of the Ronald Reagan Presidential Library. A substantial number of white law enforcement officers reside there and when the trial took place in 1992, blacks accounted for only about 1.5 percent of the population. As the people in Simi Valley read the same newspapers and watch the same television stations as residents of Los Angeles, the reason the trial was moved there seemed obvious to L.A.'s minority community. Almost all doubts that the trial would be anything but a "whitewash" disappeared when a jury consisting of eleven whites and one Filipino was seated. Fairly or not, it was pretty obvious what was going to happen. There was no way those officers would be convicted in that town.

The trial of the four police officers who brutally beat Rodney King was covered by every newspaper and TV and radio station in Southern California. The tape was shown countless times, and each time it was broadcast people seemed more and more outraged.

Twenty-seven years had past since the Watts riots, almost three decades, but once again South Central Los Angeles was on the edge of chaos. When the jury indicated it had reached a verdict the LAPD moved out in massive force, even before that verdict was announced, to try to quell any disturbance before it got out of hand. There are many people who believe it was the verdict that ignited the riots, but Clifford Mosby, one of the nation's finest private investigators and a man who has done investigations for me in several cases, discovered that they had been smoldering earlier that day.

Hours before the verdict was announced a large number of police officers responded to a disturbance at the home of a man named Damian Williams, who supposedly had thrown something at a cop. When word got out on the street, practically the whole neighborhood, including local gang members, began converging on the scene. Williams eventually came out of his house and exposed himself to the police. A fight broke out when the police tried to arrest him and the police withdrew from the scene. The mob followed them, at first throwing rocks at police cars and other official vehicles, then attacking anyone who wasn't black.

This mini-riot was already raging when the verdict was announced: The officers were acquitted of all charges. That's when the city erupted. Roving mobs began throwing rocks and bottles at passing cars, then they began pulling white people out of cars and beating them. Doors and windows of stores were smashed and the looting began.

Into this growing riot drove an innocent twenty-seven-year-old truck driver named Reginald Denny. He had no idea what was going on. But suddenly the driver's side window of his truck was broken. Several men leaped on his truck. Somebody smashed him in the side of his head with a crowbar and he was dragged out of the truck. Four black men started beating him; they punched him and kicked him, and one of the men picked up a brick and slammed it down on his head. Incredibly, a news station helicopter was directly overhead and broadcast this beating on live TV. Four other people, strangers living in the area, saw what was happening on TV and ran to the scene. At the risk of their own lives they saved Reginald Denny. When Denny woke up in the hospital five days later he had almost no memory of what had happened to him. His first thought was that somebody better call work for him "because I'm in trouble. Where's the truck?"

He had been beaten almost to death. The side of his head had been bashed in. Several bones had been broken. He had lost a lot of blood. He survived, but fifty-four other people died in the riots, another 2,383 were injured—221 critically—13,212 people were arrested, and property damage was estimated at more than $700 million.

Like so many other people who loved our city, I was outraged by both the verdict in the case and the ensuing riots. But what happened several months later surprised even me. When Reginald Denny finally got out of the hospital he was besieged by personal injury lawyers, though he wasn't even sure he wanted to sue. "My mind was consumed with doctors, nurses, medicine," he said. "All I could think about was getting better. Suing is just not a word I used. I had no idea what my options were."

Cases sometimes come to me by very circuitous routes. Denny's brother-in-law's father-in-law belonged to a Harley-Davidson riding club with an attorney I knew quite well named Dominick Rubalcava. After spending considerable time with Denny, Dominick—

who did not represent Denny because he was not a personal injury lawyer— invited me to meet him. At first I didn't think there was very much I could do to help Denny. It has been established in a lot of different cases that the government has immunity from negligence actions during riot situations. The government just isn't responsible if people get hurt in a riot. But I had read some of the statements Denny had made. He didn't seem particularly angry or bitter at anyone. He never made a single racist remark. So I was curious. I wanted to meet him.

Dominick Rubalcava picked me up at my house one morning and we drove to meet Denny at his brother-in-law's house. We took Dominick's car—he didn't want me showing up at the meeting in my Rolls.

Reginald Denny was one of the most delightful human beings I'd ever met. There wasn't a racist bone in his body. In fact, he really wasn't sure he wanted to take any legal action at all. What struck me most was his real lack of anger. "One day they're going to be accountable for their behavior," he told me. "I just wonder if they've lived in a hellhole for so long that that was just a normal day? I just don't want it on my conscience to be the guy who wants revenge, because that's just not me. What I'd like to do is shake these guys and say, 'What the heck were you thinking? What's wrong with you?' "

Another thing that impressed me about him was that he had received letters from all over the world, twenty-five, thirty thousand letters, and he wanted to answer them all. Some of them came from people in racist organizations like the Ku Klux Klan, who sent him money. "I sent those right back," he told me.

He pointed out to me that African-Americans helped get him to the hospital, that several of the doctors who operated and saved his life were African-Americans. At times during our conversation I felt like he was trying to make me feel better.

I didn't know what I could do to help him, the law was pretty well settled, but after meeting him I knew I wanted to try. In addition to liking him, I was absolutely smitten with his eleven-year-old daughter, Ashley. I began with two objectives; I thought this man should be compensated for his horrible injuries, and I wanted to do whatever I could to make sure this never happened again. Admittedly, I was quite surprised at the reaction when it was announced that I would be representing Denny. I thought the fact that a black lawyer was representing a white man might in some very small way help heal the racial rift in the city, but the only resistance I received came from within my own community. African-Americans were really angry about the Rodney King verdict, and they did not feel I should be representing a white man.

Among those people who did not want the firm to get involved was my associate and friend Carl Douglas, who would soon distinguish himself in the Simpson trial. He warned that if I represented Denny we'd have pickets in front of the office.

I told everyone that it would be tough to look at myself in the mirror if I didn't represent this man just because he was white. For decades many white lawyers had refused to represent black clients, and I wasn't about to perpetuate that racism just because I had the opportunity. I decided to represent Reginald Denny at least partially because he felt no need to get even; it would be the ultimate in hypocrisy if I didn't represent him to get even for the sins of white lawyers. "This isn't a case about skin color," I said, "this is just about injustice. Some black thugs did this to him and the LAPD just let it happen." I took some real heat, which did surprise me. Perhaps I'd become so inured to the existence of racism in the legal system that I wasn't prepared for the depth of the anger in the African-American community about the King verdict.

Many other people had contacted me after the riots asking me for help. Eventually I agreed to represent three additional riot victims; a Latino and a Japanese-American who had been beaten at the same intersection where Denny was almost killed, and a woman whose son had been the first person killed that day. But my problem with these cases was the same as it was with Reginald Denny. Legally, we had no cause of action against the city. We could have sued the people who assaulted him, but at best we would have won an uncollectable judgment; those people had no money.

The first important action to be taken in a lawsuit is to put together all of the known facts together and develop a theory about exactly what happened. That's the trunk of the tree from which all the branches grow. We needed a theory. One of the reasons the riots so quickly exploded, an element that had eluded most of the other lawyers representing people injured in the rioting, was the fact that the LAPD generally ignored South Central. My brilliant associate, Eric Ferrer, suggested that an African-American should be able to bring an action against the LAPD because the police had a policy of not offering protection to South Central equal to that received by wealthier—and whiter—neighborhoods. Maybe the law prevented us from suing the city for the negligence of the police department, but certainly we could sue them for damages resulting from dis-crimination. We were not claiming the state was liable; we were suing because the residents of South Central had been denied equal protection.

It was a great theory. And if an African-American could sue under that theory then so could a white man like Reginald Denny. So we debated suing the city not for negligence, but rather for vio-lation of his civil rights. Even Carl Douglas was supportive. "I love the irony of it," he said, "the idea that here's this white guy with an African-American firm suing the city of Los Angeles on behalf of the blacks of South Central. I just loved it."

Reginald Denny explained the theory perhaps better than any-one else. "People need to know that 'protect and serve' may mean 'protect and serve' in Beverly Hills and Westwood, but not in South Central. And that's just not right."

We filed a tort claim in Los Angeles and a civil rights suit in the U.S. District Court for the Central District of California. Our contention was that the LAPD discriminated against the people of South Central by withdrawing all its officers from that area while continuing to protect other areas of the city. As a direct result of that decision three of my clients had suffered severe injuries and one of them had been killed.

The first judge to hear the case just didn't accept our theory. He dismissed the suit without prejudice, meaning we were free to file it again with additional information. We amended our lawsuit, adding more factual evidence and legal arguments. But we also got cooperation from numerous rights groups, including the NAACP Legal Defense and Educational Fund, the Asian Pacific American Legal Center, the Southern California Civil Rights Coalition, and, among others, the American Civil Liberties Union Foundation of California. This certainly has to be one of the few cases in which the NAACP filed a brief supporting the argument that the state had discriminated against a white man. The law can truly lead you into some delicious complexities.

This time the judge accepted our argument, basing his decision on a 1989 Sixth Circuit ruling that permitted white citizens of Canton, Ohio, to sue the police department for failing to protect them because they lived in a heavily black area. Unfortunately, as the case moved forward we just couldn't satisfy the judge that the LAPD had an obligation to go into South Central. When they pulled out they basically surrendered the streets to the hoodlums. I couldn't believe they could pick and choose which neighborhoods they wanted to protect, but as it turned out the judge said that's exactly what they could do. All my cases were dismissed.

Eventually I was able to help Reginald Denny receive workmen's compensation benefits, but it was not nearly as much as he deserved. I think I probably felt worse about the inability to make a case than he did. In addition to workmen's compensation, one day I got a call from Bill Cosby who was working on his TV show *The Cosby Mysteries* in New York. "I've been watching all this," he told me, adding that he had been very impressed by Denny. With good reason, I told him, he was an impressive man. "Next time you're coming to New York," he said, "why don't you bring him with you. I want to talk to him. Does he have any children?"

Several months later Reginald Denny and I went up to Harlem to meet Bill Cosby. Without fanfare, without any publicity, Cosby established a trust fund which has paid for the education of Ashley Denny.

While the result of this case was less than satisfying, in fact I considered it time well spent. I had the opportunity to get to know a person who represents the best of what we are as Americans. I only wish I could have been more successful.

I had represented many famous and high-profile clients before Reginald Denny, celebrities as well as business leaders. In Los Angeles and in the legal community throughout the country I was well known and respected. When Denzel Washington was research-ing his role as an attorney for the movie *Philadelphia* he spent time with Carl Douglas and me. I was regularly receiving awards. I had a loving family, a strong relationship with my church, a very success-ful practice, an extremely comfortable life, and financial security. As a leader in the community I was active in many charities. I had made it. I was set. Everything I had ever dreamed about achieving had come true. I felt that I had made a difference in the lives of many people. I had seen an evolution in my city, from my formative years when African-Americans played no role at all in the daily commerce and governing of that city to the point where a black man, Tom Bradley, had served as our mayor. Things weren't perfect, there was still too much poverty in the minority community, the police still treated minorities differently, racism still existed in many places; the playing field certainly wasn't equal—but the changes had been substantial and extremely gratifying.

While I never really thought about it, I suppose I anticipated that the next few years of my career simply would be a continuation of everything I'd built. On the morning of June 12, 1994, I had finished an early-morning workout in my home and joined Dale, who was watching the *Today* show. Only a few hours earlier police had discovered the bodies of Nicole Brown, the former wife of O. J. Simpson, and an unidentified male outside her home in Brentwood. They had both been stabbed to death. From these sketchy reports it appeared to have been a particularly brutal crime.

I don't remember all of my thoughts that morning. I had a casual acquaintance with O. J.; in years past we'd had spent an occasional evening together. But we weren't close friends and I'd never met Nicole. I watched the events of that day and the next days, as O. J. moved from the distraught ex-husband to the primary suspect, mostly as a fascinated observer. I suspected that on some minor level I would be involved, as a high-profile African-American criminal attorney in Los Angeles it would have been surprising if I was not somehow involved in a high-profile crime in Los Angeles involving an African-American.

But what I never suspected, what no one could ever have anticipated in those first few days, was that it would change forever the lives of so many people. It was like feeling the first cool breezes of a hurricane. No one could possibly have anticipated the force of the storm.

The media descended on L.A. and anyone with even a remote connection to Simpson was considered a desirable interview. This was one of those rare cases that transcended the gap between legitimate mainstream media and the supermarket tabloids. My phone began ringing incessantly, and that first day I agreed to appear on several shows, among them Larry King's show on CNN and Ted Koppel's *Nightline*.

Within days O. J. Simpson began calling me from his jail cell, asking me to join his defense team. Initially, I refused. I knew how disruptive this case would be to my life; I knew it would require a real investment of time. I wasn't sure I wanted to make that commitment. I watched with interest as his primary attorney, Bob Shapiro, put together a team of experienced and qualified attorneys. Among them were people I admired, like Gerry Uelmen and forensic pathologists Michael Baden and Henry Lee.

But still the calls came from Simpson.

During the preliminary hearing I worked as an expert commentator for Tom Brokaw on *NBC Nightly News*. I hesitated to criticize other attorneys, although at times I was surprised at their actions. It didn't appear to me that they had developed a cohesive strategy; rather, it seemed like they were responding to each crisis as it occurred. But I refrained from criticizing anyone; my experience had taught me how unfair it was to sit on the sidelines commenting on people in the middle of the fray.

The pressure on me to join the defense team never eased. I remembered a speech I'd given in which I said that I had known several very competent black lawyers who had spent much of their careers preparing, preparing, preparing and never got the opportunity to prove just how good they were. I said in that speech that when you get the opportunity you can't stand on the sidelines. You have to take advantage of it.

While this certainly was not the first opportunity of my lifetime, indeed, there was a feeling that I was standing on the sidelines watching the big game being played. There was no single moment when it suddenly became obvious to me that I should get involved in Simpson's defense, but as weeks passed it just seemed the most natural thing to do. Finally I joined the defense team. Soon after that O. J. Simpson decided that I would replace Robert Shapiro as the head of the team. Admittedly, from the beginning there were some bad feelings between myself and Bob Shapiro, who made it clear he believed our client was involved in the murders, and unfortunately that situation never improved.

It was obvious from the day that Simpson was arrested that this trial had star-making capabilities. Most trials impact only the lives of the accused and, in a more general sense, the legal profession. With rare exceptions trials occupy only a few lines of newsprint and a few days' attention. But this trial carried with it a tidal wave of opportunity and there were numerous people and institutions that wanted to ride that wave: lawyers and journalists and politicians, the LAPD, the FBI. A new cable channel, Court TV, was going to broadcast every minute of the trial. Reputations would be made or broken, a lot of money was at stake. This was a coming together of the best people in numerous fields to prove their worth.

The district attorney's office went to war on this case. I had been trying cases for three decades and only once before had I seen attitudes similar to what I experienced in this case, and that was in the trial of Black Panther Geronimo Pratt, who was falsely accused of murder. In that case the government took illegal actions to insure a conviction. Among other actions, they wiretapped my telephone to listen to constitutionally protected conversations, had an informant secreted in the defense environs, and refused to inform us—as mandated by law—that the star prosecution witness was a confidential informant. It literally took three decades to prove that Pratt was innocent, and finally we did it. But it was while representing Pratt that I fully understood that the government doesn't always work for the benefit of justice, that the government can become the enemy of its people.

In the Simpson case the DA's office had a scorched earth policy—anyone who got in the way of a conviction was going to suffer the consequences. For a murder case in which two people were killed the prosecutor spent almost $10 million; forty-three prosecutors worked on this case in addition to twelve law clerks and several dozen officers from the LAPD. They used the services of the FBI and Interpol and every department of the LAPD. The DA's office had recently lost several major cases. In the Menendez brothers case, in which wealthy parents allegedly had been brutally murdered by their two sons, they had gotten a hung jury. The DA, Gil

Garcetti, whom I had known, respected, and worked with, had promised the citizens of Los Angeles that his office was not going to lose any more major cases. Prosecutors Marcia Clark and Chris Darden were rising stars in the prosecutor's office, and winning this case would make them nationally famous and probably serve as a platform for greater success. Clarence Darrow noted long ago that a trial is not a search for the truth, but rather it's an arena where contesting lawyers fight not for justice, but to win. Marcia Clark and Chris Darden wanted to win every bit as much as I did. As history has proved, their careers depended on it. At its core the O. J. Simpson case was a double homicide. The trial was to determine the guilt or innocence—and the future life—of one man, but literally hundreds of people had a substantial stake in its outcome. It was never about justice; it was always about winning.

The trial was the most sensational media event of the decade, maybe the century. The facts are known; they have been written about and commented upon endlessly. In this criminal trial O. J. Simpson was found not guilty of the murders of his former wife, Nicole Brown, and Ron Goldman, the young man who worked as a waiter at a nearby Italian restaurant. But the impact of that trial, both personally and on race relations in this country, have reverberated through the ensuing years. The passage of time has permitted participants as well as observers to put the trial into perspective. As the years have gone by it has become clear that several aspects of the trial have continued relevance. For myself, without question, the most important aspect of the trial was the discovery of audiotapes made several years earlier, supposedly in preparation for a movie script by Mark Fuhrman, the L.A. police officer who had played a significant role in the discovery of the primary evidence against Simpson.

From the day I entered the case the defense strategy was straightforward and basic. We contended that there had been a rush to judgment. That almost immediately the police decided that O. J.

Simpson had committed these murders and the objective of their entire investigation was to prove that, rather than conducting a complete and fair investigation and allowing the evidence to lead them to the killer or killers.

And to prove that they would do whatever was necessary. In the real world, as I've said, the police don't always tell the truth. They sometimes manufacture evidence. They sometimes plant evidence. They sometimes are biased. In that they are just like the rest of society. We did not set out to put the police on trial. I am not antipolice—I am for police doing their job properly, being honest—but the evidence that had been gathered by the police just didn't fit the timeline the prosecution had established. So we felt it was necessary to show that there is such a thing as police perjury, that police do plant evidence, and that police officers lie when it suits their own interests. That was our basic strategy, and the Mark Fuhrman tapes supported it.

Simply, the Fuhrman tapes are to the criminal justice system in America what Watergate was to the political system. Even before the trial began we had learned that Mark Fuhrman represented the very worst elements of the Los Angeles Police Department—and society. We were told by a witness that he was a collector of Nazi memorabilia and that on occasion he wore a hidden swastika pin on his uniform. While in public he appeared to be a reasonably articulate professional, in fact he was a lying thug. We just couldn't prove it. Before Fuhrman was scheduled to testify I approached Chris Darden, a black member of the prosecution, a person I respected, and someone who knew the truth about Mark Fuhrman. "My brother," I said to him, "I'm telling you, don't get involved with Fuhrman's testimony. You have a life after this trial. You're a black man. Don't do it." I know Chris Darden thought I was up to some trick, but he did not question Fuhrman. Fuhrman was Marcia Clark's witness. Chris Darden has never said thank you, but he knows I gave him the proper advice.

Throughout the entire trial, almost daily we received telephone calls from people claiming to have materials that would be important to our case. We investigated many of them; few of them panned out. But one day Lee Bailey's investigator, Pat McKenna, learned that a screenwriter had in her possession audiotapes of a long, long interview she had conducted with Mark Fuhrman. Supposedly these tapes would confirm that Fuhrman was a racist. Most importantly, during the trial Fuhrman had sworn under oath that within the prior ten years he had never used the word *nigger*, but on these tapes he used it frequently. If this was true, and we could play the tapes in court, Fuhrman's credibility would be destroyed.

I am a religious man. I find comfort in my faith. I have long been active in my church, and I attend services regularly. I do pray a lot during trials. I don't pray to win, but rather that I will be able to do the best that I can. That I will be strong. That I will be prepared. That I will leave no stone unturned. I pray that the Lord will use me as His instrument to achieve justice. And then I pray that whatever His will, whatever God has in store for me, I will be prepared for it and I will accept it.

Several times during the Simpson trial I prayed that the Lord would reveal to me why I had been chosen to do this, to be at the center of this storm. I always felt there was a reason I was there.

The tapes were in possession of a writer named Laura Hart McKinny living in Winston-Salem, North Carolina. Based on the description of the tapes from a young lawyer who had heard them, I flew to North Carolina with a subpoena from Judge Lance Ito to take possession of them. And as I sat in the chambers of a North Carolina judge listening to them, I finally understood why I was there.

The Fuhrman tapes supported everything I had been saying about some members of the Los Angeles Police Department since the day Barbara Deadwyler walked into my office. After spending decades of my career fighting dishonest and corrupt police officers,

I finally could show the whole world a cop who willfully committed perjury in a murder trial. I felt vindicated. This was the evidence that racism was rampant inside the LAPD. As I listened to these tapes it was very difficult not to think back to Leonard Deadwyler and Ron Settles—and the fact that in the latter's case, tapes made at the time of his arrest had been destroyed only one month after his killing—and Herb Avery, Phillip Eric Johns, and all the other African-Americans and Latinos who had been killed or maimed for the crime of being black or brown.

People contend that Fuhrman was making it up, they were just stories for a movie script. But I contended he wasn't talking about a movie script; he was describing the culture inside the LAPD. He was talking about his life as a cop. Framing people, setting up people, killing people. And Internal Affairs, the branch of the police department charged with investigating and stopping this behavior, did nothing. We are like God, he said, we can do whatever we want. It was a confession; choke holds, murder, lying, and nigger this, nigger that, coming from the man, the Los Angeles detective, who swore, took an oath and swore, that he had never used that word. On these tapes he talked about bombing and burning all African-Americans. He said he loved working in the police station in the 77th Division because it had the smell of dead niggers who had been killed there. These tapes were chilling. They completely destroyed his credibility, they made his previous testimony about the evidence he had supposedly discovered at Simpson's house absolutely worthless.

After we heard portions of these tapes and read the full transcription, we asked that Fuhrman be recalled. Many times in my career I had been asked, "Do you really believe that a police officer would lie in a murder case?"

And each time I had replied, "Did the sun rise this morning?" And after more than two decades, we were going to prove it.

Chris Darden was not in court that day. The traps that my colleague F. Lee Bailey had so brilliantly laid for Fuhrman during his initial testimony, when he put him squarely on record as claiming he had never used the word *nigger* in the previous decade, were now sprung. Among the questions Fuhrman was asked was whether or not he had planted evidence.

It should have been a simple question. But Fuhrman refused to answer it, claiming his constitutional right against self-incrimination. For me, his refusal was the answer.

Only very brief portions of the tapes were permitted to be placed in evidence by Judge Ito. The judge was worried that their inflammatory nature would prejudice the jury, and perhaps bear more emotional weight than necessary. By playing small portions he felt the defense would be able to make the significant and necessary point that Fuhrman was a liar and that his testimony should be evaluated with that in mind. Fuhrman was eventually fined $200. That's the price put on lying under oath in a trial that could have resulted in a man losing his freedom for the rest of his life: $200. And as far as I know, he never even paid the whole fine. It doesn't seem sufficient. We proved he committed perjury; he should have gone to jail for it. And for those people who clung to the fantasy that Fuhrman was making all of it up, that a Los Angeles police officer would never do anything like that, it all was proven true several years later when it was revealed that in the Rampart Division of the LAPD, officers routinely made false arrests, beat up whomever they felt like, stole drugs held in evidence and sold them, engaged in illegal shootings, planted "evidence" to justify arrests and killings, framed innocent people, and committed perjury. As the *Los Angeles Times* concluded, "An organized criminal subculture thrived within the [Rampart Division of the] LAPD."

For years we had known that was true, and finally we had Detective Mark Fuhrman on tape admitting it. I wonder how all those people, including reporters and columnists, who defended him, who criticized the defense team for claiming that the police had planted evidence, reacted to reports about the Rampart Division?

The complete Fuhrman tapes have still never been made available to the public. These many years later I fail to understand why. As I said in my summation to the jury, "(B)oth prosecutors have now agreed that we have convinced them beyond a reasonable doubt that Mark Fuhrman is a lying, perjuring, genocidal racist, and he has testified falsely in this case..." Yet he's gotten away with it, he's emerged with his reputation generally intact. He's been rehabilitated. Since the trial Fuhrman has written several best-selling books and been embraced and defended by respected authors like Dominick Dunne. This is one of the worst people I have ever known, so what possibly could possess Dunne to defend him? It's sad, very sad. At one point ABC intended to hire him as an expert commentator until a network news vice president stood firmly against it. If people were permitted to hear these tapes I feel confident Fuhrman's career would end quite abruptly and he would be forced to crawl back into his hole, never to be heard from again.

As important as these tapes proved to be in the trial, I knew that finding them was the reason I was led to become involved in the Simpson case. After these tapes and the Rampart scandal I don't believe any rational person could still harbor doubts that racism was woven into the fabric of the LAPD.

I have never accused every LAPD officer of being racist or committing illegal actions. I have had many friends—and still do—who had served there long and honorably. I have long had great respect for many police officers—it is a difficult and dangerous job and many of them do it extraordinarily well; but not for the Mark Fuhrmans, and not for those officers who knew what was going on and failed to come forward. After the trial an L.A. cop took me aside and lamented, "Did you have to humiliate us?"

To which I replied, "You did it yourself."

For many people the single phrase with which I became forever associated was my reminder to the jury concerning the bloody glove found at Simpson's house that the prosecution claimed belonged to him, "If the glove doesn't fit, you must acquit." Not only was that the most memorable line in the entire trial, it's the line that eventually will be cited by *Bartlett's Familiar Quotations,* the line endlessly quoted to me by people, the line by which I'll be remembered, and I suspect it will probably be my epitaph.

The actual line came from a member of our "dream team," Professor Gerald Uelmen. In our strategy sessions we were continually commenting on the fact that the prosecution's case just didn't make sense. They had gathered a mountain of evidence but under careful examination it was more like a pile of dirt. The parts just didn't fit their version of how the murders were committed. In the past I had often used rhymes in my summations; I'd found that juries enjoyed them, understood them, and most importantly, remembered them. It was a unique way of summing up a case. When I was involved in a major pollution case in Louisiana, for example, I warned the defendant, "If you pollute, we'll file suit."

In the Simpson case when the hour got late and we all got tired, we'd create rhymes to describe our strategy. Among the early candidates was, "If it doesn't make sense, you must find for the defense." But when Gerry Uelmen told us, "If it doesn't fit, you must acquit," it became shorthand for the case we were putting together. So it fit perfectly in my summation of our case. The prosecution's evidence just didn't fit.

I am unhappy to admit that few people have done as much for truly bad rhyming as I have. For a time it seemed like everybody was parodying that phrase. When Indiana University's legendary basketball coach Bobby Knight was fired for a series of offenses, a writer speculated that eventually he would be tried and as his defense attorney I would tell jurors, "If you do not sin, you cannot win," and "If the team's a hit, you must acquit."

When a Columbus, Ohio, radio station publicly invited O. J. Simpson to call them and they would send him a ticket to come to Columbus for a round of golf, they suggested, "If he makes the call, he can hit the ball!"

A *Cincinnati Enquirer* columnist, bemoaning the fact that newspapers often opt for catchy headlines that sometimes are more clever than truthful, suggested, "Johnnie Cochran's Rule of Headline Writing is, 'If you can't alliterate, don't pontificate.'"

A disc jockey in Atlanta suggested that in my summation in the Sean "Puffy" Combs trial I might remind the jurors, "If Puffy didn't shoot, you ain't got poot."

And, admittedly, even I was not above a bad parody. During a mock trial in which I represented a woman whose husband had died aboard the *Titanic*—and won $1.5 million damages for her—I told the jury, "If you design and build a boat, it must be able to stay afloat!"

But obviously the most controversial charge that emerged after the verdict was that I had "played the race card" to win the trial, I had "inflamed racial passions" by persuading black jurors to vote their skin color rather than their belief based solely on the evidence presented in that courtroom, that I had urged them to "send a message with their verdict" and that by so doing I had set back race relations in this country.

People worked themselves into an emotional fervor over this verdict. They lost any semblance of objectivity. Even years later many people remain so certain they know what happened that night in Brentwood that they refuse to look at the facts, preferring to rely on their emotions. As one columnist wrote bitterly in *Commentary*, "Cochran operated at the very margins of competence ... and in general presented a case that certainly would have lost before any jury not chosen for its prejudices and ignorance."

It is a vile charge. It is the most preposterous thing in the entire world. It is absurd to charge an African-American with playing the race card in America. As Bill Cosby wondered, "Who owns the deck? Who dealt the cards? What are you talking about?"

To deal with the criticism Cosby suggested I remember an old joke. "There was this black guy in the middle of the desert," he said. "He's buried in sand up to his neck. He can't even move his arms. There are a bunch of white guys on horseback, and they ride toward him swinging their swords. As they swing their swords at his head, somehow he manages to move his head out of the way. And with that they started screaming at him, 'Fight fair, nigger!' "

Until this trial I don't remember ever hearing the term *race card*, and, in fact, I despise it. It trivializes the racial problems we have in this country. Racial intolerance isn't a card game, it's reality. It has been the single most divisive issue in this country for two centuries. At different times over two hundred years it has ripped apart this country, race has been the primary factor in countless deaths, and I take the racial problems we have in America much too seriously to use race to help defend a single client.

The charge that I could convince black jurors to vote to acquit a man they believed to be guilty of two murders because he is black is an insult to all African-Americans. Day after day in cities all over this country, in Cleveland, Detroit, Atlanta, black jurors vote to convict black criminals. Statistics show that the conviction rate for juries that include black jurors is just as high as it is for juries consisting mostly of white people.

The charge against me was that I persuaded the jury to use this trial to "send a message" to white America. In fact, while the jury was predominately African-American, it included several white people. Coincidently, not too long after the Simpson verdict Clint Eastwood sued the *National Enquirer* and won, and the media reported that the jury "had sent a message to the press." Juries always send messages with their verdict. What I asked the jury to do was, "Look at this evidence. There is reasonable doubt in this case. If you don't find there is a reasonable doubt, the message you will send is that police perjury, police corruption should just continue. It's the order of the day. . . . Otherwise, in my judgment, the cover-up continues."

Not surprisingly, when Simpson was found liable for the deaths in a second, civil trial by a predominately white jury in the fashionably white city of Santa Monica, few people dared suggest that this mostly white jury had voted along racial lines.

The primary advantage that I had with this jury was that they were familiar with the history of the Los Angeles Police Department. They'd lived it. Several of these jurors knew from personal experience that police officers do not hesitate to lie—even under oath—or plant evidence when it suits their needs. So when we showed that Fuhrman had collected significant evidence—had the opportunity to plant significant evidence and then had gotten on the witness stand and lied—these jurors knew his testimony was worthless.

Fuhrman lied because he felt comfortable lying in a courtroom, because the system had always tolerated his lying; judges looked the other way and jurors were supposed to accept it. But not this time, not this time.

Mark Fuhrman was the prosecution's witness. They put him on the stand, they vouched for his credibility; in essence, they told the jury, believe this man and you'll have all the evidence you need to convict Simpson. My job, my job as with any witness, was to deal with his credibility. That's all we did; we impeached him and proved he was a liar. If we had not attacked him we would have been guilty of malpractice. But it was easier for the prosecution to describe that as "playing the race card."

Of course race played an important role in this trial, as it has in just about every significant event involving a black man in this country's history. The allegations in this case were oddly reminiscent of those made against Emmett Till, a black teenager lynched by a mob for allegedly whistling at a white woman. Half a century later a black man was accused of killing his beautiful blonde ex-wife and it became the dominant media event in the entire world. I wonder—although I'm confident I know the answer—would this trial have attracted as much attention if the victim had been O. J. Simpson's first wife, who was an African-American?

The verdict did not surprise me. I knew we had won the night before the decision was announced simply because the jury returned its verdict forms in eight minutes. These are somewhat complicated forms that juries must fill out after deciding on guilt or innocence. On those forms numerous determinations need to be made; the only possible way jurors could have completed the forms so quickly was by checking the not guilty box.

What did surprise me, however, was the reaction to the verdict—not by African-Americans, but by white America. There has been tremendous criticism of the entire African-American community for the reaction of some people, many people in fact, who celebrated when the verdict was announced. The fact that many black people rejoiced at the verdict engendered tremendous resentment from the white community. That white anger surprised me much more than the response of the minority community. That anger was somewhat inimical to the American way. In this country, if an accused person is truly cloaked in the presumption of innocence and there is a jury of one's peers—this was not an all-black jury—and he is acquitted, then I would expect the people would be more than willing to accept that verdict.

Many people did not. But the minority community cheered because we've had a history in which the justice system hasn't always worked for us. From the time of Emmett Till, from the time of the Scottsboro Boys and murdered civil rights leader Medgar Evers, from the little girls killed in Birmingham, Alabama, when racists blew up their church, from the Simi Valley trial of the officers who beat Rodney King, when white people have been accused of murdering and maiming blacks and the jury stayed out for fifteen minutes before acquitting them and members of the jury knew all the accused by their first name, black people accepted the rule of law. In fact, all along African-Americans have been among the staunchest supporters of the Constitution because they believed that it held the best hope of ever getting relief. This time I think there was a belief that it worked in our favor, the presumption of innocence had pertained. Justice had been denied blacks in America for a long, long time. And finally they saw someone who looked just like them get the benefits of the system.

The night of the verdict I celebrated with about twenty-five people by going to dinner at a popular Los Angeles restaurant. Someone immediately phoned the restaurant with a bomb threat. There were many people who blamed me because justice was done in that courtroom—and they did not agree with that verdict. Some of those people have never resolved those feelings and remain embittered about it. Several months after the trial ended *The New Yorker* ran a cartoon captioned, "Extra! Extra! O. J. Simpson's still not guilty!" And while eventually he was found liable in the civil trial—in which evidence of Fuhrman's racism was not permitted to be heard—he is going to be not guilty of all criminal charges forever. That isn't going to change.

Within the African-American community I was a hero. The Reverend Dr. Calvin Butts, the dynamic pastor of Harlem's famed Abyssinian Baptist Church, explained, "Our people were cheering because a black man had used his talents, his gifts, and his ability to upset the system and bring forth a verdict no one thought possible." Black people often come up to me simply to say thank you. They say, "Thank you for standing up for us," "Thank you for showing the world that competence comes in all colors." At a dinner in 2001, Jesse Jackson commented that we had "de-Calhounized the legal profession."

But as time passed I could see the feelings many white people had about me were mellowing. It happened gradually, but in distinct stages. Initially they simply recognized me: "There's O. J. Simpson's lawyer . . ."; "Hey look, there's Johnnie Cochran." Then it became, "You got that murderer off—I didn't agree with the verdict, but you did a heck of a job." And that evolved into, "Maybe I didn't agree with the verdict, but if I needed a lawyer you'd be the person I'd call." And finally, "Hey Johnnie, how you doing today?"

Most members of the defense team went through the same process, but not O. J. Simpson. It is striking to me how desperately some people really want to punish him for not being convicted of murder in his criminal trial. They just can't let him be. In Florida, for example, while driving his car in December 2000, he got into an argument with another motorist. This type of thing is so common it has a name; road rage. But because O. J. Simpson was involved the case gained national attention. Simpson was charged with felony burglary for allegedly reaching into another man's car and a misdemeanor battery charge for pulling that man's eyeglasses off his face. If he had been convicted of both charges he would be facing sixteen years in prison. Sixteen years—for an incident in which no one was hurt. After a monthlong trial he was acquitted because, as one juror explained, "Our decision was because of a lack of evidence."

In December 2001, a squad of federal agents invaded Simpson's Florida home because his name was mentioned in a conversation between dealers of the drug ecstasy.

None of the members of the criminal trial defense team is currently advising him. He doesn't need us; he's a grown man. I have spoken with him on an irregular basis. While I think it is impossible for anyone to know how they would respond if they were in his unique situation, I do think it is fair to say that some of the things he's said and some of the schemes in which he's gotten involved were probably not as well thought out as they should have been. But none of that is sufficient reason to continue to harass him. Threatening sixteen years for a road argument is simply vindictive.

On those rare occasions when I look back on the trial, admittedly I have one regret. The Simpson family sat on one side of the courtroom and Fred Goldman, Ron Goldman's father, and his family sat on the other side. It was only a few feet, but it was an impossibly long distance. When I looked at him, when I looked at his family, I saw their pain. I'm quite sure Fred Goldman hates me; I'm not thin-skinned about that. I can deal with it. I had my job to do, I did it, and I would do it again. I will always be proud of my efforts and that of the entire defense team in this case. But I wish there was some way I could have spoken with him. I would have said to him, "I have to do this job because this is the way our system works. You can't just think someone is guilty, it has to be proven." I would have liked to express my sorrow for the loss of his son. I'm certain he doesn't want to hear that from me, but I regret not having had the opportunity to do so.

Finally, on occasion I am still asked my own opinion about the guilt or innocence of O. J. Simpson. Supposedly I've told a few very close friends that I thought he was guilty of the crimes. That is simply not true. I can state unequivocally that I have never, ever said to anyone that O. J. Simpson was guilty. Only once in my career has a person I was defending confessed to the crime of which he was accused, and it was not O. J. Simpson. From the first conversation I had with him till the last, he claimed to be innocent. He never wavered. I wasn't at the scene on June 12, 1994. Only the victims and the killer or killers were there. The rest of us can only speculate—and that includes me. What I do know for certain is that every single thing O. J. Simpson told us that we could investigate turned out to be true. If he told us there was a letter in a safe deposit box, we were able to find that letter. If he told us he had spoken with someone, that person verified it. Every time.

If the prosecution was correct that the murders occurred at approximately 10:40 P.M., it would have been just about physically impossible for Simpson to be neatly dressed and on his way to the airport less than a half hour later. The prosecution could never explain what happened to all the blood the killer or killers must have gotten on their clothing. I also believe, based on evidence presented during the trial, that LAPD officers planted Simpson's blood on both the back fence at the murder scene and on his socks found in his bedroom. Did they try to frame a man they believed was guilty? All I know is there were too many things about their theories of the case that made no sense.

While I understand all the reasons people believe O. J. Simpson committed these two murders, the case presented by the prosecution didn't come close to proving that without a reasonable doubt.

In addition to finally proving that an LAPD detective would lie in his zeal for a conviction, the trial exposed at least two extremely important problems that we need to deal with, and while we've made some progress since the end of the trial, these problems have not been solved. The Simpson case did not create the division between the races, it exposed it. Most white people still can't understand the depth of feeling in the African-American community about this trial, about the criminal justice system in general. Most white people don't understand that African-Americans do not believe we are afforded equal opportunity in this country. There is a reason based in history that although 12 percent of the population of this country is black, in my lifetime there have been only two African-American United States senators, only 3 percent of the lawyers and doctors are black, and 95 percent of the top-salaried jobs are held by white males. The institutions of this country had been sealed against African-Americans for so long that while the laws may have changed, the traditions haven't. Blacks were thrilled to see that the criminal justice system, with all its idiosyncrasies, could be made to work in their behalf.

The trial also revealed problems in that criminal justice system. The tools of crime solving have progressed much faster than the abilities of the people who use them. Police officers simply are not properly trained to employ the most recent advances in forensic science. Imagine trying to dig a hole with the wrong end of a shovel. The way the LAPD collected, identified, and processed evidence was dreadful. It was unprofessional and led to much of the evidence being tainted.

As a direct result of the Simpson case a national movement has developed in forensic science to regulate crime labs—to accredit them, license them, hold them to higher standards, give them proficiency tests, and raise the quality. Even the FBI crime lab has since become accredited. Unfortunately, there is still a tremendous lack of crime-scene training for police officers, the people who usually arrive first at the crime scene and collect much of the evidence. As Peter Neufeld and Barry Scheck have proven numerous times with their Innocence Project, innocent people are sitting in our prisons—some of them on death row. We now have many of the weapons we need to prevent more innocent people from joining them—and for putting guilty people in prison—but there is an unfortunate hesitancy on the part of law enforcement to implement them. That remains a danger to all of us.

Perhaps the final lesson we've learned is the cost of justice in real dollars. The state has at its disposal almost unlimited resources, and can spend just about whatever is deemed necessary. If experts are needed the prosecution can hire them. Few defendants have the resources to compete. It's very difficult for a poor man to get a fair trial in this country, very difficult. There is little question that O. J. Simpson would have been convicted if he were not a wealthy man. He couldn't have hired a team of lawyers, we couldn't have done our own investigation, we couldn't have proved someone had tampered with the evidence. If a person lacks the finances to level the playing field he cannot mount a credible defense.

Many people in this country will never forget where they were on December 7, 1941, September 11, 2001, and October 3, 1995, the day the verdict in the Simpson case was announced. For a few hours that day the entire country paused to listen as Judge Ito's clerk read the jury's verdict. And then, thrilled and infuriated, we went back to work. The verdict divided the country, primarily along racial lines. I was and I still am very concerned about that. But a wise man named John H. Johnson, of Chicago, Illinois, the founder and publisher of *Ebony Jet*, advised, "You remind me of Thurgood Marshall with *Brown v. the Board of Education.* The white people were angry with him. They thought that their daughters were all going to marry black guys. This was the worst thing that could ever happen. He got death threats.

"John, it's time to move on."

Move on. We have a system of justice in this country. We have rules. We played by those rules. We had a jury. They worked for one year for five dollars a day and made their finding. That's the American system. People may not agree with the verdict. They may not like it. But that is the system and once the jury has reached its verdict, the only thing to do—as I have learned in victory and defeat—is move on.

FIVE

On comedian Chris Rock's first show for HBO his guests were
myself and "The artist formerly known as Prince."

"Let me ask you this," Chris Rock began our interview, "does
O. J. owe you any money?"

I nodded. "I think he owes me about eight-point-six million
dollars—no, I'm only kidding, only kidding."

"Yeah," he said, "just slightly kidding."

"No, no, no, I'm only kidding."

"Yeah, you better be kidding," he warned, " 'cause you never
know what might happen." A few minutes later he asked, "Everybody talks about race in the trial. You think looks had anything to
do with it? 'Cause O. J. is a good-looking guy now."

It was actually a good question. Appearance can matter in the
courtroom. "You know, I've had cases with good-looking defendants. I once had a case where we had pictures of the defendant in
his briefs. And you should have seen this jury. They were just mesmerized by pictures of this man. And so looks did have something
to do with it."

Finally he asked me if I thought the media in this country had
treated me unfairly. "I accept what takes place, but let me put it
this way. Under the circumstances there are a lot of people in the
media who prejudged the Simpson case, and they prejudged everything we did. And I think if I were white it would be a different situation."

"If you were white," Chris Rock agreed, "you'd be like Tom Cruise in *The Firm*."

When I appeared on Keenan Ivory Wayans's program he asked, "You have sort of a love-hate thing going on with the public. Did you ever regret doing that trial?"

"Not at all. I would do the same thing in a minute. I did my job. Love me or hate me, but respect me."

On the sitcom *The Hughleys*, I was the surprise attorney for a nasty neighbor who was claiming the sad dog Darryl Hughley had found had bitten him. "You know what I always say, Mr. Hughley," I read my lines, "Why put the pedal to the metal, when it's friendlier to settle!" And in my summation to the jury I pointed out, "I would conclude my remarks by saying, A dog is no longer a friend to man, once he bites you in the can."

On *Roseanne*, I appeared in a skit with my friend and confidant, defense attorney Leslie Abramson, as opposing counsel on a parody of all the new court shows, *Judge Roseanne*. I even made the soap operas, playing myself on *Guiding Light*. It was a typical soap opera plot involving human cloning, a comatose police officer, and a woman accused of murder. When I first walked into the "courtroom," the prosecutor said, "Oh my God, they have Johnnie Cochran."

Truthfully, I did not recall hearing those words from Marcia Clark or Chris Darden.

But that's what the Simpson trial did for me. My transformation from a Los Angeles attorney to a media celebrity—and a lawyer asked to become involved in some of the most important civil litigation taking place in the country—had begun. What helped a lot, I believe, was my willingness to go along with the jokes about me. About my rhymes, the flashy way I dressed, my sometimes skillful use of the English language. "A designer in Oregon is introducing a line of neckties inspired by the neckties Johnnie Cochran wears," David Letterman said in his monologue. "The guy says they come in fifty different varieties . . . kind of like O. J.'s alibis."

On Barbara Walters's *The View*, comedienne Joy Behar's dog Max supposedly was "getting married" and she went with him to "the best lawyer money could buy," for a prenuptial agreement. "Everything looks good," I explained seriously, "the doghouse, dish, and bone are all in his name . . . and his squeaky toy." And then I gave him some advice: "Remember, Max, if the bone ain't buried, you ain't married."

When Jerry Seinfeld and friends were "arrested" for watching a holdup without aiding the victim, they hired a lawyer who looked like me, talked like me, and dressed . . . at least he looked like me and talked like me.

A popular Internet joke listed suggestions for the closing argument I would make if I was representing President Clinton in his impeachment: "The economy's great, let the white boy skate."

I heard all the jokes. I laughed at a lot of them. I have always taken my work completely seriously, I take my responsibility to my family, my church, and my clients seriously—but I've always been able to laugh at myself.

In addition to the comedy shows, I did all the interview shows, all of them, some several times. *Today, Good Morning America, Nightline, 60 Minutes*, all the cable shows, I was on the cover of *Time* and *Newsweek, Jet* and all the other black magazines. Most Americans knew me from only that trial, and I wanted people to understand there was a lot more to me than that. I did not want to be defined by any one case, even a case with a successful conclusion.

The trial had made me just about the best-known attorney in America. A poll taken at the Million Man March on Washington, D.C., found that the two most influential black men in the country were Louis Farrakhan and myself. The phones in my office rang continuously. My career took on almost mythical proportions, as if I had never lost a case—and I have lost cases. The media sometimes made it seem like I was invincible.

It was flattering, most of it. As long as I never permitted myself to forget exactly what I was, a practicing lawyer, and my goal, to change this country. And just in case I did forget, I continued to receive considerable hate mail as well as the occasional threat on my life. Believe me, I knew very well, as Katie Couric pointed out to me on the *Today* show, "A lot of people despise you. They think you're a snake oil salesman. They think you're slicker than slick."

For a practicing attorney the positive publicity I received was invaluable—and it began to pay off almost immediately. Long before I joined the Simpson defense team I had been retained by a young man named Sean Abrams. Abrams, rap star Snoop Doggy Dogg, and Snoop's bodyguard, McKinley Lee, had been charged with murder for a 1993 drive-by shooting.

I had represented and gotten to know several prominent hip-hop stars, including Tupac Shakur, Shuge Knight, and even Snoop, on other cases. The violence in that world sickened me, but there wasn't much I could do about it. The Snoop Dogg murder trial was scheduled to begin less than two weeks after the Simpson trial ended. I didn't have any time at all to savor the success in the Simpson case; I barely had time to change my suit. Then I had to go right back to work. As desperately tired as I was, I felt a young man had put his future in my hands.

I was hot copy. Just about everything I said ended up in the newspapers. I told reporters, "Once again, in this case the evidence is going to be a problem." I warned that the LAPD was going to be embarrassed again.

Perhaps the last thing the DA's office wanted was to lose another case to me. They approached me and offered to dismiss the case against my client. They knew he wasn't the shooter, they said, he was just in the car. I was thrilled, and my client reluctantly accepted the DA's offer. Loyalty was very important to him and he did not want to appear to be abandoning his friends.

The DA proceeded against Snoop and Lee, and after a four-month trial both men were acquitted of murder, as the jury believed they had acted in self-defense.

Among the biggest beneficiaries of the Simpson trial was the struggling cable TV channel Court TV. It had been founded in 1991 by *American Lawyer* magazine publisher Steve Brill for the purpose of broadcasting trials live. By covering the Simpson trial gavel-to-gavel just about all day, every day—and when the trial recessed for the day broadcasting shows on which lawyers analyzed, dissected, predicted, and argued about each day's events—it had gained tremendous recognition and millions of viewers. This was the channel that O. J. Simpson built. It was also a descendant of the Deadwyler coroner's inquiry, which had been broadcast live in Los Angeles a quarter century earlier.

Steve Brill invited me to a gala dinner celebrating the fifth anniversary of Court TV. At the panel discussion during the festivities I was seated next to a lovely, conservative female prosecutor from Atlanta, Georgia, named Nancy Grace. I knew her work—she was among those many lawyers-turned-TV-analysts who had spent considerable time criticizing my work in the trial—and she had reacted with disgust to the verdict. As Brill may have planned, Nancy and I really got into it that night. At one point she said something I thought was incorrect and I told her so. "You really don't know what you're talking about," I said about as politely as it is possible to say that.

She took umbrage at that, pointing out, "Well, I've never lost a case."

"That may be true," I responded, "but you've never tried a case against me or you wouldn't be saying that."

From that discussion Brill decided that Nancy and I should cohost a TV program. It was planned to be the legal version of CNN's popular *Crossfire;* this would be defense attorney versus prosecutor, liberal versus conservative, man versus woman, black versus white. We would be to the law what Siskel and Ebert were to movies. He offered me a guaranteed three-year contract worth millions of dollars. In addition I would be able to continue to practice law. But to do the show I had to spend considerable time in New York City, although I could maintain my Los Angeles practice. Keeping my practice was essential. After the trial Marcia Clark had quit the DA's office to host a TV program, claiming the Simpson trial had "ruined" any chance she had to get an impartial jury. But the practice of law was what I did, what fulfilled me. It was the essential element of my life. It's where I control the agenda, I control the playing field. There has not been a day when I haven't loved being a lawyer, even on the worst of my days in a courtroom, and I certainly would not have given up the law for a television show. But Brill was offering me the opportunity to do both.

The Simpson trial had created a market for lawyers and programs about the law on television. The networks had learned the value of treating law as entertainment; trials could be packaged as live soap operas and attract a substantial audience—and cost very little to produce. While a lot of people were against this, I actually thought it was a pretty good trend. I've never seen anything wrong with giving people access to the legal system as observers. I figured the more people who are watching the system the less chance anyone will have to abuse it. To me, it shined the light on the system.

I had received several other offers to host television programs. I was asked to be the judge on a *People's Court*–type show. I couldn't see myself adjudicating disputes of ruined laundry and who gets the goldfish in the divorce, so I turned that down. I was asked to be the lead attorney on a show analyzing whatever big cases were in the courts, but as I had little respect for most legal analysts who found it so easy to criticize while not knowing the California code of criminal procedure or understanding how to try a murder case, I turned that down. But Brill's offer appealed to me—except for that part about moving to New York City.

That was a challenge. I had spent considerable time in New York, and Dale certainly loved it, but I had grown up and spent my professional life in Los Angeles. My practice was based there. My family was there, my mother was buried there. I knew all the major players there—the mayor, the chief of police, the legal establishment—and I was known and respected there. I'd served on the Board of Airport Commissioners, I had been the president of the Black Business Association, I was involved in several charities. I was very happy in Los Angeles. Steve Brill wanted me to uproot my entire life and move to New York City to host a TV show. It didn't make a lot of sense, but there was something about it that was difficult to resist.

I recognized that this was a tremendous opportunity. Hosting a TV show would enable me to reach a mass audience and talk about whatever I wanted to talk about. I was also feeling quite misunderstood by people who knew me from only the Simpson case—there were quite a few people who thought of me as sort of the devil incarnate—and I felt this would give me the opportunity to show those people that my real objective was to fight for justice. I wanted them to see me as an advocate of the rule of law.

In addition, Peter Neufeld and Barry Scheck offered to provide space for me in their office in Tribeca, just as I had done for them in Los Angeles. Maybe we would even work on a few civil rights cases together. That prospect excited me; we had formed a strong bond, they had become soul mates and brothers. Both Peter and Barry are extraordinary lawyers whose politics mirror mine, but they were also loyal friends who kept a steady eye on my back. The chance to work with them again was particularly enticing for me.

When I was younger I had been a skydiver. I climbed mountains. I never turned away from a challenge. No one had ever won a police abuse lawsuit against the LAPD until we did it. I've always found it difficult to refuse a challenge, particularly a challenge as enticing as this one. Basically, I was being offered a national forum to argue for my own ideas. Now how could I not accept that?

It was time to move on. I thought I would quietly move to New

York and see how Dale and I enjoyed living there. After making headlines for two years, perhaps I could keep a low profile, or at least a lower profile. But as soon as Court TV announced that I was going to be spending substantial time in New York City co-hosting the show *Cochran & Grace,* the *Village Voice* ran a cartoon on its front page showing me as a giant bursting into the city pushing buildings out of the way. So much for making a quiet entrance.

I liked Nancy Grace. She's a very intelligent, articulate woman who became an attorney after her fiancé had been murdered. But coming to the law that way made her a strong advocate for the state. So we approached the middle from opposite sides. Because of that, Steve Brill thought there would be sparks between us every night, that I would argue every defendant was innocent and she would claim they were all guilty. When we were promoting the show it seemed like it might be that way. "He is the legal talent of our time," Nancy told reporters, "but I don't necessarily agree with anything he says."

The reporter then asked me how someone might hire me. "Well, you know . . ."

"First," she replied, "you have to be a famous football star. Then you've got be a billionaire."

"See," I said, "see how little she knows about me? She doesn't know about all those whom we call 'No Js' that I represent."

When I was asked if I continued to give advice to O. J. Simpson I said, "Yeah, when solicited. When he was on the stand [in Simpson's civil trial] I gave him some advice—just be succinct and tell the truth."

"That hurts, Johnnie," Nancy said, "that really hurts—that thing about telling the truth . . ."

Hosting a television show was new to both of us, so we were both sort of feeling our way. There was no training period, we had very little rehearsal, just a lot of advertisements wondering, "Has Johnnie Cochran finally met his match?" In January 1997, Nancy and I sat down shoulder-to-shoulder in the studio, they turned on the camera, and we were on the air. The problem with our program, as we discovered soon after going on the air, was that neither one of us believed the law was always black and white. It isn't quite that basic. Many times we found areas of agreement on the issue of the night, which softened the supposedly sharp edges of the show. The "intense verbal jousting" that Court TV had promised too often became a friendly conversation. The producers were always pushing us to be more passionate, telling me, "Show the same kind of passion you showed when arguing Pratt." They wanted me to be more theatrical; as a result, initially I felt stiff and uncomfortable.

But Steve Brill was correct in his assumption that I would bring a lot of attention to Court TV. Within months of starting the program I had received more virulent hate mail than any of the other attorneys on the network.

On the show we discussed the main legal issues of the day, which more and more were revolving around President Clinton, and we had occasional guests, but the show lacked the fire the network had anticipated. Unexpectedly, after a few months my patron saint Steve Brill sold Court TV to Time Warner. Within weeks the decision was made to reassign Nancy to trial coverage, which she loved. Eventually, Brill was replaced by the very astute Henry Schleiff, a lawyer who had produced a variety of shows, among them the Maury Povich and Montel Williams talk shows. He was an experienced TV producer.

The show was renamed *Cochran and Co.* and for the next six months I was the sole anchor. It gave me time to experiment, to learn what I should have known before I'd started. I had on a wide range of guests, and I found that the show worked best when I had on smart right-wingers, real hard-line conservatives. I invited all of the people from the Federalist Society, Ben Ginsberg, Barbara Olson, all of them. What surprised me was how much better prepared these people were than my more liberal guests. The liberals always wanted to speak from their hearts, while the conservatives would cite page numbers in obscure books. Liberals would paraphrase Thomas Jefferson; the conservatives would quote verbatim from the Federalist Papers. These conservatives were ideologues, they wanted to win, they wanted to be in charge. When the 2000 presidential election ended and Bush took charge, a lot of these people surfaced—and they were serious. Liberals sometimes seemed like they were just out there playing around, but these people meant exactly what they said. They're serious! They are focused. They believe! They've taken control of the airways and too many people seem to have caved in to them. It's a disgrace. Nobody stands up to them, nobody speaks out. It's astonishing to me. If you have an adverse thought these people are going to jump right on you. But because I disagreed with the right-wingers so completely it made for a very good debate—some nights we rubbed each other so badly we created the kind of friction Steve Brill had originally envisioned.

I also took telephone calls. I remember particularly the lady who called during a debate about reparations and said flatly, "I never had any slaves. I'm not apologizing."

Eventually Court TV paired me with the very respected Boston attorney, Rikki Klieman—who eventually married former New York City police commissioner Bill Bratton—to co-host the show with me. Like so many of us, the Simpson trial had brought Rikki to television as an analyst for Court TV. We were a good match. Our show covered serious legal topics, we did several shows about the misuse of the death penalty with Barry Scheck, focusing on cases in which apparently innocent people might have been put to death. We also covered the Jon Benet Ramsey investigation; one night we had on a group of Orthodox Jewish Yale students who had sued the university over its policy that forced freshmen and sophomores to live on campus, claiming that made it impossible for them to follow their beliefs; I remember the show we did with the attorneys representing the Texas Cattle Association who were suing Oprah Winfrey, claiming its members had suffered substantial damages due to a show she did about mad cow disease; and naturally we covered the legal problems of Bill Clinton.

Hosting a television program did not come naturally to me. Rarely, if ever, have I read directly from prepared notes in the courtroom, but for television I had to learn how to read a prepared script from a TelePrompTer and make it sound natural. Basically, most of the time I sounded like I was reading from a TelePrompTer while trying to sound natural. The one thing I did not sound was natural. I also had to learn how to ad lib, how to fill time by speaking.

Now, speaking publicly and extemporaneously is one thing with which I have never struggled. Words come easily to me. In addition to having made countless prepared speeches, several times I've been in situations where the scheduled speaker failed to arrive and I was asked to give the keynote speech . . . and I had about five minutes to prepare. I never panicked in those situations. I knew from experience that when I opened my mouth the proper words would come out. In fact, often my mind is several paragraphs ahead of my mouth, and those who know me well are used to hearing my voice speed up to try to catch up with my thoughts. In fact, only one time in my entire life do I remember being somewhat speechless. Unfortunately, that was while taking my wedding vows with Dale.

Dale and I had agreed that we would each write our own vows. Truthfully, I hadn't really prepared for the ceremony. I had always been able to find the words I needed when I needed them and I was confident that on this occasion it would be no different. I would simply tell her I loved her. Dale spoke first. Her words were poetry; they were beautiful and they were heartfelt. She mesmerized the entire audience.

And when she was done, everybody looked at me, waiting expectantly to hear a cascade of mellifluous words rolling gently off my golden tongue. Uh. . . . "Oh yes," I said, or something equally mundane, "and I pledge my love to you, too."

Rikki Klieman helped me considerably. Working with her, I became much more comfortable, much more me. The problem was that while we were having intelligent discussions, on other channels people were throwing stools at each other. Court TV's ratings had gone down considerably after the conclusion of the Simpson trial, and management was experimenting with new programming. For the first time the channel began re-running network series like *Law and Order* at night, cutting back on live programming. Eventually Henry Schleiff asked me to host my own program, a half-hour show entitled *Johnnie Cochran Tonight,* on which would interview a single guest.

My first guest on that show was Bill Cosby, the wonderful Bill Cosby, whose son, Ennis, had been murdered less than a year earlier. "I remember the last time I had dinner at your house," I began.

"Me, too," he agreed, "stuff's still missing."

Later on that show, while discussing the difficulties of parenting, Bill Cosby pointed out, "Remember, God was a single parent."

My guests on *Johnnie Cochran Tonight* were pretty much anybody I wanted to interview. We had Barbara Walters, Katie Couric, and Maya Angelou; Jenny Jones discussed the lawsuit against her show in which it was claimed she had triggered a murderous rage by introducing a man to a homosexual who had a crush on him. Spike Lee responded to critics of his movie *Summer of Sam*. Colin Powell appeared twice, I had conservative congressmen Newt Gingrich and Bob Barr and Democratic senator Joe Lieberman. I had Quincy Jones and Sean "Puffy" Combs and Russell Simmons. I had Larry King and Greta Van Susteren. On my show Chris Rock wondered, "Do you think ants should have abortions?" and then said the best thing about his career was that, "I've become a person my parents can be proud of." I spent several days in a maximum-security prison for a two-part interview with Wilbert Rideau, who had spent thirty-eight years in prison for a crime he'd committed when he was nineteen years old. I did several shows with white supremacists, including a man named Matthew Hale, who criticized me bitterly for "representing a murderer." I even put on Dennis Rodman's hat and Miss Universe's crown and wondered if that made me Mr. Universe. Geraldo Rivera (who had spent more than a year attacking me night after night, night after night, during the trial) and I made back-to-back appearances on each other's shows; the Simpson trial had rescued his career, it enabled him to get a $7 million contract at MSNBC. Travis Smiley got us together, telling Geraldo, "Cochran's not that bad. On the issues you guys are very similar." Geraldo is an interesting person and I respect him. He was man enough to come on my show and apologize for many of his remarks, admitting he finally understood I was doing my job. I got into a big argument with Ward Connelly, who had benefited greatly from affirmative action and then turned on it, suggesting we close the door after he got inside. And I did many, many shows about the Clinton impeachment hearings.

Overall I did 511 shows in three years on Court TV, including 139 nights of *Johnnie Cochran Tonight*. For most people, hosting a daily television show is a full-time job. More than a full-time job. But for me, it was something I did after I finished my day job, being an attorney. It was the ultimate moonlighting experience, but it was absolutely exhausting. I like to believe I have an endless reservoir of energy, I do like to believe that, but admittedly there were times when that reservoir was running mighty low. For three years I was the ultimate commuter. On Monday morning I'd catch an early flight from L.A. to New York, arriving about 3:00 P.M. and racing to the studio to do that night's show. Then as soon as the show ended Thursday I'd take the Delta red-eye back to L.A. I felt like I lived on an airplane, constantly going back and forth, back and forth. I couldn't just relax on those flights, I'd spend my time reading background material for upcoming shows or briefs and depositions for upcoming cases.

Every weekday, whether I was in New York or Los Angeles, I'd spend part of my time in the office doing legal work, but I'd have to stop several times for conference calls to arrange that night's show. There was never a moment to rest. If I was in L.A. I'd do the show at 4:30, so it could be broadcast live on the East Coast at 7:30. Conducting trials was impossible; when I couldn't avoid a trial I had to explain to judges why I needed to leave the courtroom early. Although many of them were understanding, there were some judges who believed that the American legal system was more important than my cable television show. And usually, when I finished the show, instead of going home I'd go back to the office to do a few more hours of legal work.

That was the glamorous life of a television personality.

I survived because I had an incredible staff. Just incredible. Our ratings were acceptable for cable TV, but Court TV wasn't carried by local cable companies in several important areas—among them my own Los Angeles neighborhood. When my contract expired I was not unhappy to end the show. Three years of coast-to-coast commuting, three years of working two time-consuming and difficult jobs had worn me down. It was time to move on.

I loved the show. Loved it. I have no regrets at all. In fact, there are many things about it I miss, but as I learned, it was impossible to be at my best every day on the show and still practice law. Given the right circumstances, I would do that again. I would particularly savor the opportunity to speak up against the right wing, because somebody should be defending the Bill of Rights, somebody should be speaking out loudly. The political climate in this country has changed, and many people seem to be afraid to stand up for their beliefs. I'm not. I don't care if people love me; I've already been one of the more controversial people in this country. I'm not afraid of getting fired or silenced, but I would like people to respect me as I respect them.

Court TV gave me a wonderful opportunity. As I had hoped, my program had provided tremendous visibility, it had enabled people to see me on a nightly basis cast in a very different role, to see my true personality. And most importantly, it brought me to New York City.

It took me some time to adjust to New York. There was a steep learning curve. That cartoon of me pushing aside buildings as I barged into town was so ridiculous. The impression was that Big Johnnie was coming to town ready to knock down anything that stood in my way. That couldn't have been any further from the truth. I just wanted to get to know a bit about the city and eventually find those places where my presence and abilities might be able to make a difference. I was well aware that there was an entrenched power structure in the African-American community and a lot of those people were looking at me warily. I knew that, and I was very careful to make it clear to everyone that I was in New York to do a TV show and I wasn't going to topple any structures. I didn't want anyone resenting me, or feeling threatened by me. This wasn't my place.

The fact is that when I got here I knew very little about New York, I didn't know what bank to use, where to get a good meal, where to get my hair cut. I certainly didn't know the intricacies of New York state law. I really didn't even know Harlem. Imagine that, a black man knowing almost nothing about this extraordinary African-American community. Harlem surprised me. It was much larger than the black community in Los Angeles—with a lot of churches. The primary difference between South Central and Harlem was that in Los Angeles people lived in houses, they had front lawns, they had at least a little control over their immediate environment. But what was obvious to me right from the very beginning was the unrealized economic potential of Harlem. It was in the air. It seemed to me right from the very beginning that if the residents of Harlem could harness the energy and the desire and the power that I saw on the streets, Harlem could be an engine of prosperity. It could become a tremendous place to live.

This was four years before Bill Clinton opened his postpresidential office there. And five years before I would become chairman of the Upper Manhattan Empowerment Zone—an economic entity that uses public funds and tax incentives to encourage private investment. It provides economic support for people who want to locate businesses there or make investments in the community.

When I began working in New York I only knew a few people; among them Neufeld and Scheck, Earl Graves, the publisher of *Black Enterprise*, Elaine Williams of *Essence* magazine, and Terrie Williams, the public relations maven. They began to take me around the city, they introduced me to their friends. Gradually, my circle of acquaintances grew. My pastor in Los Angeles, Dr. William Saxe Epps, had come from the Abyssinian Baptist Church in Harlem, so when I stayed in New York for the weekend I would attend services there and I got to know Reverend Dr. Calvin Butts and members of the congregation. I began to learn about the city. Although I've been a lifelong and passionate Lakers fan, I started going to Knick games at Madison Square Garden. I began eating the big, thick pastrami sandwiches at the Carnegie Deli. I found out where to buy my ties and where to get my hair cut.

The city welcomed me with honking taxicabs and buses and trucks. Admittedly, when I began doing the show I didn't know what to expect from New Yorkers, and maybe I was even just a little wary. But from my first day New Yorkers made me feel at home. Wherever I went people recognized me and waved or shouted a friendly greeting or asked for my autograph. Not everybody, of course, but most people. Dale and I very quickly felt at home in New York.

Among the very first cases in which I became involved in New York was a negligence lawsuit concerning a fire in an apartment. What made it unusual was that it was the apartment of the legendary eighty-nine-year-old jazz vibraphonist Lionel Hampton and the fire had been started by an ordinary halogen lamp. Not a faulty halogen lamp, but rather a lamp little different from the millions commonly used in homes around the world. Who wouldn't want the opportunity to represent Lionel Hampton? If you appreciate music, you admire Lionel Hampton. As I learned, a halogen floor lamp had tipped over onto his bed and ignited his bedclothes. Hampton managed to escape unscathed, but his memorabilia from eighty years in show business had been destroyed.

The case was referred to me by an outstanding New Orleans lawyer named Tim Francis. Peter Neufeld and I then brought in Jethro Eisenstein, who was very experienced in product liability matters. The lawsuit was based on a truly startling fact, something that everybody should know—those tubular halogen bulbs can be extremely dangerous. A three-hundred-watt halogen torchère bulb typically reaches temperatures near a thousand degrees, almost four times as hot as an ordinary seventy-five-watt bulb. Paper, fabrics, clothes, even wood will burn if in contact with a bulb for seconds. Apparently these lamps can be tipped over pretty easily and more than one hundred fires and ten deaths had been attributed to them.

Peter and I served as co-counsel to Eisenstein in Hampton's lawsuit against the company that had imported the lamp. Eventually we settled for six figures, as well as protection from liability lawsuits brought by other neighbors. But I think the most important thing that came out of this lawsuit was the publicity that made people aware that these bulbs were extremely dangerous. Imagine that, a lamp could heat up to one thousand degrees. People didn't know that, so they put these lamps in their children's bedrooms or they'd leave their house with them on.

The publicity generated by this lawsuit might well have saved lives. The lamps were subsequently redesigned with a safety cage constructed around the bulb.

During the first year I did the show I turned down most of the cases offered to me, but in December of 1997 an Oakland attorney called and asked me to serve as an advisor to Golden State Warriors basketball star Latrell Sprewell. In a rage during practice one afternoon, Sprewell had grabbed his coach, P. J. Carlesimo, by the throat and threatened to kill him. Then he left, but returned fifteen minutes later and again confronted his coach. It was an ugly incident, and there had never been anything like it in sports.

National Basketball Association Commissioner David Stern called the second confrontation "a premeditated assault" and suspended Sprewell for a full season. This was the longest nondrug suspension in pro basketball history. The Warriors, citing a morals clause, terminated his contract, costing Sprewell $25 million.

I'm a big sports fan. Big. I've been to almost every Super Bowl—the only times I missed the games I was in the middle of a trial and couldn't get away. I've been to most recent heavyweight championship fights—even if I've had to travel around the world to get there. In Los Angeles I can usually be found at Lakers games—sitting way behind Jack Nicholson. I've represented several prominent athletes in my career, among them football Hall of Famer Jim Brown, former heavyweight champion Riddick Bowe—and O. J. Simpson.

I had never met Sprewell, but everyone I asked told me that this was completely out of character for him, that he was one of the good guys and had just lost it. There was no excuse to be made for what he did, there was no justification—but it seemed to me that based on other incidents maybe the penalty was excessive.

Long before I got involved this story moved from the sports pages to the front pages of newspapers. Sprewell's actions were being cited by many people as the inevitable result of an overly permissive society. Editorial page columnists were writing about it as if it marked the beginning of the end of civilization. Sprewell had become the poster child for every wealthy, pampered, selfish athlete.

I was in the enviable position of being able to pick from a lot of offers for cases on which I wanted to work. For me, it was a question of where I wanted to invest my time. I had no specific formula for making those decisions; if I felt there was a substantive issue at stake I would certainly be interested, if the case itself was interesting or unusual I would be interested, if I believed a wrong was being committed that I might help make right I would be interested. I didn't overlook the opportunity to pay my bills, either, but fortunately I didn't have to make choices based solely on my bottom line.

The Sprewell case seemed like a good fit for me. It wasn't going to be a prolonged case which would have taken a lot of time. It involved pro basketball, which was a passion of mine. I really did believe that the penalty was unreasonable. And for a long time I had been thinking about representing professional athletes. It seemed unusual to me that about 90 percent of the players in the NBA were black while probably 99 percent of their agents were white. It brought back to me memories of Mrs. Dickerson, the black woman who'd hired a white lawyer because she'd heard they got better settlements. It didn't make sense to me that there were so few black player agents and I wanted to do something to change that. I've always believed that in most cases agents who did little but negotiate contracts were basically ripping off their clients because the league's salary structure and the market determined their value, not their agent. Eventually I did become an accredited agent for both the NBA and the National Football League and founded Cochran Sports Management. It isn't a very active company, but I represented Ray Allen when he signed a $70 million contract with the Milwaukee Bucks—for which I charged him $500 an hour rather than taking a percentage.

So I agreed to work with Latrell Sprewell and his agent, Arn Tellem. And even after everything that had been written and said about me after the Simpson case, admittedly I was a little surprised at the response of the media when I appeared with Sprewell and several other players at a press conference. This was, according to one writer, "an ugly incident Sprewell made worse by bringing in Johnnie Cochran and playing the race card . . ." In various newspapers and columns I was "the unctuous Johnnie Cochran," "the famous scumbag Johnnie Cochran . . ." who brought with me "the pious racial posturing of the master bottom-dealer."

None of these insults was new or particularly creative. Nor did they bother me.

Most of the work I did was with Billy Hunter, the very capable executive director of the NBA Player's Association. Often the best thing an attorney can do for his client is keep him out of the courtroom. Our objective was to make it possible for Sprewell to resume his playing career as quickly as possible, then he could work on rebuilding his reputation. In this case the penalty was almost an athletic death penalty. If an employee at General Motors had attacked his boss and been fired, he could go down the block and try to get a job at Ford. If he had an otherwise spotless résumé and unique skills that Ford needed, they just might hire him. But there was only one National Basketball Association.

It was not a complicated case. The foundation of the legal system is precedent. What had judges decided in other, similar cases? Knowing that allows attorneys at least a little bit of predictability by extension. So one of the first things a good lawyer does is try to find out what the going rate has been, what's the bottom line? Obviously nothing exactly like this had happened before, but we found several other cases in which athletes had lost control. In 1996 baseball player Roberto Alomar had spit in the face of an umpire, for which he had been suspended five games and voluntarily donated $50,000 to charity. In 1965 baseball player Juan Marichal had hit catcher John Roseboro over the head with a baseball bat and was fined $1,750 and suspended for eight games. College basketball coach Bobby Knight had hurled a chair across the court. Players had brutally attacked opposing players. Players had thrown towels and other objects at officials and gone into the stands after fans— but no one had been penalized as harshly as Sprewell. There simply was no precedent for this penalty.

That's what we wanted to say.

After spending time with Latrell Sprewell I believed that he really did feel awful about the entire incident. He knew he was wrong, he didn't look for excuses. He couldn't even explain his actions, like many people under terrific stress, he just lost it. We agreed that the most important thing that Sprewell had to do was admit he was wrong, take responsibility for his actions, and apologize publicly to Carlesimo. With most of his teammates standing behind him to show support, Sprewell told reporters, "I know this conduct is not acceptable in society or professional sports. I accept responsibility for what I've done . . . I feel that ten years of hard work shouldn't be taken away for one minute."

"The question is one of fundamental fairness for Latrell," I said, adding later, "This man was deprived of any kind of due process. Nobody heard from him at all. That's not the American way." I made a point of stating clearly that this was not about race, no one was claiming that the actions taken by Carlesimo, the Warriors, or the league were racist, but several columnists reported that "the presence of Johnnie Cochran alone sent a message that this was about race."

Apparently there were people who believed the race card was the only one in my deck.

Rather than a courtroom, the case went to arbitration. I did not represent Sprewell in the arbitration, but a neutral arbitrator reduced the penalty to seven months and forced the Warriors to take him back, which meant that they had to pay most of his salary.

The proof that this assault was an aberration currently resides in Madison Square Garden. Immediately after Sprewell was reinstated, the Warriors traded him to the New York Knicks. Sprewell became one of the Knicks most productive and popular players. He redeemed his reputation and has had no additional problems. It would be nice if every legal situation in which I got involved turned out so well.

But they don't. My life has taken many sharp turns; I've gone through some amazing changes. Los Angeles mayor Tom Bradley certainly initiated change in my life when he appointed me to the Airport Commission in 1981; that gave me the opportunity to travel around the world and see different cultures. I learned about business. I learned about chairing an important body. I certainly learned about big-city politics. And I met my wife. It was an incredibly broadening experience. The second substantial change in my life was coming to New York. It was almost like reaching the top of a great mountain only to look into the distance and discover a whole new mountain. I was close to the pinnacle in Los Angeles, and then I found this new challenge, this new adventure, this city.

I often look to the Lord for guidance. When I needed to find my purpose as a young lawyer Barbara Deadwyler walked into my office. When I wanted to understand why I had become involved in the Simpson case we discovered the Fuhrman tapes. And when I needed to find the means to understand New York City, I met Abner Louima.

The Abner Louima case introduced me to the fabric of New York. While representing Abner Louima I got involved with most of the institutions that hold the city together. The case thrust me right into the midst of the legal and law enforcement communities, it forced me to learn the realities of city politics, and made me fresh meat for the New York media. It even got me my first ride on the subway.

Like everybody else, I first learned the details of the Louima case by reading about it for several days in newspapers. On the night of August 9, 1997, Louima, a Haitian immigrant who had been living in Brooklyn for eleven years, walked out of the Club Rendez-Vous, a Haitian nightclub, into a brawl. Several police officers were already on the scene. During the fight, Officer Justin Volpe was sucker punched by an unidentified black man wearing a vest. Louima wasn't doing anything illegal, he was simply watching the fight when a cop grabbed him. Louima, who was also wearing a vest, was charged with assaulting an officer and resisting arrest; he was handcuffed and thrown into the back of a squad car by Officers Charles Schwarz and Thomas Wiese. On the way to the 70th Precinct the cops stopped and, joined by Officers Thomas Bruder and Justin Volpe, beat him with their fists and radios, telling him they were going to teach him to respect cops. Volpe had misidentified Louima as the man who had hit him.

At the 70th Precinct, according to the testimony of several police officers, Schwarz "escorted" Louima toward the bathroom where Volpe sodomized him with a broken wooden plunger handle. Volpe then shoved that stick, covered with feces, into Louima's mouth, then warned him, "If you tell anyone I'll kill you and your entire family."

This torture took place in New York City. It was done by a police officer who had all the power he needed because he wore a badge. And none of the other officers in that precinct at the time did a thing to stop him.

His hands still bound by handcuffs, his pants and underwear hanging at his ankles, Louima was tossed into a holding cell, where he was slowly dying from his injuries. Nobody did anything to help him, nobody cared if he lived or died. This was just business as usual for these people. Volpe, meanwhile, paraded around the precinct holding the bloody stick and boasting, "I had to break a man tonight."

About an hour and a half later EMS technicians arrived and examined Louima. After an unreasonably long delay, they rushed him to Coney Island Hospital in critical condition. A hole had been torn in his colon, his bladder had been punctured, and he was bleeding internally. Doctors performed emergency surgery to save his life. In the hospital the cops claimed that Louima had been injured during consensual homosexual sex.

A nurse named Magalie Laurent knew that wasn't true and called NYPD Internal Affairs. This woman was a hero. The officer who took her call was so uninterested he didn't even assign it a case number. The police did not respond. She then called Louima's family and told them, "He didn't injure himself that way. They did this to him." The family then began calling reporters and also found very little interest. Just another immigrant claiming that the cops beat him up. Apparently that was no big story in New York City. But a mysterious caller, never identified and assumed to be either a cop with a conscience who was afraid of the NYPD's legendary "blue wall of silence" or an EMS technician, called *Daily News* columnist Mike McAlary. After investigating McAlary wrote, "This is a story to stop the city." The Louima story finally broke wide open, and for his reporting McAlary was awarded a Pulitzer Prize.

A lot of New Yorkers were outraged. These people had just had enough. A crowd estimated by police at seven thousand and by organizers at fifteen thousand marched on City Hall. New York Mayor Rudy Giuliani tried to calm demonstrators by appointing a special commission to study police brutality. Forming committees is just a wonderful political ploy; it buys time with the hope that when a report is issued the reason for it has long been defused or even forgotten about. I would suspect that no one was surprised that when the report was delivered to Giuliani a year later he claimed its recommendations were impractical and pretty much ignored it.

For several days the Patrolmen's Benevolent Association, the cops' union, refused to allow the four officers who participated in the beatings and torture of Abner Louima to answer any questions.

Five police officers were eventually arrested, the fifth cop charged with lying to cover up the incident.

Welcome to New York. I had seen too much police abuse to be shocked. But even I had never seen anything quite as depraved as this act. This was truly barbaric. Volpe had said it, he had it right, he had tried to break a man sexually. If this had taken place in Los Angeles I knew my phone would have been ringing. The reporters would have been calling and eventually the victim would have reached out for me. But this was New York and I was new in town. I expected to watch this from the sidelines. I also recognized that like the Simpson case this one was going to make or break reputations and careers. It was the kind of case that potentially could rip apart the city. As I was learning, the people of color in New York did not trust Giuliani and they were watching him closely to see if he supported the torturers or the victim. Politicians hate cases like this, for them it contained all sorts of dangers. It was clearly going to be a major problem for Brooklyn DA Charles J. Hynes, whose office was going to have to decide whether or not to prosecute the cops.

The initial legal strategy was extremely important. Any mistakes an attorney makes at the beginning of a case will haunt him until its end. Pretty much whatever is said those first few days is written in stone. In the Simpson case his first attorney allowed Simpson to go alone with police officers in a car. The police asked him all sorts of questions and locked him into his defense. This is a basic police tactic, they want suspects to answer questions immediately, before they have a chance to calm down and really grasp their situation, and, most importantly, before they have an opportunity to consult an attorney.

The police definitely know this—and that's why in New York the PBA was firm that prosecutors and police department officials could not speak to police officers about cases in which they were suspected of misconduct for two days. They had to wait until a forty-eight-hour "cooling off period" had passed. It was an outrageous abuse of the legal system. No other police force in the country has that rule. The real reason for it, I knew and every decent defense lawyer knew, was that it gave the cops time to get their stories straight with each other. It gave them time to make sure everybody told the same story to investigators. It gave police officers time to do exactly what the cops wanted suspects *not* to do.

About two weeks after the assault I received calls through my California office from a woman named Janie Washington, the general manager of WLIB, an extremely liberal radio station, and Club Rendez-Vous bandleader King Kino telling me that Abner Louima wanted to meet with me. At that time Louima was represented by two Afro-Caribbean attorneys, Carl Thomas and Brian Figeroux. It seemed pretty obvious he wanted to speak with me about getting involved in some way in this case. Before meeting with him I called Peter and Barry and asked Peter to come with me to the hospital. If I was going to participate I wanted them to be with me.

Abner Louima's entire family, with the exception of his wife, was in his hospital room the day we met. His father, his brother, his cousins, some uncles, it was a big concerned family. Abner speaks in a heavy Creole accent, and he was speaking very softly. What surprised me was that he didn't seem very angry. He was hurt, he looked weak and wounded, and clearly he was dismayed that this had happened to him, but there was little anger. He told me that day that he wanted to make sure the police never did this to another person. That was his objective, make sure it couldn't happen again.

Also there that day was Sanford Rubenstein, a tough, experienced New York personal injury lawyer.

Louima asked me to meet with his uncle, Reverend Nicolas, at a Haitian evangelical church in Brooklyn. After that meeting he asked me to join Thomas and Figeroux and Sandy Rubinstein in representing him.

The Abner Louima police abuse case was my real welcome to New York.

SIX

"As if being plungerized weren't bad enough, he's [Louima] now going to be Cochranized," according to conservative broadcaster Tony Snow.

"The man who cynically turned West Coast justice on its ear in service of the guilty is now poised to do a similar number on the city of New York . . . (H)istory reveals that he will say or do just about anything to win, typically at the expense of the truth . . . Louima deserves better . . . Most of all, he deserves to see the truth come out. And so do the rest of us. This is not L.A.," a columnist named Andrea Peyser wrote in the conservative *New York Post*.

Obviously not everyone in New York greeted my involvement in the Louima case with enthusiasm. Nowhere was it written or said that I'd spent more than three decades fighting police abuse, that I brought with me extraordinary experience in police abuse cases. The facts were that I knew the national experts on police procedures who would testify; I knew the forensic doctors best able to testify that Louima's injuries were not caused by "his face coming into contact with the ground"; and I certainly knew how to cross-examine police officers.

Most criticism I simply ignored, but I couldn't permit anyone to claim that I lied in the courtroom. That's a pretty serious charge to make against an attorney. Although most people advised me against it, I sued the *Post* for libel, asking for $10 million in damages. That was a nice round number, I thought. I didn't sue to make a point, I did it to win. I've never objected to being insulted or called all kinds of names, but I didn't believe ignorance about my professional conduct should be constitutionally protected. So $150,000 later, the court decided that those comments were considered opinion and therefore were not libelous. It was an expensive point to make. There was a lot of work to be done to prepare Louima's civil case. For a time we had six lawyers working on it, until Thomas and Figeroux resigned. That still left plenty of work for Peter, Barry, Sandy Rubenstein, and me. One of the very first things we did was develop the theme. This wasn't simply a case of a cop beating up an innocent person, it was much more perverse than that. This was a sexual assault on a man. These police officers had to be sick to do something like that, but they also had to feel so empowered by the system that they felt confident they could do whatever they wanted and get away with it, that nobody was going to stop them. When Peter, Barry, and I agreed to work together in New York we had decided to take cases that would allow us to go after problems in the system. If there was ever a case that was going to generate real change, this was it. Not only had several police officers participated in the beatings, many more had to be aware of those beatings and the sexual assault and they hadn't done a thing to stop it. For police officers to stand by passively as a cop shoved a wooden stick up a man's rectum and do nothing about it demonstrated a massive failure of the system. That's what we wanted to go after, not just Volpe. It took us some time to figure out how to do that.

Initially the case was handled by Brooklyn DA Charles Hynes's office. We were concerned about that. There was a tremendous amount of pressure from all sides being put on that office. Even before completing the investigation they put the case in front of the grand jury. Abner Louima was put through the discomfort of testifying in the grand jury—*twice*—only days after surviving emergency surgery. With the case on the front page of newspapers around the country, the DA was unwilling to wait for at least a partial recovery.

After the four cops were indicted, we were really afraid that they would waive their right to a jury trial, preferring to let a judge decide their fate. This is an old and, unfortunately, very successful tactic cops have often used in misconduct cases. In New York about 95 percent of cops who had waived juries had been acquitted by the judge. Even if Volpe was prosecuted successfully, the system would be protected. Volpe would fall on his sword, take the rap for all the other cops involved, and nothing would change. That would have been a disaster for New York City.

Peter met with prosecutors from Hynes's office several times and it was clear to him that they were making tactical as well as legal mistakes. Hynes sent assistant DAs to the hospital to interview Abner Louima under oath while he was still hooked up to tubes. There was no reason to put Abner under that pressure. He was no longer in critical condition, he wasn't going to die. They could have waited, given him some time to recover.

Hynes's office also took the position that the police didn't need to interview the accused officers. How can you interview the victim while he's lying in the hospital and not attempt to interview the people who put him there? It made no sense. It is a fundamental rule of police procedure that the first thing you try to do is get a suspect to make a voluntary statement before a lawyer orders him or her to be quiet. Hynes specifically told the police not to talk to Volpe, Schwarz, Wiese, and Bruder. Peter, Barry, and I felt, bottom line, that Hynes was not going to be successful.

We decided to do everything possible to get the case moved from the DA's office to the federal level. Although federal prosecutors had agreed to take a good look at this case, no decision had been made whether or not they would get actively involved. We believed that a federal prosecution would be much better for Abner Louima, as well as for the city. We asked local legislators and community and spiritual leaders to lobby the Justice Department. We made the phone calls we could make and ultimately we were successful. The Office of the U.S. Attorney for the Eastern District took control of the prosecution.

It was the best result for everybody. Hynes was an elected official. He was going to run for reelection and this case really could have hurt him. Federal prosecutors don't have to please voters. They can take as much time as necessary to develop a case. Maybe even more important, police officers fear federal prosecutors because they can't influence their work. One visit from an FBI agent is potentially far more career threatening than an interview with a fellow cop during his rotation in the Internal Affairs unit—cops have no influence with federal agents.

Federal prosecutors have basically unlimited resources to draw upon. They have a lot of experience trying civil rights cases and federal sentencing guidelines are much stronger than state penalties. When the Eastern District got the case we went to pay our respects to the people who would be handling it; Kathy Palmer, a superb lead prosecutor, Zach Carter, Loretta Lynch, and a young African-American lawyer named Ken Thompson. I didn't know any of these people but I gained great respect for all of them. During that meeting I pledged Abner Louima's complete cooperation. Whatever these people needed for their investigation and prosecution we would try to provide. Within the appropriate legal guidelines, we gave Palmer all the information we found. Not long after we got involved, Palmer resigned from the U.S. Attorney's Office to enter private practice, and was replaced by a gifted trial lawyer I would come to really like and greatly respect, Alan Vinegrad.

Because I had considerable credibility within the minority community, I was able to encourage witnesses to cooperate completely with federal investigators. I told them that they had an obligation to their community to step forward and tell what they had seen, and I reassured them that these were people they could trust. There just isn't a great reservoir of trust for any type of law enforcement in the minority community.

Our job as personal injury lawyers is to get as much money as we can for our client. I'm not the slightest bit embarrassed to write those words. People who do the wrong thing should pay for it, and the more they pay the more certain it is that they won't do it again. Our fee comes out of that money, but we also want to see justice done. A criminal conviction will most certainly help us in our civil case. A lot of young lawyers don't understand that. If I were training young lawyers I would tell them it is imperative to work with the prosecutor. It makes a substantial difference.

Eventually we began our own investigation of the crime. I never trust the police to investigate the police; I always do my own investigation, either hiring private investigators or doing some of the work myself. I really got involved in this case. I was assuming that eventually we'd go to trial and I intended to be prepared. As always, one of the first things we did was go to the crime scene. At the Club Rendez-Vous, we interviewed several people who had been there the night of the assault. We stopped on the street where Louima had been beaten on the way to the precinct. We drove the same streets. At this stage I was more of an investigator than an attorney, but to prepare for a trial I needed to see every location, I needed to hear the voices. I wanted to know the truth. We conducted at least fifty interviews, I probably did a dozen of them by myself and participated in many more. I spoke with Abner Louima's brother, I spoke with the nurses at the hospital, and I spoke with the club's bandleader, King Kino.

Finally we got a court order to go into the 70th Precinct station house to take photographs. We wanted to have photographs to show the jury. I remember being struck by how small it was. We tried to re-create that night through the camera. How exactly had they marched Abner Louima in front of the desk where the sergeant was sitting? What could the sergeant see? Were there any areas in the station house out of sight of that desk? Abner's pants were already down around his ankles. Then they marched him through the station into a cell. Finally they brought him into the bathroom. The door to the bathroom couldn't have been more than twenty-five feet from the sergeant's desk. That bathroom was frightening. It was filthy. This was where they made Abner bend over near the toilet, and Volpe rammed the stick into his body.

Standing there, I could hear him screaming. That place was so small that anyone in the building must have known what was going on in the bathroom but nobody did a damn thing about it. They ignored it. It took five days before one officer, a probationary patrolman named Eric Turetsky, had the courage to come forward to reveal what had happened; and breaking the NYPD's legendary blue wall of silence forced him into protective custody.

The police officers who were present when we did this walk-through watched us with curiosity, but I didn't feel any real sense of hostility. Any questions we asked were answered without hesitation. But I was glad to get out of there.

Within days of beginning our investigation it became obvious that a massive cover-up had taken place. We heard about a lot of phone calls being made, and then apparently there were several meetings, including a meeting with PBA representatives in the basement of the precinct. None of the officers was hurt, but for some reason they all went to the hospital together. This was a pattern I'd seen before. As far as we were concerned, this was clearly obstruction of justice. But knowing that and proving it in a courtroom are entirely different things, and these cops had almost a week to concoct their story and learn it. There wasn't much we could do about it, but then we got a big, unexpected break.

Tommy Wiese's attorney, Joe Tacopina, asked to meet with us. I'd known Tacopina for several years and had always found him to be an honorable man and able advocate. Peter, Barry, and I met him and a second lawyer for breakfast at the Cupping Room, a SoHo restaurant. As we sat there, Tacopina tried to convince us that his client had actually assisted Louima and had certainly not participated in any assault. Tacopina laid out a perfect chronology. Whenever anything happened to Louima, Wiese was there, but he wasn't really *there*. He didn't actually see any crimes being committed. Wiese and Schwarz were driving Louima to the precinct but stopped and Wiese left the car. When he returned, Schwarz was in the backseat with Louima and he saw that Louima was bleeding— but Wiese never saw Schwarz assault Louima. At the station house Wiese happened to be standing right outside the bathroom door when he heard a banging noise, not screaming, a banging noise. Because several years earlier in that same bathroom a prisoner had wrestled a gun away from an officer and shot her, Wiese entered the bathroom to check on the noise and found Louima on the floor with his pants and underpants pulled down and Volpe standing there alone holding a stick covered with feces. The possibility that Volpe had sodomized Louima with that stick was so terrible that it didn't even occur to Wiese. But Wiese then helped Louima to his feet.

The story continued like that. Supposedly Wiese was so troubled by what he had seen that three days later he tried to contact Internal Affairs, but whoever answered the phone put him on hold for twenty minutes and then suggested he call back in a few days. But before Wiese could do that Turetsky revealed what had happened. Wiese supposedly had taken two lie detector tests; but the first one really didn't count because he was so nervous the machine registered he was lying when asked his name, but he passed the second one.

Sitting there listening to Tacopina, we were dumbfounded. He was laying out the whole scenario for us. He was telling us what each officer was doing. Wiese, for example, was outside the door, meaning he was obviously the lookout. That meant Schwarz was inside with Volpe.

Tacopina's intent was to convince us that his client was really a good guy, that he was out of the car when Schwarz assaulted Louima, that he assisted Louima when he realized he was hurt, and he didn't realize Volpe had done anything wrong because it was too terrible to imagine. He was trying to make us believe that Wiese was a lesser player, that Schwarz had not been in the bathroom, and that the obviously deranged Volpe had acted alone, knowing that if Louima accepted his version of the events he could be of great help to Wiese in the criminal case.

We didn't believe any of it. As soon as breakfast ended we went back to the office and wrote down everything we could remember. We had four typed pages of notes. Tacopina had taken a real gamble, he was betting we would believe his story, and he lost. His thinking made sense; if the victim isn't antagonistic to your client you're in a much stronger position in terms of liability, and if there is a conviction, in terms of punishment.

Joe Tacopina tried, but we never believed one word Wiese said.

Eventually Vinegrad's office subpoenaed our notes. The defense challenged their accuracy, but we knew they were accurate to the very best of our recollection.

The Louima case enabled me to learn about New York City. About the only place I didn't go was City Hall. Rudy Giuliani stayed as far away as possible from this case. But after a court appearance in Brooklyn one afternoon, Peter suggested that the fastest way back to Manhattan was by subway. The subway? This was my first ride on the famed New York City subway system. I'd certainly heard a lot about it. But as we were sitting on the #2 train I noticed that a woman sitting across from us was reading the Bible. She looked right at me for a second and then returned to her Bible. Then it must have clicked in: Johnnie Cochran was sitting directly across from her on the subway. I've seen this happen before. She looked up again, giving me what I've learned is the New York subway glance, the object of which is to look at someone without ever meeting their eyes. It was clear she wasn't certain it was me. So I smiled at her and asked, "How you doing today?"

Eventually I asked her what she was reading and she told me. I don't remember chapter and verse, but I read the Bible and I know parts of it quite well. I actually was able to quote a few words from the section she was reading. I could just imagine the surprise when she got home and told someone in her family, "I ran into Johnnie Cochran on the subway this afternoon and he quoted Bible passages for me." She asked me to autograph her Bible, which I was pleased to do.

The New York City subway didn't seem quite as ferocious as its reputation.

Working on the Louima case also allowed me the opportunity to work with New York City's most controversial African-American leader, the Reverend Al Sharpton. When I came to New York I was very mindful that Reverend Sharpton was the leader, without office, of the black community. He was the guy out front on just about every issue concerning minority interests in the city, but I didn't know much about him. I knew Jesse Jackson much better. But soon after I began working on the Louima case I was invited to speak at Reverend Sharpton's House of Justice up in Harlem.

White people tend to underestimate Al Sharpton. But make no mistake about it, he is a very smart man and he is committed to the cause of justice for minorities. He is an extraordinary organizer and knows how to keep the attention of the public on an issue. He has the ability to bring together everybody, from white movie stars to blacks with only one pair of shoes. Al Sharpton is a very complex person; there's a lot more to him than the caricature that appears in the media.

I understand that there are people who are never going to accept him. That some people will never forgive him for his participation in the Tawana Brawley case. But I think he's learned from that, I think he's learned from his mistakes. Along with Earl Graves and other people, I helped him pay the judgment levied against him in that case because New York needs Al Sharpton. He's that squeaky noise in the wheel, the stone in your shoe, he's going to do whatever he has to do to make certain that important issues, issues that nobody else wants to talk about, like police brutality and racial profiling, get the attention of the media. He has a real following, so if he wants to fill up a courtroom he can fill up that courtroom.

Maybe he's in the press a little too much, he probably knows that, too, but he plays an important role in race relations in this country. There is no question that he has made huge contributions to the African-American community. So when I got to New York City I paid due respect and homage to all the African-American leaders. To Earl Graves and Representative Charlie Rangel, to Al Sharpton. I didn't come here to supplant anybody. I didn't come to New York to run for political office, I came here to do a television show and practice law to the best of my ability. Reverend Sharpton and I have worked together on several cases and he is someone I genuinely respect and like.

In the Louima case Peter, Barry, and I spent a great deal of time talking and planning our strategy. A lot of lawyers don't take the time to meet to really discuss their cases. We spent a lot of time together. It was obvious that Abner Louima had been a victim of police brutality and that the city was legally responsible; proving that was the easy part, I couldn't wait to get in front of the jury in this case, but we also saw the opportunity to accomplish a lot more for all the people of New York. Before I came to New York I wasn't aware of the "forty-eight-hour rule." This was the rule that made the blue wall of silence possible. For forty-eight hours after an incident in which police officers are involved only their union, the PBA, was permitted to speak with them. Other cops investigating the case couldn't even ask for assistance, prosecutors couldn't ask questions. It was a dangerous, absurd regulation.

During that forty-eight hours following the torture of Abner Louima, officers from the 70th Precinct as well as PBA representatives had been very busy with phone calls and meetings. They had to find a way to justify beating Louima, they had to dirty up the victim. That's when the scurrilous lie that Louima's injuries had been the result of being sodomized during gay sex was first born.

Legally the forty-eight-hour rule applied only to administrative investigations. Basically, it meant that cops didn't have to speak with Internal Affairs, the police force unit responsible for investigating police behavior. It was put in the union contract with the city to prevent police officers from being fired. It was about job protection. But police officers have always interpreted it to mean they didn't have to speak with anybody for forty-eight hours. That was ridiculous. The rights that police officers have in criminal investigations can't be different from those rights enjoyed by citizens. Like any other American citizen they have their Miranda rights. They have the right to remain silent. They have the right to consult an attorney. If they can't afford an attorney they have the right to a court-appointed attorney. Those rights are guaranteed by the Constitution, not by the PBA contract. But the Constitution was now being abused.

Here's how it worked: Just about a year before the Louima case, a twenty-six-year-old black Gulf War navy veteran named Nathaniel Gaines was riding home on the subway after watching Fourth of July fireworks. A police officer accused him of stalking a woman and pulled him off the train in the Bronx. Nathaniel Gaines was unarmed and had no criminal record. The police officer, Paolo Colecchia, shot and killed him on the subway platform. Originally the NYPD and Medical Examiner's Office announced that Gaines had been shot in the front, but later they admitted he had been shot in the back.

One of the first people to arrive at the crime scene was the union delegate, who refused to allow Colecchia to speak with his superior officers. Colecchia specifically invoked his right under the police union contract to wait forty-eight hours, two working days, before talking to other police officers investigating the case. When Colecchia finally testified in front of a grand jury he claimed that there had been an argument and Gaines had refused to follow his orders. The two men struggled over Colecchia's gun, which accidentally went off. Fortunately, Colecchia testified before his lawyers had received the ballistics and forensic evidence reports.

Those reports proved that Colecchia was lying. Gaines had been shot in the back from a distance of at least twenty feet. He was leaving the scene, probably running away, when he was shot in the back. It was manslaughter—the unlawful killing of a human being without malice—but the police did everything possible to protect one of their own. Without a warrant they opened Gaines's locker at his job at the Triborough Bridge and Tunnel Authority, looking for anything that could be used to dirty him up. Drugs, pornography. But they didn't find a thing. In my opinion, Colecchia should have been charged and convicted of murder.

On the other hand, Colecchia had a poor record. A week before this happened he had apparently flipped out in the precinct and had his gun taken away from him. But without any treatment or real analysis of his psychological state, they gave him back his gun.

As usual, in the criminal trial Colecchia waived his right to a jury, meaning he put his fate in the hands of a judge. The judge found him guilty of second-degree manslaughter—and sentenced him to one and a half to four years in jail, then released him on bail pending his appeal. This case was so egregious that even the PBA didn't want anything to do with it; the union refused to pay his

legal expenses. At a special congressional hearing about police brutality in New York City convened by black representative John
Conyers (D-MI) held in the Bronx, Nathaniel Gaines's sister, Tracy,
asked the question I'd been asking over and over for so long: "What
is the price of the life of a black man in this country?"

Mayor Giuliani didn't bother to come to this hearing, supposedly because it was not an official congressional session.

It was obvious to us that in the Louima case, just like in the
Gaines shooting, the forty-eight-hour rule had been misused by
police officers with the full approval of the PBA. During one of our
strategy meetings Peter suggested we go after that rule. But then he
went further; pointing out that all the evidence indicated that the
union was an active participant in the attempted cover-up. Union
delegates weren't just advising the cops of their rights, they were
arranging meetings, they were making sure everybody knew the
story—they were active participants in trying to cover up a brutal
crime. Peter suggested we sue the union.

The New York City Patrolmen's Benevolent Association is a
very, very powerful union. Basically, the PBA ran the station houses
and through its rules maintained the blue wall of silence. There
were no holes in that wall. Even good cops, which is the great
majority of the 42,000-member force, were afraid to come forward
with information about rogue cops.

But sue the PBA? No one had ever tried to sue a police union
before. None of us was even sure if it was possible. Peter believed
we could sue them under what were known as the Ku Klux Klan
statutes, which were federal civil rights laws enacted at the end of
the Civil War to stop law enforcement officials from preventing
newly freed blacks from exercising their rights as citizens. Those
laws had been used to sue police departments, but never police
unions, for acts of brutality. But it was our contention that the PBA
was acting like an organized gang. In almost every situation they
immediately took the officer away from the scene, usually bringing

him to the hospital under some pretext. A ringing in the ears, for example. We also had information that suggested that the PBA would only hire those lawyers for their members who agreed that they would not let their client testify or provide information against other officers. And we knew that even if an officer wanted to report misconduct by another cop he could speak only to a union representative or an attorney paid by the union—and those people would do everything possible to prevent any report from being made. We knew the union was intimidating people. And finally we had anecdotal evidence that by organizing meetings at which the cops got their stories together, the union was obstructing justice.

If we wanted to attack the blue wall we had to go after the union and its leadership. Peter and Barry spoke to attorneys all over the country and most of them thought we were out of our minds to try this. When we finally did file our lawsuit, the PBA found it laughable. That's what they called it, laughable. We didn't think so; we thought we could make a strong case against the union.

We decided in the civil case to go after dollars and change. By law we could not go after the city for punitive damages, money paid in addition to real losses to punish the wrongdoer, but nothing prevented us from getting punitive damages against the union. The union had deep pockets. And an angry jury could punish the PBA by making it dig deep into those pockets.

A criminal trial preceded the civil action. I didn't attend the criminal trial because I didn't want to draw attention to myself. I understand I'm a controversial figure, particularly in a trial in which four white police officers are accused of beating and torturing a black man and a fifth officer is accused of covering up their actions. I also didn't want to have a defense attorney point at me and tell the jury, "Look, there's Johnnie Cochran over there. He's only here because he's interested in money."

I *was* interested in money—I wanted the police department to pay for its crimes. I wasn't in the courtroom but I read every page of the trial transcript. The testimony verified that everything we had claimed happened had indeed happened. Cops used phrases like *We met...We had this meeting...We were down in the basement...We got together and talked* ... Without meaning to, they laid out the blueprint of the conspiracy.

So I didn't go to the trial, but Peter or Barry or Sanford Rubenstein were there almost every day. I did attend the closing argument. During the trial Michael Immitt, a PBA official who testified reluctantly for the prosecution, admitted that he'd visited the roll calls at the 70th Precinct and told the officers, "Sit tight. Don't talk about it. Don't talk to anyone unless something official comes down." But he denied that he had conspired with the four accused officers to conceal information.

As the trial began Volpe's lawyer, Marvin Kornberg, began laying the groundwork for his theory of the case; that Abner Louima had received his injuries during an act of consensual homosexual sex. It was beyond absurd. No one believed it. No one. Four other officers testified that they had seen Volpe carrying a plunger and leading Louima into the men's room. After three weeks of testimony, when it had become obvious that Justin Volpe was going to be convicted, he pleaded guilty. He confirmed almost every aspect of Louima's story—including the fact that Schwarz and Wiese had assaulted Louima—although he claimed that Wiese rather than Schwarz had been in the bathroom with him during the assault, and that contrary to Abner Louima's testimony, Schwarz didn't take part in it. The trials of Schwarz, Wiese, and Bruder continued.

The Louima jury, consisting of six African-Americans, five whites, and one Latino, took three days to reach its verdict. Schwarz was found guilty of violating Louima's civil rights by holding him down while Volpe sodomized him and participating in the cover-up. Wiese and Bruder were acquitted of beating Louima on the way to the police station. Volpe was sentenced to thirty years in prison; Schwarz got fifteen years and eight months and was ordered to pay Louima $277,495.

Subsequently Schwarz, Wiese, and Bruder were tried for their participation in the cover-up. This second trial went to the jury during a tense time in New York. Just a week earlier another jury had acquitted four police officers in the killing of immigrant Amadou Diallo, an innocent man who had been shot forty-one times in the vestibule of his apartment building. The police officers claimed that in the darkness they had mistaken Diallo's wallet for a gun. New York's minority community was outraged and was focused on this trial.

The three men were convicted of conspiracy to obstruct justice. While there was substantial evidence against them, the key evidence was phone records introduced by Vinegrad that proved these officers, who testified that they rarely had spoken with each other before this incident, had made numerous phone calls to each other. They were talking about something. Wiese and Bruder were each sentenced to five years in prison.

Several years after the trials, Charles Schwarz and his many supporters continue to insist he was never in the bathroom with Volpe and Louima. Even Volpe identified Wiese as the second man in the bathroom. Another hearing was held in 2001 to hear supposedly new testimony, and after hearing it the court found no reason to question Schwarz's guilt. But in early 2002, an appellate court found that Schwarz's attorney had a conflict of interest because in addition to Schwarz he also represented the PBA, and released Charles Schwarz from prison. While I always applaud actions by the court to zealously guard the rights of defendants, something I have always fought for, I must say I'm at least a little concerned by the interest the appellate court has taken in this case. This is a very technical reason to reverse a jury verdict, two guilty jury verdicts, actually. This potential conflict of interest isn't something new, something someone suddenly discovered. We had pointed it out to the court and the prosecution, we had even filed a lawsuit claiming that the PBA had created this conflict. Schwarz's attorney had a $10 million contract with the union, how could he represent this one guy? Prior to the first trial, there was a three-day hearing at which the U.S. attorney brought this problem to the attention of the court. Schwarz knew about it and accepted it, he waived his right to an appeal—yet the appellate court said he did not have the right to do that, calling it an "unwaivable conflict."

Quite frankly, I don't think the court would go to this extreme for any other defendant. I don't believe they would have done it for Schwarz if he hadn't been a cop. That's the thing I find most offensive. Police officers should be held to a higher standard of responsibility, not a lowered standard. I've seen my client Abner Louima testify five different times and he has told the truth each time. Now he will have to testify at least once more, perhaps two or three times. The system continues to assault him. When does Abner Louima get closure for one of the worst injustices in the history of New York State?

Obviously I have some real concern about this, I don't want to see an innocent man spend years in prison. I've already watched Geronimo Pratt, an innocent man, spend half his life behind bars. But in the Louima case I believe they have the right man. In reversing Schwarz's conviction on a technicality, the court never claimed that the evidence failed to prove his guilt. Abner Louima admitted he could not positively identify the second man in the bathroom, although he was certain it had been the driver of the patrol car that brought him to the precinct. But other white police officers who were there positively identified Schwarz as the man who led Louima toward the bathroom. And Wiese's lawyer, Tacopina, placed Wiese outside the door, which always made sense. I have always believed he was the lookout, his job was to prevent anybody else from going into the bathroom.

Supporters of these police officers have tried to portray them as victims of the criminal justice system, victims of an out-of-control prosecutor. That's unbelievable. These are the same police officers who parked their squad car on the way to the station house to beat Louima. These officers were out of control that night and it wasn't just Volpe. It seems obvious to me that anyone who was in that police station that night and did nothing to stop the torture of Abner Louima is guilty of obstruction of justice, aiding and abetting and covering it up—and Schwarz, Wiese, and Bruder have all admitted being there. I'd certainly like to see Wiese and Bruder tried for lying and obstructing justice.

The U.S. Attorney's Office in Brooklyn has been remarkably good and strong. To the great credit of Alan Vinegrad the prosecution isn't backing down. Not at all. A message has to be sent to police officers that you can't lie and get away with it.

After these police officers were found guilty in the criminal cases the city knew it couldn't win a civil action. They knew that we were well prepared to fight the case in court. The only real question was the terms of the settlement. What is the price of Abner Louima's physical and psychological damages, as well as that to his reputation? I wanted the city to make him whole again, to make him like he was before that night in August. But that was a miracle that no one could accomplish, so I wanted them to pay for it.

Dollars and change, that's what we decided to sue for. A lot of dollars and substantial change. I'd started suing police departments in Los Angeles thirty years earlier when nobody had paid any attention to our demands, nobody cared what the LAPD did to African-American citizens—when we had no power. Now we had thousands of people marching in the streets, front-page newspaper coverage, and all the power of the law.

In the initial lawsuit against the city and the PBA, we claimed officers of the 70th Precinct "conspired to create a blue wall of silence and lied to obstruct justice," that the PBA specifically "condoned an environment in which the most violent police officers believed they would be insulated from prosecution," and that the city and the union together "have promoted an atmosphere in which the very worst police officers feel assured that evidence of misdeeds depriving citizens of their civil rights, no matter how awful, will be hidden by the PBA representatives and 'the code of silence.' "

The amount of money we asked for had no real bearing on reality. At one point, before I joined the case, Rubenstein filed a claim demanding $155 million. It could as easily have been a billion. The number is there because many jurisdictions require an amount of money be included in the initial filings. I'm never shy about picking a number. The real purpose of it is to make sure the people being sued know we're millions-of-dollars serious. Nobody ever expects to actually get that amount of money. In this case the only reason that I didn't put down really big numbers was that I didn't want the newspapers pointing out that the amount of money we demanded was enough to hire ten thousand teachers. How much money did we expect to get? Enough to make the point that the city couldn't afford to tolerate anything like this ever again.

In addition to money, we wanted to force the city to make some permanent structural changes regarding police abuse and police brutality. We wanted the city to eliminate the forty-eight-hour rule, we wanted to find a mechanism in which a police officer who wanted to report a bad cop had a neutral advocate who would protect his identity, we wanted officers and union officials retrained. We wanted to force changes that would make the NYPD a less secret organization. We even considered requesting that video cameras be installed in every precinct. In prior cases we'd found that the police officers are likely to act professionally if they know their actions are being videotaped. For example, if there had been a camera in the 70th Precinct that night, Volpe would not have dared parade Abner Louima around with his trousers around his ankles.

The union was determined to fight us. Union lawyers insisted that it had done nothing wrong and legally had absolutely no liability and, frankly, were kind enough to tell us we were wasting our time and their money with this action. Among many other people I met with were Patrick Lynch, a very articulate union representative, and attorney Tom Puccio, the union's attorney, to discuss the case. Puccio's a tough lawyer, he doesn't give an inch. Less than an inch.

Negotiations were very tough. I truly wanted to take this case to court and unless the city and PBA made an extraordinary offer I intended to do exactly that. One day, I remember, we were in court with lawyers representing the PBA and three lawyers representing the PBA's insurance company. The PBA wanted its insurance company to contribute to a settlement rather than allow us to go to trial, where damages could be massive. These were classic insurance company attorneys; white and buttoned-down. Peter described them as people who wouldn't give a ninety-year-old widow a nickel if her house burned down. Peter and Barry both tried to explain to them why it made sense to settle. They listened impassively, evidently not impressed by the logic of the argument. Then I said simply, "It's real simple, you can take the position that you're not going to settle and we'll go ahead and try this case."

They wouldn't even discuss discussing an offer. But when the meeting ended the three insurance company attorneys handed me their business cards and asked me to autograph them to their wives and daughters. When that happened, Barry turned to Peter and said, "This is over."

After literally years of negotiation, the city offered Abner Louima $7.125 million, and the PBA agreed to pay an additional $1.625 million, for a total of $8.75 million. It was, by far, the most ever paid to a victim of police abuse in New York City. Attorney fees came to about $2.9 million. As important, this was the first time in American history that a police union had successfully been sued and forced to pay damages. But the union would not agree to any procedural changes as part of the settlement.

It was a very tempting offer. It was a significant amount of dollars, but not enough change. It was enough money to guarantee a comfortable life for Abner Louima, but it didn't accomplish the original objective. When the details of the proposed settlement leaked to the media we got a lot of pressure to reject it from the minority community.

The decision to accept a settlement always rests with the client. In many cases in which I've been involved, the settlement represented more than money to a family; this was payment for the loss of a loved one. Finally accepting a settlement, ending a lawsuit, means ending a connection with that person. It's extremely difficult. I always explain to my client, always, what the law is and what is a reasonable expectation. I make it absolutely clear that I am willing and prepared to take the case to trial and I expect to win a substantial judgment, probably more than is being offered. But that means there will be at least another year or two of appeals, and a judge or appellate court can simply reduce the award if they feel it's excessive. The benefit of a settlement is closure—finally, there is a resolution—but there is also the chance that a substantial amount of money will be left on the table.

We laid it all out for Abner Louima. We had a lot of discussions about it. While at times he was tempted to accept the payment— and who wouldn't be?—he was insistent that more changes in police procedure be made. If the city wouldn't agree to additional reforms, then we would try to force the PBA to change its methods. So we continued to negotiate while preparing for the trial.

Negotiations went on for several more months. The real hangup was that the union did not want any changes we requested to be part of the settlement agreement. Rather than allowing us to claim that we had successfully forced them to change their procedures, they wanted it to be known that they had voluntarily made such changes because they realized it was the right thing to do—even though these changes evidently hadn't been the right thing to do in the past. It was a tricky bit of language. It didn't matter to us who got the credit for these changes as long as they were made.

When Abner Louima felt comfortable that certain changes in police union procedures were already in place and more would be instituted to dismantle the blue wall, he agreed to the settlement.

I was extremely ambivalent about settling. I'm a trial lawyer, I love going to trial. But I didn't try to talk Abner out of it because, ultimately, the client needs to be satisfied. He had a family, he had already been through three trials, he had told his story five times and it was difficult for him to go through it again and again, and he had been living with police protection for so long. I also knew that settling was much better for the city. Another trial would have exacerbated already badly frayed feelings. There are situations where it's important to consider the greater public good, to be a good citizen.

The judge put a gag order on the negotiations. When the settlement was finally announced and the gag order was lifted, Abner Louima told reporters, "Since that day almost four years ago I have vowed to do everything I can to ensure that the torture and cover-up I suffered will not be inflicted on my children or anyone else's children in the future . . .

"As a result of what happened to me . . . several changes for the better have taken place at the Patrolmen's Benevolent Association and in the New York City Police Department, and more, I hope, will be instituted in the future."

Thomas Puccio said that the PBA had not agreed to make reforms as part of the settlement, as Louima had demanded. He continued to insist that the PBA had "no liability," adding, "The PBA felt that it would assist the city in putting this case behind everyone. We never believed from the beginning that there was any real liability on the union's part, but in order to achieve a result here, it was necessary for the PBA to come to some sort of compro-

mise. So, fortunately, our insurers were willing to kick in to the settlement, so to speak, and that's how it resulted."

The nineteen-page settlement agreement did not include a single sentence mandating change. But, in fact, several vitally important changes were implemented during this period—although
legally I am bound to point out that these changes may not be
directly linked to our lawsuit. Among those changes were the cre-
ation of a civilian panel, rather than one composed of members of
the NYPD, to prosecute police brutality; training procedures concerning the use of force were drastically improved; the union
agreed to provide independent legal counsel to police officers desir-
ing legal advice, but who fear a conflict of interest with other police
officers under investigation or with the union itself; and the city
agreed to phase out the forty-eight-hour rule as police contracts
expired. The forty-eight-rule was ended for sergeants, lieutenants,
and captains and "taken off the table" in negotiations with the
PBA. The PBA has fought this, but the city has remained resolute.

According to the city's public advocate at that time, Mark Green,
since the Louima and Amadou Diallo cases, "(T)he NYPD has
been the subject of virtually constant independent, external over-
sight . . . more resources were provided to the Civilian Complaint
Review Board . . . the NYPD began to take substantiated CCRB
complaints more seriously, with the disciplinary rate for officers
with substantiated complaints tripling between 1996 and 2000."

These reforms didn't hurt the police department at all; in fact,
they made the job easier for the good cops and they helped restore
some of the confidence in the police department that had long ago
been lost by the minority community.

As soon as this agreement was announced, all of our telephones
started ringing. And ringing. The fact that for the first time in a
brutality case we had been able to hold a police union financially
responsible for the actions of its membership, we made them pay,
excited lawyers and civil rights organizations all over the country.

We were inundated with requests from NAACP chapters, from victims of police abuse, from attorneys, all of whom wanted to take similar actions. As Peter told Matt Lauer on the *Today* show, "All around the United States what's going to happen is, just as the PBA here [in New York City] decided on its own that it had to engage in certain remedies to prevent itself from being held liable again, we expect other police unions around the country will follow suit."

Rather than simply handing Abner Louima a lump sum payment, one big check, we worked with financial advisors to structure a long-term plan that would provide security for him and his family for the rest of his life. In essence, an annuity. Providing that service for clients is not unusual.

In almost all substantial settlements the payment is by far the most money the victim has ever had at one time and he or she probably isn't sure how to handle it. It's guaranteed there will be plenty of people around willing to help "invest" it, and at least part of our job is to prevent that from happening.

We've been responsible for some very creative settlements. I represented sixteen eight- and nine-year-old African-American schoolgirls in a shocking case. The Los Angeles School District assigned a white male teacher who had a history of exposing himself to teach in a predominately white elementary school in the San Fernando Valley. When he was accused by parents there of deviant behavior, rather than bringing charges against him or firing him, district officials transferred him to a school in Watts. Just imagine that. Their method of getting rid of a pervert was putting him into a classroom with African-American children. A known pedophile. At that school he was accused of sexually molesting two little girls. Again, instead of bringing legal charges against him, they transferred him to the Sixty-Eighth Street School, another black elementary school. Predictably, during recess he would send the boys out to play and masturbate in front of these little girls. Eventually the teacher was convicted of his crimes and sentenced to forty-four years in prison.

The school district understood we could demand an astronomical payment. The psychological damage done to these children was incalculable—yet we had to try to put a price on it. Representatives of the district claimed that any large payment would bankrupt the school district. They were basically accusing us of trying to destroy the educational system in Los Angeles. To help structure a settlement I asked Syd Irmas, who had a lot of experience in setting up long-term trusts, to help me forge a resolution. We eventually settled for $6 million—of which $1 million was put in a "special needs" trust. Nobody in the country was doing anything like this. This settlement, which eventually grew to be worth more than $25 million, was to be used to pay for any emotional counseling the girls needed as they got older. And we added a provision that after the girls reached a certain age the fund was to be distributed by a trustee according to a formula everyone agreed upon. That agreement benefited both the school district and the victims.

At Syd Irmas's suggestion, I donated $250,000 of my fee to the L.A. Family Housing Corporation; Syd donated land, and with government support we helped build ten units to house formerly homeless families. Named after my parents, the Johnnie L. Cochran Sr. and Hattie B. Cochran Villa stands proudly as an example of what can be accomplished when private citizens work with effective government agencies to solve public problems.

There simply isn't any means to determine the real value of an injury or a life. It's like trying to put a price tag on love. I had a heartbreaking case in which I represented the parents of an autistic child. He was very special, a savant. This was their only son. He attended a special school and he was very difficult to control. In fact, he was so difficult that his mother never allowed him to have play dates. But the parents of a classmate invited him to come to their home, promising he would be safe. The child's parents were extremely reluctant, though they eventually agreed.

The classmate's parents went to the movies, leaving the children in the care of their housekeeper, an immigrant who spoke little English. She couldn't handle both boys, and my clients' son jumped in the pool and drowned. The parents were devastated. Devastated. They loved this child completely.

But he was autistic, he would never be fully independent, he was going to need special care for his entire life. What was the value of his life—in legal terms? When I first began practicing there was a doctrine known as "the worthless child" that basically stipulated that certain children had no economic value. In this case the defense argued that rather than earning a living this child would be a drain on his parents and society. That there was no economic harm done, and cold as it might be, that is the measurement used in court cases to determine damages.

I spoke at great length with the defense about the love a mother has for her child. Eventually we received $2 million. It seems like a lot of money—until you imagine the impact of the loss on these parents. They didn't see their child as a drain on their finances, he was their son and they loved him. Try to put a dollar value on that love. Eventually they sent me a plaque designating me "Attorney for an Angel." I keep it in my home.

Probably the most successful settlement in which I've been involved was the death of Junious Roberts, an innocent, unarmed black man shot to death by a white policeman in Montgomery County, Maryland. One night in April 1999, Roberts was just talking with another man. A police officer thought he looked suspicious, that his eyes appeared "glassy," and that the ignition of his car appeared to be "punched out," meaning the car had been stolen. Junious Roberts was just talking to another man. Finally he got into his car and drove away. The cop followed. When the police officer put on his red flashers Roberts didn't stop, he kept driving, eventually pulling into a McDonald's parking lot and stopping.

The police officer took out his weapon, a nine-millimeter semi-automatic Beretta. When Roberts refused to get out of his car the police officer reached in with his free hand and tried to pull him out. The gun went off, a bullet ripped through Roberts's liver. He died three hours later. More than three decades after the death of Leonard Deadwyler, white police officers are still shooting unarmed black men.

This was the second such killing by a Montgomery County police officer within a two week period and, again, the community was enraged. A grand jury cleared the police officers in both cases. Roberts's family refused to accept the official version of the events and paid for a private autopsy to be performed. I was asked to join the team representing the family by two excellent lawyers, Billy Murphy and Walter Blair.

County officials met with us long before we reached the trial. They pointed out that Roberts was disabled, he suffered from heart problems, and couldn't work, so in purely economic terms there was no substantial loss to his family. And they also pointed out that Roberts had been drinking that night and was legally drunk. We responded that the police officer had no reason to suspect him, no reason to tail him, and absolutely no reason to shoot and kill him. But clearly these officials were sensitive to the problems in the county and wanted to do something positive about them. They acknowledged that there was a serious problem, although they refused to admit any liability. They did voluntarily initiate a program to compile statistics to determine the extent of racial profiling in the county.

We hammered out a settlement that could serve as a model in police abuse cases throughout the country. As I told reporters when it was announced, "Out of a dark cloud we found a silver lining."

The family received $2 million, from which we took our share. But in addition the county paid another million dollars to be used to make significant changes in the police department. The family didn't share in this money and we did not take a fee. The funds were used to begin a pilot program to install video cameras in patrol cars to tape all encounters between officers and civilians, to support a new training program to teach officers how to deal properly with issues concerning racial, ethnic, and gender diversity, to pay for a minority recruitment program for the police department, and to institute other programs "aimed at achieving greater racial harmony and respect between Montgomery County Police and all minority groups within Montgomery County."

And while it was not a formal part of the settlement, a new chief of police, an African-American, was recruited from Portland.

I learned some time later that the federal Department of Justice was aware of serious problems within Montgomery County law enforcement and had been monitoring the situation, so perhaps their willingness to settle had as much to do with timing as the facts of the Junious Roberts case. Whatever the reason, putting these changes into effect proved that the county was committed to improving relations between the police department and the minority community.

Measured in black lives, the price of progress remains very high.

SEVEN

When I first became involved in police brutality cases in Los Angeles in the mid-1960s it often was a pretty lonely fight. Just a victim and his family, me, and sometimes a few community activists against an entrenched bureaucracy confident the police could do no wrong. And even if on occasion it was clear that the LAPD did maim or kill an innocent black man, well, nobody seemed too upset.

Times have changed: not the incidence of abuse or deprivation of civil rights by police officers—that remains a serious problem—but the way society responds to it. Now these cases make front-page headlines. Now the police can't hide behind the claim that they were just doing their duty. Now thousands of people get out in the street and protest. Now politicians know they have to get involved. Of course, none of that guarantees that justice gets done.

The killing of Amadou Diallo by four white police officers was one of those cases. Amadou Diallo was a twenty-three-year-old African immigrant living in the Soundview section of the Bronx. He was working as a street vendor, selling videos, CDs, and audiotapes on a corner of East Fourteenth Street in Manhattan, sharing a small apartment with two other Africans. He had no criminal record, he didn't own a gun, he was just a hardworking young man. And just before midnight on the night of February 4, 1999, he walked into the dimly lighted vestibule of his apartment building.

Four white police officers, members of an NYPD unit known as the Street Crime Unit, were cruising the neighborhood looking for a serial rapist. They were dressed in civilian clothes, driving an unmarked vehicle. There was no way of knowing they were cops. The SCU was an "elite" unit whose motto was "We own the night"; it was even reported that several members of the unit had designed a T-shirt bearing a quotation from Ernest Hemingway: "Certainly there is no hunting like the hunting of man, and those who have hunted armed men long enough and liked it never really cared for anything else thereafter."

Those police officers apparently got a tip that "a suspicious-looking man" was hanging around in front of Diallo's building. They got there just about the time Amadou Diallo was opening the front door. According to these police officers, two of them began walking toward him, ordering him to "come out and keep your hands where we can see them." At this point they were probably less than ten feet away from him. Their lawyers later claimed that Diallo was "acting strange" and exhibited "aggressive behavior," which according to their interpretation means that instead of raising his hands he reached into his pocket and began pulling out a black object. In the darkness, supposedly it looked to the police officers like a gun. "Gun!" one of the cops shouted. A second officer opened fire, firing three shots, and then began retreating. As he backed up he slipped and fell—making it appear to the other cops that he had been shot at point-blank range. They opened fire with their sixteen-shot nine-millimeter semiautomatic weapons. They fired forty-one shots in less than eight seconds—forty-one shots. *Forty-one* shots. Amadou Diallo was hit nineteen times; bullets ruptured his aorta, spinal cord, lungs, liver, spleen, kidneys, and intestines. He was hit in his legs and even in the bottom of his feet. He was dead before the shooting stopped.

When the cops searched his body they discovered he did not have a gun. The black objects they claimed that they saw were his wallet and his pager. Four white cops had killed a completely innocent, unarmed man just walking into his own home. It was, as Reverend Al Sharpton said, "a police slaughter."

These police officers, realizing they'd killed an innocent man, began searching for evidence that Amadou Diallo wasn't so innocent. Without the legal formality of a search warrant they went into his apartment and searched—desperately, one might assume—for drugs, weapons, anything that might help them justify this killing. They also took Diallo's roommates to the station house to question them—forcing them to walk past Diallo's bullet-punctured body without bothering to tell them that the police had shot him—and kept them there for hours without explanation. These were all immigrants, people who didn't know their rights. One man was grilled by several different officers over a twelve-hour period—SCU officers, sergeants, detectives, and finally Internal Affairs officers, probably to see if maybe they could poke a hole in his story. It was an outrage, it was disgraceful. When relatives of the men being questioned went to the precinct they were told they could not speak with them, that technically those men were in custody.

These police officers were desperate to find a scapegoat and they couldn't do it. Amadou Diallo was exactly what he appeared to be, a hardworking immigrant who did nothing wrong, who simply wanted to live his life peacefully and had been shot forty-one times by four police officers. These people lacked the common decency, the courage to admit that they'd messed up, shot an innocent man. They never thought, We shouldn't have shot him, we shouldn't have kept shooting, but we did and we regret it terribly. There was not a word said like that; instead, they searched for an excuse.

Three days after the killing, more than a thousand people—black and white, among them one hundred rabbis and rabbinical students—showed up for a protest demonstration. Over the next few weeks more than 1,200 people were arrested during protests outside police headquarters. Mayor Rudolph Giuliani, long before he became a hero on September 11, 2001, was still a small, mean-spirited man looking to protect every cop. Although he expressed regret to Diallo's family, he pointed out that the cops "all had good records." Good records, in this case, meaning that of the four officers only one, Richard Murphy, had not previously had complaints—although unsubstantiated—filed against them with the Civilian Complaint Review Board. The other three had also been involved in prior shootings for which they were cleared of wrongdoing. Good records? What would qualify as a bad record? If forty-one shots was not considered excessive, how many times would they have had to shoot him before someone decided it was too many?

The cops weren't even suspended. Their nine-millimeter weapons were confiscated, replaced by standard service revolvers, and they were placed on administrative duty—with pay.

Within days Kadiatou Diallo, Amadou Diallo's mother, arrived from West Africa to take her son's body home. Madame Diallo called me, probably on the advice of Reverend Sharpton, and asked to meet me. We met in her room at the Rhiga Royal Hotel, where she was staying with her new husband. Madame Diallo was a very impressive woman, well spoken and very regal. "I think my son was wronged," she said to me. "I want you to represent me. I want you to look out for my interests. I want justice for my son."

Although the usual chorus of critics complained when it was announced I would represent Madame Diallo, few people in the media dared claim that I was going to "play the race card." Even to the most rabid of them all, it was obvious that the police had already played that card.

"This isn't only a case of driving while black," I said at a press conference, "it's walking while black, it's living while black, it's breathing while black." Once again, there was absolutely no question in my mind that this would not have happened if Amadou Diallo had been white. If he were white, he would still be alive. If

Diallo had been white these cops wouldn't have been so frightened. They wouldn't have been so ready to shoot. And they wouldn't have kept shooting. But they lived in a culture where it is assumed that a young black man must be doing something wrong. They began with the assumption of guilt. And when he didn't respond that heightened their fear. I understand the scenario; these officers didn't leave the precinct that night planning to kill a black man, this wasn't Mississippi in 1967. This wasn't premeditated. They didn't get out of their unmarked car intending to shoot him. I understand that police officers are frightened and often overreact, I really do understand that. I am fully aware of the reasons for that. I can rationalize and even justify that fear.

But I know one other thing: Amadou Diallo is dead, he shouldn't be dead, and if he weren't black he wouldn't be dead. I believe that with all my heart.

After being retained by Madame Diallo I began putting together a legal team. I think teams properly constituted accomplish much more than lawyers working independently. My first calls were to Peter Neufeld and Barry Scheck, who joined me. I felt we needed a lawyer known to the community, so I invited Michael Warren to become part of our team. Michael Warren is a very good, experienced New York civil rights lawyer, who'd long ago earned the respect of the minority community in police abuse cases. There are always politics involved in cases as sensitive as this one and he knew how to chart a course through these waters. We also asked Reverend Wyatt Tee Walker, who had been one of Reverend Martin Luther King Jr.'s closest aides during the 1960s, and who was then pastor of the Canaan Baptist Church in Harlem and chairman of Reverend Al Sharpton's National Action Network, to serve as administrator of Amadou Diallo's estate. There was nothing in the estate at that time, but we intended to file a civil lawsuit that would have filled it. Also, Madame Diallo's former husband and Amadou's father, Saikou Diallo, hired an experienced lawyer named Kyle Watters to represent his interests. It was a very fine team, a lot of experience, and we all got along quite well.

Just about the first thing I did was go to the scene of the shooting with Peter. The vestibule felt like an execution chamber. It was cold and even though it was outdoors, it felt airless. Bullet holes pocked the walls and door. It was difficult to stand in there without imagining the night of the killing, without sensing Amadou Diallo's presence, without thinking about the confusion and the sense of horror he must have felt when they started shooting. It was so still in there I could almost hear him. That place smelled of injustice. He was twenty-three years old, just trying to get home. What risk, what danger was he posing? I saw the ghosts of cases past coming along. Ron Settles, I always see Ron Settles. People told me, "You don't have any witnesses, you can't prove a thing, you're crazy." But as I had learned many years earlier, forensic evidence is the best witness.

A grand jury had indicted all four officers on charges of second-degree murder. These men had been well advised not to appear before the grand jury to tell their version of the story. Under existing police department regulations they didn't have to speak with anyone—including their supervisors—for at least forty-eight hours. By the time they told their stories, I'm convinced that they knew exactly what had been learned from the forensic evidence, so whatever they said was compatible with that evidence.

They were going to be tried in the Bronx, where the shootings had occurred. That was very important. The people who would sit on that jury lived in the Bronx, they knew from their own experience about the elite Street Crime Unit. They would best be able to judge the officers' credibility. I met with the Bronx DA Robert Johnson and told him we were going to conduct our own, independent investigation and would share with his office any worthwhile evidence we developed. Then we hired Kevin Hinkson to lead our investigation. Kevin Hinkson was a former police officer who had become an outstanding private investigator. He's a big guy with a soft manner who inspires confidence. People feel comfortable talking to him, and sometimes they tell him things they would not tell police officers. They trusted Kevin. So did I, completely.

We hired a forensic pathologist to learn as much as we could about how Amadou Diallo died. We hired a criminalist and a ballistics expert. We wanted to know as much as we possibly could about what really happened that night.

The police were desperate to prove that Amadou Diallo was less than an honest, hardworking man. "Cops Look for Dirt," one headline read. Finally they found a thread "Amadou Lied in His Claim for Asylum." Apparently he claimed that if he returned to Guinea his life would be in jeopardy because of his political beliefs. That probably wasn't true, although it is a claim made by many immigrants. Making his immigration application public was simply the city's attempt to dirty up the victim. We were all sitting around my office one afternoon trying to figure out how we were going to respond to this. True or not, it certainly didn't justify shooting him forty-one times. After we all had voiced our opinion, Al Sharpton answered the question, very quietly reminding us, "It's not how he got here, it's how he left here. And he left here with nineteen bullet holes in his body and he hadn't done anything wrong."

Having been involved in so many police brutality cases similar to this one, maybe it seems like it would get harder and harder for me to feel truly outraged. But it doesn't. I can't begin to describe the outrage I felt. The anger and frustration. Reverend Sharpton had been right, this was a slaughter, that's all it was. And I wanted to see justice done.

It was obvious the officers would claim they fired only in self-defense, believing their lives were in danger. With no eyewitnesses, that would be very tough to disprove.

Initially I wanted to hire Michael Baden, the pathologist with whom I had worked for so many years. But because he was employed by the state of New York, the potential for a conflict of interest made that impossible. Instead we hired Dr. Cyril Wecht, from Pittsburgh, to conduct an autopsy for the defense. Working with the New York City medical examiners, he made an important discovery. The officers claimed that Diallo did not fall down until the shooting ended, giving them at least a flimsy excuse why they continued to fire. But Dr. Wecht found that two bullets had hit Diallo in the bottom of his right foot, one of them entering right through the ball of the foot, the other one hitting the bottom of his middle toe. Even more telling, Wecht found that a bullet had entered Diallo's calf and traveled up his leg, lodging in the back of his knee. If he was standing, that bullet would have had to enter his body and make almost a ninety-degree turn. That is not impossible—when bullets fly, anything is possible—but it is highly unlikely. The path of the bullets made it obvious that the police officers continued to fire after Amadou Diallo was on the ground, long past the point at which they believed they were defending themselves. If we could prove that they lied about something as important as that, their credibility would be destroyed. It was an important first step.

There were a lot of other questions to be answered. The policemen had stated that the lighting in the vestibule was very poor, which is why they had mistaken a wallet for a gun. We wanted to find out just how dim it was—or how brightly it was lit. Kevin Hinkson was working the block for us within days of the shooting. Police investigators were there, too, but everyone in the neighborhood believed that the police were searching for evidence that would justify the shooting, not put other cops in jail. So people who were afraid to talk to the police spoke willingly with Hinkson.

It didn't take long to find credible witnesses to the shooting. I interviewed several of them. There was an invalid living almost directly across the street, a man confined to a hospital bed with twenty-four-hour nursing care. His bedroom window faced the entrance to Amadou Diallo's building. When the police asked his wife if she had witnessed the shooting she told them that she had not—but she didn't tell them that she had a home attendant, a nurse, who had seen just about the whole thing.

This nurse told us that the first shots got her attention and she saw the fusillade of bullets ripping into Diallo's body. She had an almost perfect view and provided helpful information. Another man who lived on the block was on his way home when he heard the first shots and watched as the police fired into the vestibule. Most importantly, he did not see anyone stumble backward as the police claimed. We gave all of the information we developed to the prosecutor's office.

We approached this case as if we were going to try it in criminal court. It was obvious that sometime years in the future the city would be paying a substantial sum of money to the estate of Amadou Diallo, but in addition to making the city pay enough to better supervise this group that claimed they "owned the night," I wanted to see the officers pay for their recklessness.

This case also carried enormous political consequences. The family had refused to meet with Mayor Giuliani. They were being advised by Reverend Al Sharpton, who day by day was becoming a powerful figure in New York City.

There were a lot of people trying to get close to Madame Diallo and her former husband. Those two people, who seemingly had been getting along just fine, began fighting over control of their son's estate.

Madame Diallo and I had established a good relationship, but she just didn't understand why I wasn't available to her at every moment. I explained to her that I had obligations to several clients and that I had to travel back to L.A. often to run my office there. She was not impressed by the fact that I was so busy, that I had so many other clients. She didn't want to speak with my partners on this case, she wanted to speak with me. At one point she complained that she had been trying to get in touch with me for more than a day. "I didn't know where you were," she said.

"I had another client I had to see in Los Angeles," I told her.

She shook her head. "You shouldn't have other clients," she told me, "you should just have this one client."

This was a complaint I had heard before. When someone becomes involved in a legal case, even a minor case, it often becomes the focal point of his or her life. Sometimes it even becomes an obsession. And that isn't limited to criminal cases, either. At any given time I am actively involved in about fifty different cases. Each of them is at a different point in what is always a lengthy process. The Geronimo Pratt case lasted twenty-seven years. The Donald Scott case, in which police killed an innocent white man whose land the government wanted, lasted almost eight years. Legal cases are rarely predictable and never run evenly. Usually they require time in great gulps separated by long periods of waiting. Ike Odoi-Kyene, a male model from Ghana who I successfully defended in a murder case, told reporters, "It can be hard to get Johnnie on the phone, and before the case started I am getting very upset. I am paying him all this money and I'm thinking, Where is he? When you talk to him, sometimes you think Johnnie is not listening. But he is. And then in the trial he is sitting back, calm. Meanwhile, I'm sitting there shaking, worried about my life. And, oh boy, he is making it seem like being a lawyer is nothing. But trust me, he saved my ass."

There is only one way to work on so many cases simultaneously— and that is to work. I only know one way to work, full speed ahead. I haven't really changed that much from the young lawyer who simultaneously tried a civil case in the morning and a murder case in the evening. What helps is that I am organized to the extreme and have a tremendous support system.

I am organized. I am neat. I am neat in everything that I do. Every suit and shirt in my closet is neatly lined up. When I finish work I hang up my suit neatly and change into something comfortable—and neat. That's me, that's who I am. I like order; my wife claims that if a room is a mess I can't sleep in it. That's probably a bit of an overstatement, but only a little bit.

What I don't do as well is focus on minor details. I depend on other people to do that. I wouldn't be able to correctly remember the specific dates on which I argued specific cases without looking it up, for example.

But Madame Diallo just never understood that this is the way I work. In July, she sent me a nice letter explaining that she had decided to retain a new lawyer. Her brother told the media that she "wants someone who has enough time for her." And Kyle Watters said that there was a disagreement between Madame Diallo and her former husband about how to manage their son's estate, explaining, "We're in the middle of a matrimonial dispute."

Whatever the reasons, I was fired. That hadn't happened to me very often in my career. And admittedly, my pride was hurt. I didn't like it, I didn't agree with the reasoning, but I understood and accepted it. She hired a good New York lawyer named Robert Conason. "Madame," I told her, "you have an absolute right to do whatever you want. He's a fine lawyer and we'll cooperate with him totally." We handed over all the materials we'd gathered to her new lawyers.

What happened after that was a travesty, although I don't know that even if we had remained involved we could have done anything at all to change the situation. I doubt it. In December the State Supreme Court Appellate Division moved the trial to Albany, claiming that it would be impossible to conduct a fair trial in the Bronx. When I heard the news there was just an empty feeling in my stomach. This seemed to me to be the elevation of politics over justice. People in the Bronx know how police officers act in the Bronx. They would have been best able to determine how the police had responded that night. These are people who want to live in a safe neighborhood, who want their children to be safe—and who time after time after time have served on juries that have convicted and put African-Americans in jail. Obviously the people in Albany want to be supportive of the police, too, but too often they accept the most broad definition possible of "necessary force" and turn a blind eye toward some of their actions.

Those people who wonder why African-Americans and other minorities complain that the justice system is rigged against them should carefully examine what happened in this case. Granting the defense motion for a change of venue was an insult to the people of the Bronx. This was the legal system telling the minority community it could not be fair in this case. This was the legal system playing the so-called race card, determining that white police officers accused of killing an innocent black man could not get a fair verdict from a multiracial jury in the Bronx. Bob Johnson claimed he fought hard against this, but lost, Kadiatou Diallo said quietly, "We don't want our agony to be prolonged. We are here, we seek justice, we respect the rules. It's not fair."

It was not fair. One person who was not going to get a fair trial in Albany was Amadou Diallo. Albany is the capital of New York State, the heart of the political system. It is overwhelmingly white. It's not quite Simi Valley east, but it is a conservative city. As soon as I heard that the trial was to be held there, I knew that it would be extremely difficult to convict the officers of murder. I don't think anyone was surprised when the four officers were acquitted of all charges. Actually, I think pretty much everybody expected it. The prosecution didn't call the witnesses that we had found; the nurse, the man walking down the block. I never found out why. I'm not sure it would have made any difference in the outcome. Race never became an issue during the trial. It was like there was a big pink elephant in the room and everyone politely stepped around it like it wasn't there. I'm not criticizing the way Johnson's office tried the case, once it landed in Albany they didn't have much of a chance. That's a pretty frightening thought, but I believe it to be true.

As far as the law was concerned, it was just a forty-one-shot mistake. Some sort of terrible accident. In *New York Trend,* an online magazine, Dr. T. Taylor-Williams pretty accurately described the feelings in the black community: "... I know exactly where I was when Orenthal James Simpson was cleared of the double murder, most African-Americans do. Why? Because it was the first time most of us had witnessed a person of color ... prove that with access to resources, strategy, and money, [that person] can lodge a successful defense. ... Whether or not O. J. Simpson committed this crime, the prosecutor's case did not prove his guilt. ... And what were the repercussions of this verdict? There was a resounding cry from a majority white population that the 'system' had failed. They complained that the legal system they had constructed had flaws. They charged that there should be a complete overhaul of the courts and laws ...

"The [Diallo] trial's relocation to suburban Albany resulted in exactly what our fair leaders planned, didn't it?"

There was not even the pretense of shock or surprise from the white community when the verdict was announced. The four officers who killed Amadou Diallo have gone on with their lives. One of them, in fact, resigned from the police force and joined the New York Fire Department, and when a black fireman refused to work in a firehouse with him, it was the black fireman who was harshly criticized—for not accepting the jury verdict.

I wish my team and I could have continued with this case. Would the officers still have been acquitted? Maybe so. Could we have gotten a substantial settlement for the family when the civil suit against the city finally goes to trial? I like to believe so, although the family is represented by good lawyers. But I would have loved the opportunity to stand in front of a jury and describe in detail what I believe happened that night. It would have made me feel better.

I think Madame Diallo wishes we were still representing her interests, too. I see her occasionally at various events and we always speak. For a woman who grew up in Africa to be thrust into a situation as difficult as this one and respond with such strength of character—and then grow stronger as time passes—is a truly remarkable thing. But that's what happened to her. She seems more impressive each time I see her, more confident, more determined. At one of these gatherings, a march in Washington, D.C., she said quietly to me, "I wish you were still my lawyer."

Hearing that, I felt somewhat vindicated.

Following the killing of Amadou Diallo the Street Crime Unit was reorganized. It was reduced in size and split into eight groups, each under the control of borough commanders. And finally in April 2002, new mayor Michael Bloomberg's police commissioner Ray Kelly announced that the Street Crime Unit was being disbanded. Kelly made a point of telling reporters that this was not being done in response to the Diallo case or other pending litigation against the NYPD. Whatever the reason for its demise, no one I know will mourn its passing.

Just a few days after the jury in Albany had acquitted the officers in the Diallo killing, on March 16, 1999, twenty-six-year-old Haitian-American Patrick Dorismond was killed. The brief description is chillingly familiar: an innocent, unarmed black man doing absolutely nothing wrong was shot and killed by a police officer. When does a series of isolated incidents become a pattern of behavior? After two killings, three, four? The people of Los Angeles refused for decades to acknowledge the existence of a law enforcement culture that permitted police officers to lie in the courtroom, to plant evidence, to frame suspects, and to violate basic constitutional rights—almost always involving minority suspects—until the Rampart scandal broke that system wide open.

No one can deny that Mayor Giuliani distinguished himself and brought honor to the city with his response following the September 11 terrorist attack, but his actions prior to that toward New York's minority community could accurately be described, at best,

as mean-spirited. Most members of New York's minority community did not believe the mayor ever acted in their interests. A lot of
people considered him very dangerous. It was Rudy Giuliani, they
point out, who sent the police into homeless shelters on the coldest
night of winter to arrest homeless people with outstanding misdemeanor warrants. Maybe the well-publicized events of his personal
life, the very public dissolution of his marriage, being diagnosed
and treated for cancer, rallying the city after the attack, have
changed him. I have always believed strongly in redemption.

The knee-jerk response by the establishment in almost every
case in which police officers act irresponsibly is to blame the victim,
to dirty up the victim—Louima supposedly hit a policeman, Diallo
acted suspiciously, Settles was on drugs—but rarely has that tactic
ever been used as crudely by a political leader as in the killing of
Patrick Dorismond. Dorismond was a responsible, hardworking
father of two little girls working as a security guard for the midtown Business Improvement District. In fact, he actually wanted to
become a cop. After work one evening he stopped at a bar on Eighth
Avenue and Thirty-Seventh Street in Manhattan with a friend for a
beer, possibly two beers. When the men left the bar slightly after
midnight an undercover police officer, involved in a "bust and buy"
drug sting, approached them and asked Dorismond if he wanted to
buy some crack cocaine. Differing reports of the incident indicate
that the officer asked Dorismond where he might buy some marijuana. This officer, and his two backups, were involved in a controversial antidrug program known as Operation Condor. Whatever
the question, Dorismond turned him down. He didn't want to get
involved. Period. As Nancy Reagan had advised, he just said no.

Firmly, and repeatedly, he warned them to get out of his face.
This had started as a normal street encounter, the kind of thing
that happens countless times every day, but it quickly escalated.
According to the man with Dorismond, the police officer persisted.
Dorismond became angry and the two men began arguing. At this

point Dorismond apparently did not know he was arguing with a cop. The two backup officers rushed to the scene, one with his gun drawn. During the ensuing altercation the gun fired, Dorismond was hit in the stomach and was killed. No drugs or contraband of any type was found on his body. He was just another young, innocent, dead black man.

Those facts are pretty much indisputable. No one is claiming anything significantly different took place. That was another tragedy, but what happened after that was reprehensible. This came at a bad time for Giuliani, who was just beginning his run for the United States Senate against Hillary Clinton and had to solidify his conservative base. He had to show how tough he was.

Patrick's anguished mother, Marie Dorismond, a pediatric nurse, cried out, "Every one of you that used to have a sick kid coming to Kings County Hospital, every nurses, every doctors, every lawyers, stand up! This is Mrs. Dorismond from Pediatric D-72. They got my son now."

Without a shred of evidence that the police officer had acted responsibly, Mayor Giuliani leaped to his defense. Initially Giuliani claimed that the cop who fired the shot had been wired and that his conversation with Dorismond would probably be made public. Theoretically that tape would prove that the cops had identified themselves to Dorismond as police officers—as they claimed—rather than the muggers they probably appeared to Dorismond to be. If they had not identified themselves, as others claimed, then Dorismond was simply doing what any brave man would do—resisting drug dealers trying to mug him. That tape that Giuliani mentioned apparently didn't exist. No transcript was ever made public.

Giuliani then claimed that "at least one version of the facts suggests that Mr. Dorismond acted in a way that was very aggressive toward the police," and that he had a "propensity for violence." He added that Dorismond "was no choirboy." In fact, as it turned out, Dorismond had indeed been an altar boy in his church.

Then Giuliani got serious. He ordered Police Commissioner Howard Safir to unseal Dorismond's juvenile record, explaining that his record "may justify, more closely, what the police officer did."

There is a law prohibiting any juvenile record from being made public. Giuliani broke that law attempting to protect the cop. Dorismond's record consisted of several misdemeanor charges, cases that were dropped. When he was thirteen years old, for example, he had been arrested for robbery and assault—for a fistfight over a quarter. He had never been convicted of a crime. Defending this illegal action, Giuliani, who is a lawyer and should know better, said that rights of privacy end with an individual's death.

As an adult Dorismond had been involved in several encounters with police officers, among them a domestic dispute with the mother of one of his little girls. Ironically, although the public would never learn about it from City Hall, precisely that same charge had been lodged against the police officer who had killed him. That officer had also been cited on several occasions for drawing his weapon too often and without sufficient provocation.

In addition, and perhaps to deflect some criticism, Mayor Giuliani publicized the toxicology report showing Dorismond had traces of marijuana in his system when he was killed.

Among many, many others, Giuliani's attempted character assassination infuriated Democratic Speaker of the New York State Assembly Sheldon Silver, who said, "I am compelled to go on record in saying that Mayor Rudy Giuliani's actions following the death of Patrick Dorismond are egregious, reprehensible, and a complete abdication of his moral and legal responsibilities as a public servant . . .

"[In releasing these sealed documents Giuliani] violated a public trust, state law, and let down the people of New York. Mayor Giuliani has responded to a suffering, grieving family . . . by victimizing them."

Finally Giuliani personally visited the families of the cops involved in the shooting—but did not bother to contact Patrick Dorismond's family. Weeks later, after being excoriated in the media about his behavior, he finally allowed an intermediary to make arrangements for a meeting with Mrs. Dorismond, but then refused to schedule that meeting when Mrs. Dorismond said she wanted me to be present.

I got involved almost immediately. Because of the Louima case I had a strong connection to the New York Haitian community. I'd been to the churches. I think the Haitians respected the work I'd done for Abner Louima and knew I would fight hard for their rights. The family called my office and I went to Brooklyn to meet Marie Dorismond. "Mr. Cochran," she told me, "I am so vexed." So terribly, terribly vexed. I went with the family to the funeral. There was a heavy police presence at the funeral to control the large, angry crowd. Unfortunately, some people began throwing bottles and other objects at the police and a brawl broke out; twenty-seven people were arrested and twenty-three policemen were injured. Although Mayor Giuliani did not dare attend the funeral, he did visit the injured police officers in the hospital, where he praised them for their "measured response to provocations."

This really is the poster case for dirtying up the victim. I can't think of another situation in which an elected public official so blatantly—and illegally—attempted to destroy the reputation of a completely innocent man. I don't know Rudy Giuliani. We've never really met, although we've attended several of the same functions. I suspect I remain too controversial to his strongest conservative supporters for him to be seen talking with me. The same is true for Al Sharpton. Giuliani and Sharpton never even appeared in the same photograph. I found it extremely pleasing that Reverend Sharpton was invited to Mayor Mike Bloomberg's inauguration—by one of Bloomberg's new commissioners—and that Bloomberg has pointedly allowed himself to be photographed shaking hands with Sharpton. And one of the first actions taken by Bloomberg's new police commissioner, Ray Kelly, was to greatly scale back Operation Condor. These are strong messages of inclusion and awareness to the minorities of New York City.

Within weeks a grand jury convened by Manhattan DA Robert Morgenthau cleared the police officers of any wrongdoing. A completely innocent man was shot down on the streets of New York in 1999 and no one was going to be punished for it. In response to the grand jury decision, Giuliani finally said that he wanted "to extend my sympathy and my prayers to the people most affected by this: the Dorismond family, who will have a very hard time accepting this."

As there was no indictment there would be no criminal trial. That meant there would be no substantial investigation by the city. We would have to uncover all the evidence ourselves. We began investigating this case just as we had all the others. We hired Kevin Hinkson. Hinkson is a former police officer who pointed out that department rules allow police officers to use the same level of force as is presented against them. If someone is brawling with only fists cops are not permitted to use a gun, for example—which is exactly what happened. We built our case.

In May 2000, we filed a notice of claim, a lawsuit, against Mayor Giuliani, Police Commissioner Bernard Kerik, and the police officer who shot Dorismond for $100 million, for violation of Patrick Dorismond's civil rights, wrongful death, and pain and suffering. Essentially we were suing New York City for creating a climate and allowing the situation to take place in which an innocent, tax-paying citizen could be killed for turning down an offer to buy drugs. And we said at that time that we had specifically included the mayor in our lawsuit "to take him to task for demonizing a person who was an altar boy." Giuliani was actually reasonable in the Louima case because the attack was so heinous that even he couldn't defend the actions of the police officers, but he has to be held accountable for his actions in the Dorismond case.

This lawsuit is very slowly moving through the court system. The city has fought just about every motion we've filed. We've gathered documents, found witnesses, and taken numerous depositions. When the trial finally begins we will be ready.

Assuming there is a trial. I would like very much to try this case, but if city's attorneys are smart it will never get inside a courtroom. An innocent man is dead. Former Mayor Giuliani has tremendous legal exposure here, as there is no legal justification for his actions. There are other aspects of the case, including racial profiling, that make it difficult for the city to defend. We're waiting, patiently.

I know I will feel very confident arguing this case in front of a jury—so long as it is a fairly constituted jury. The fact is not all juries are created equal. Even in twenty-first-century America. I was reminded of this reality when we tried the Cynthia Wiggins case in Buffalo, New York.

This was a case that just infuriated me. Cynthia Wiggins was a seventeen-year-old high school student living in a very poor suburb of Buffalo. She was an African-American single mother who wanted to go to college one day and perhaps become a doctor. She had real goals. To support her child she worked part-time as a cashier at a fast-food restaurant, Arthur Treacher's Fish and Chips, in a very upscale mall, the Walden Galleria in Cheektowaga. But to get to her job she had to take a bus, and rather than going directly into the mall the bus stopped across Walden Avenue, a heavily traveled seven-lane road. Basically, it was a highway with traffic lights. One December day in 1995, when a seven-foot-high snowbank made it impossible for the bus to stop at the curb, Cynthia was let out of the bus into a lane of traffic. This stop had no sidewalk, crosswalk, or bus shelter, nothing to offer any protection. While crossing the street to get to her job, she was crushed by a dump truck. The driver never saw her and kept going. Someone wrote down his license plate and police tracked him down. Cynthia Wiggins survived on life support for several weeks before succumbing to her massive injuries. She was survived by her grandmother, her mother, her sister, and her two-year-old son, Taquilo.

The facts didn't surprise me; poor people depend on mass transit and because poor people use public transportation, upscale neighborhoods and stores restrict access to buses and trains. They want to make it harder for poor people to get there so they'll choose to shop elsewhere. It's a subtle but pervasive form of discrimination against America's biggest minority, the working poor, and it's true all over America.

I got involved in this case when the lawyer representing the family of Cynthia Wiggins, a Buffalo attorney named Bob Perk, wrote a letter to my firm that attracted my associate Carl Douglas's attention. "Boss," Carl told me, "you ought to take a look at this one." In the letter Bob Perk laid out the facts in a straightforward manner, but it was obvious that he was truly passionate about this case. That's why he reached out to me. Later I saw a report about the case on Ted Koppel's *Nightline*. The more I learned about the death of Cynthia Wiggins, the angrier I got.

Bob Perk welcomed my call. He told me he had disliked the report done by *Nightline*, and had not really participated. He felt the show had misrepresented Cynthia Wiggins. Among other things, they had claimed she was jaywalking, which was apparently inaccurate, and had identified her as "an unwed teenage mother," a phrase that carries with it a negative connotation. "This was a good person," he told me, "a hardworking young woman getting her life in order." He told me he would need help to try this case. "There are going to be who knows how many witnesses and countless depositions, we're going to need expert testimony, and somebody has to plow through a mountain of documents." Then he invited me to join him in trying this case.

Bob Perk had done a fine job preparing his case. His excellent investigator, Don Fuhrman—"the Good Fuhrman," as we later referred to him—had dug up some potentially devastating documents. It wasn't simply poor planning that caused the Niagara Frontier Transportation Authority #6 bus to drop off its passengers across a busy street from the Walden Galleria, it was an attempt by the mall to keep out "undesirable" people. The #6 ran right through the heart of Buffalo's inner city, the predominately black east side, but pretty much everybody who rode this line qualified as poor.

While bus lines from other areas, even those large tourist buses from across the Canadian border, were permitted to drive right into the mall, the #6 was denied access. The Galleria welcomed Canadians, but they did not want poor Americans. Documents obtained from NFTA by Fuhrman and a reporter for the *Buffalo News* proved that the bus company knew the stop was dangerous and had been requesting permission for its buses to enter the mall for the past four years—permission that had been continuously denied.

Initially Bob Perk assumed there had to be some logical reason the #6 bus didn't pull into the mall, some sort of crazy lease provision or traffic regulation. But a *News* reporter found a memo stating flatly that there would be no #6 bus service into it because the mall didn't want it on their property. There were no strange provisions, no odd restrictions, they just didn't want "those people."

The Pyramid Management Group, owners of the mall, denied it was discriminating against black and poor people. They came up with all kinds of silly reasons why the #6 bus had been banned. It was to relieve traffic congestion. It was to ease wear and tear on the roads. It wasn't convenient. When they ran out of excuses they blamed the victim. They claimed that no one had forced Cynthia Wiggins to take the #6, that it was her choice to jaywalk across a seven-lane road. As one of their attorneys said, "The mall should not be held responsible for how employees choose to get to work."

I had an answer for them: "If you design and build a mall, it must be open to one and all!" And to make sure they got the message, we sued them for $210 million. This wasn't just an accident, this was an avoidable tragedy. It happened because the mall wanted to make it hard for poor people to get there. The mall didn't want these undesirable elements disturbing their more affluent patrons. And because of that Taquilo Wiggins was going to grow up without his mother.

I had never before been to Buffalo in winter. It was cold. It was *very* cold. My connections to the city were somewhat tenuous; Dale had gone to college in Rochester, which is only a few hundred miles away, and O. J. Simpson had earned his place in football's Hall of Fame playing for the Buffalo Bills. It was one of the few places in the country where some people still talked about "The Juice" as a football player.

I spent a considerable amount of time there. I'm sure many people assumed when I joined Bob Perk that I was going to be a figurehead, that I was just going to show up for cameras and trust that my reputation would cause the mall owners to surrender in fear. It didn't exactly work that way. I was passionate about this case. I was there for numerous depositions. I was there for pretrial hearings and strategy sessions. When I wasn't physically there Bob and I would be on the phone often late into the night. As the trial approached I basically moved to Buffalo. I got to know, and like, that city very much. I knew where to eat breakfast, where to get the best hot dogs, the best Buffalo wings. I met a lot of friendly people. For such a cold place, it's an awfully warm city.

We probably took sixty depositions. Some of them were memorable. I remember a NFTA bus driver who told us that everybody knew the stop was unsafe—and then she added that the drivers had warned their supervisors that the stop created a very dangerous situation. I remember asking the executive director of the bus line, "Did you have concerns about the safety of your passengers?" Of course we did, he replied. You knew it was an unsafe situation, I continued, if you were concerned about the safety of your passengers, what did you do about it?

Nothing, he admitted.

I just let that answer hang in the air for about forty seconds. Nothing. Once again, the silence was deafening. Nothing.

The Pyramid Management Group was represented by the very fine, white corporate firm Williams and Connolly. The case was handled by its one black partner. He was a very nice man, I liked him, and he was competent, but it was obvious he was there to counterbalance me. It's an amazing coincidence how often I find myself sitting across a courtroom from the only African-American partner in a firm. That happens to me quite a bit; as we get ready to go to trial, a black lawyer suddenly shows up representing the other side. Good. I applaud that. I think it's great. I'm always confident I'm going to beat them, but I'm glad they're getting an opportunity.

The first thing that happens in a trial is jury selection. And this is where the real problem in this case began. We had a wonderful judge, one of the finest judges I have ever had in my career, named Jerome Gorski, who did everything possible to ensure that everyone received a fair trial.

We were going to try this case in front of a six-person jury, with three alternates. In many jurisdictions only six people sit on a jury in a civil case. Those six jurors and three alternates were to be selected from a panel consisting of about ninety-five people. I remember sitting in the courtroom as these potential jurors came in. It was just one white person after another. It was astonishing. I certainly have nothing against white people, some of my very best friends are white, but the panel was hardly representative of the city of Buffalo. Of the ninety-five panelists, ninety were white.

This was really troubling to me. I love the jury system. Thomas Jefferson said rightfully that it is the anchor of our liberties. Picking a jury is probably the most important aspect of a trial. If you don't have a jury with people who have come into the courtroom with an open mind—people who are really willing to listen to your presentation and consider the evidence—then you have little chance of winning.

When selecting a jury I try to ensure that its makeup reflects the balance found in society. That means economically as well as racially—and in some cases, the economic factor is even more important than racial balance. People who have never ridden a bus to work are going to have a hard time understanding the actions of a person who depends on public transportation just to leave her neighborhood. Poor people understand each other, they know the hardships, they know what they have to do to survive, they know how demeaning it can be.

I always want at least a few African-Americans on a jury when the victim or the accused person is black. I want somebody in the jury room to be able to speak up for my client, to make sure that the case is decided on the facts rather than skin color, whether the final verdict is for or against that client.

I've heard the complaints that I try to stack juries with African-Americans—although I've rarely heard any complaints when prosecutors systematically try to exclude blacks from a jury specifically because of their race. Of course, when prosecutors do it, it's known as strategy.

Jury selection is done differently in each jurisdiction. Usually, as each prospective juror is interviewed one side or the other can bring a challenge for cause—meaning the way that person answered a question proved he or she could not render a fair verdict—and if the judge agrees, that person is dismissed. In addition, each side usually gets a limited number of "peremptory challenges," meaning it can dismiss a potential juror without stating a reason. But a lawyer can't challenge someone because of his or her race. I don't care if I'm going to trial against a close friend, as soon as they start kicking off black jurors without having a really good reason, we're going to be heading for a fight. When we were picking the Simpson jury ten of the first eleven jurors excluded by the prosecutors were black, but there were so many blacks on the panel that eventually we were able to get a diverse, representative jury.

The Simpson trial was the only time in my life I've used an expert to help select the best possible jury. Usually I can do it myself. I've certainly had enough experience. I know that black women make extraordinarily strong jurors because of what they have endured in society; if a black woman tells me she will be fair I know I can depend on that. Conversely, if I see a white male juror wearing white socks and a conventional suit with a string tie, he isn't going to be sitting on my jury. That's Archie Bunker style. I don't even have to ask him any questions, he's out. Some of the clichés are true: Younger people tend to be a little more open, older people are more conservative. I've usually done better with women than men.

I've argued cases in front of hundreds of juries, but no lawyer forgets his first jury trial as a defense lawyer. I was representing a young man charged with first-degree murder. He was with a gang when the crime was committed. I made what I believed to be a brilliant final argument, even I was impressed by the majesty of my words, I carried the jury on a magic carpet of truth and justice; well, at least that's what I believed. The jury acquitted my client while convicting some of the other gang members. I had done it! I had captured the minds of the jurors. I was feeling great—until I got a note from one of the jurors, a nice lady who sat in the front row, which read, "Tell Mr. Cochran's client he'd better not do anything like that again."

Contrary to what many people believe, I'm not always searching for racial implications, but in Buffalo when I looked at a large courtroom crowded with potential jurors and could count the number of black faces on one hand—literally—it was obvious that something definitely was wrong. When we began questioning these people, the five African-Americans admitted they knew all about the case and had already formed opinions. The judge properly dismissed them. That left us without a single African-American on the jury.

We dismissed a lot of white jurors, too. It was not difficult to identify those people with strong opinions; there were probably an equal number of people who thought the mall was the devil or that Cynthia Wiggins was responsible for her own death. If we didn't challenge these people the other side did. But there was one lady I won't forget. She didn't want to serve on the jury and had a reasonable excuse, so the judge dismissed her. She started to leave but suddenly turned around and came back. "Tell me, Mr. Cochran," she said, "did the gloves fit?" Everyone in the courtroom started laughing.

We did not get a representative jury. It consisted of five white people and one East Indian; all three alternate jurors were white. That was pretty outrageous. It was hardly a cross-section of the community. As reporter Donn Exmonde wrote in the *News,* "It would be nice if it [the jury] included people who haven't just shopped at the mall, but who got there on the bus. Or, as in this case, didn't get there."

But Bob Perk explained that this was not some sort of racist setup; no one was stacking the deck to get even with Johnnie Cochran. The lack of minority jurors was a problem lawyers in western New York had been struggling with for a long time. For whatever reason not enough minorities served on juries.

But five out of ninety-five? I wasn't going to accept that without a fight. We met with the judge in his chambers. "Judge," I said, "there's something wrong here. Just how is this possible? We've got an all-white jury. I've tried cases all over the country and this is the worst panel I've ever seen."

The judge was sympathetic; he admitted it was a problem, but legally there wasn't anything he could do about it. He summoned the commissioner of jurors, who went through the entire selection process to us. He showed us his lists. He definitely had followed state law. I think everybody in the judge's chambers knew this wasn't a representative jury, but there was nothing that the judge could do to change a bad situation.

Bob Perk and I made a motion to supplement the panel to include some more blacks and Latinos. The judge turned us down as we knew he would. We knew this was a fight we couldn't win, but we wanted to be on record as protesting the makeup of the jury in case we had to file an appeal.

I've spent many years of my life standing in front of mostly white juries, so that prospect did not frighten me. For years blacks and Latinos had been systematically excluded from participation in the jury system. It isn't any big secret that many communities intentionally kept blacks off juries. Now I knew that this wasn't that type of situation at all, there didn't seem to be any kind of sinister motive or an organized or even disorganized effort to exclude African-Americans, it was just the way the system worked.

Well, I was there to tell them it wasn't working. I was there to remind these people that they faced a serious problem that had to be addressed. When I sat back and tried to understand what I was doing in Buffalo, New York, in the middle of winter the answer was, obviously, I was there to make it very clear that the old ways of doing the people's legal business no longer applied. That they had better find a way to encourage inclusion.

In fact, Bob and I actually liked this jury. There was one man in particular, a seventy-year-old retired union plasterer, who we felt would be sympathetic to our case. I'd found in previous trials that men who have worked in the construction trades understood that you don't pick on women and you don't hurt kids.

Conversely, there was another juror that I felt we couldn't reach with a tent pole. During the initial questioning he'd sat there with his arms crossed, his mouth closed, responding to my questions with brief, almost abrupt answers. Our problem was his answers didn't disqualify him. He told us he knew nothing about the case and was certain he could be fair. I wondered about that, but Bob and I didn't dare use one of our three challenges on him. Knowing when to spend a challenge is always a tough call, because the next person to sit in that chair might be many times more damaging. So we ended up with him on the jury, where he sat with his arms crossed and his mouth closed.

I knew when I stood up to make my opening remarks during jury selection that most of the people in that courtroom recognized me from the Simpson trial. And at least some of them certainly expected me to "play the race card." I had to address it without specifically mentioning it, a neat little exercise. I began by asking the jurors the simple question, "Why do you think the mall refused to let the number-six bus let off its passengers inside?" I told them that this case wasn't about race, it wasn't only black people, it was poor people, it was disenfranchised people. At one point we played a video shot by one of the local news stations showing people getting off that bus across the street from the mall. "All of the other buses were allowed in there," I told them, "buses from Amherst, buses from Canada, but not the number-six bus from a few blocks away. Why was that?" Look at those people, I said, they're poor, they're old, some of them are handicapped. They were all put in the same dangerous position. Unfortunately, it was Cynthia Wiggins who died because of it.

I never said a word about race, although Bob and I did put a large photograph of Cynthia Wiggins with her baby up in front of the jury. And left it there.

During a trial lawyers pretty quickly get a sense of whether or not they're making emotional contact with the jury. You can see the way they watch you as you walk across the courtroom, or whether or not they avert their eyes when you look right at them, or maybe they smile easily in response to something you say. I love juries. I remember watching the Simpson jury walk back in to announce its verdict. There was only one African-American man left on that jury and he had made it known that he wanted to go home. He'd had enough. He'd told Judge Ito he was tired and he wanted to go home and watch Notre Dame football, but the judge had refused to release him. By that point we couldn't afford to lose another juror. As the jury returned with its verdict he looked right at me and almost imperceptivity nodded. Just a little tip of his head. But it was enough. Later Carl Douglas, who was sitting behind us, told me he had seen it, too.

Robert Shapiro was standing on the other side of Simpson. "It's going to be bad news," he said to him.

"Shut up," I snapped at Shapiro, then told Simpson, "You're going home."

After the first few days of the Wiggins trial, Bob Perk and I felt we'd successfully made contact with the jury. We'd bonded. It was obvious they liked us. We were building the trust we needed. They were willing to listen to our case. Things were going very well. But on my way to court on the fourth day I picked up a copy of the *Buffalo News,* and I was stunned. Absolutely 100 percent stunned. There was a large headline reading, "Cochran Says, 'This Is the Worst Jury I've Ever Seen.'"

That is not the exact headline, in actuality it might have even been worse. One of the people who had been in that closed session with the judge several days earlier had leaked the story to a reporter. I was pretty sure I knew who it was, an attorney representing one of the defendants. While technically it was accurate, I had said those words, it was completely misleading. I had been referring to the racial makeup of the jury pool, not the members of the six-person jury we'd selected. But that didn't matter; as I read the story, I could almost see our case disappearing.

The jury was not sequestered, so the jurors were probably reading the story just about the same time I was. And some of them, at least, were probably feeling betrayed. I know if I were in their situation I'd certainly be upset. "Cochran looks me in the eye and makes me believe I can trust him and then he turns around and tells the whole world that I'm no good? He smiles at me in the courtroom and behind my back he's telling people how awful I am? That'll be the last time I'll trust him. I won't believe a word he says."

Bob Perk was equally upset. By the nature of the profession lawyers tend to be crisis managers, but this was a difficult situation. The fact that we trusted the judge made a huge difference. We discussed the situation with him, and admitted we were thinking about making a motion for a mistrial. In court that day the judge questioned the jurors, asking them if they had seen the story. I think they all answered negatively. We simply had no legal grounds for a mistrial.

As I told Bob, "Who knows, maybe it's a good thing it came out. Maybe some good'll come of it, maybe something'll change around here." And who really knows, maybe I even believed it when I said it.

I never found out if or how much the jurors really knew about the story. But I didn't sense any change in their response to our case. This was a relatively basic personal injury case. A single mother working at a low-wage job had been accidentally run down by a truck driver who never saw her as she crossed a busy street—at least partially, the defense argued, against the traffic light. The truck driver who hit her had not been malicious, it really was an accident. Realistically, this was not a case that would be settled for a substantial sum.

But we didn't argue that case at all. Our contention was that this hardworking young lady who was struggling to raise her son and go to college was in that street only because the owners of the mall didn't want black people, poor people, handicapped people in their mall. If the jury accepted our argument that she should never have been forced to cross that street to get to her job, we would be in a position to provide for her son for the rest of his life.

We were working all day and into the night. It was cold in Buffalo. Dale came up for a few days and the cold didn't seem to bother her, but I was freezing all the time. After the first week of testimony I knew the jury was still involved in the case, they were paying close attention to the witnesses. That's always a very good sign.

Many times as a trial progresses after each side presents its case, settlement discussions begin; how much is it worth to stop right here, how much are you willing to gamble? Not this time, though. There were never any serious settlement negotiations. We had great confidence in our case, we didn't believe they could offer us enough to settle. We wanted to go through the whole trial and put our fate in the jury's hands. We were going for a knockout.

Instead the judge offered us a technical decision. One afternoon he quietly told each side, "If this little boy doesn't get his future secured I'm going to be very upset." Then he began nudging us toward a settlement. A really good judge can do that, he can run a fair trial while making it clear to both sides that he wants a fair settlement. If one side or the other tries to play rough he can be a little tougher in his rulings, a subtle way of letting them know he isn't satisfied. Judge Gorski did that.

Eventually we settled for $2.55 million. The mall paid $2 million, the driver of the bus—who was driving with an expired license—paid $250,000, and the NFTA paid $300,000. Neither Bob nor I really wanted to settle, but our obligation was to secure the future of our now four-year-old client. We didn't have the right to turn down that offer. Properly invested in annuities that money will be worth ten times that amount by the time Taquilo Wiggins grows up. We could have continued to argue the case and I believe we would have won a very large verdict, but this was the right thing to do.

Bob Perk and I also donated part of our fees to help establish a daycare center in Cynthia Wiggins's honor, a place where teenage mothers can safely leave their children while they're working.

Long before the trial began—and admittedly after community leaders had threatened a boycott—the Walden Galleria began letting the #6 bus drop off its passengers at the mall. In complete safety. That did not seem to cause additional wear and tear on the bus, the roads, or the mall. The fact that they made that change before the trial began might be seen as evidence of wrongdoing, but postincident remedial actions are generally not admissible. If they were, nobody would ever make changes before a trial. So we couldn't tell this to the jury. That didn't matter, what mattered was that people from Buffalo's east side could now get safely to this lovely mall.

The issues we had raised about the makeup of the jury did not end with this trial. Nor are they limited to Buffalo. This is a serious problem affecting the entire legal system of this country. But Buffalo tried to do something to change things. The chief administrative judge appointed a commission to investigate jury selection in upstate New York; she wanted to find out if there really was a problem getting minorities to sit on juries. Definitely, the commission reported. That led to changes being made in the way juries are picked. According to *USA Today*, Buffalo is leading the nation in trying to find ways to promote racial diversity in the jury box. The city recognized a problem and is dealing with it, trying to create a standard that might become the model for the rest of the country.

It turned out to be one of the greatest experiences of my career. Our young client is financially secure for the rest of his life. Substantial changes are being made in the jury selection system. Judge Gorski was named Judge of the Year. I was invited back to Buffalo to speak when the judge was honored. I was also asked to speak by the local chapter of the NAACP. Even though I'm a guy from the warm West, I came to love freezing Buffalo. And Bob Perk and his wonderful legal staff.

EIGHT

This is what it's like to be black in America: In 1980 I was the assistant district attorney, the third-ranking person in what then was the largest law office in the world. I even had a gold badge bearing a large number three. I was a success, a big success. I had made it by playing by the rules, by participating in the system. As was probably said at that time, I was a credit to my race.

On a beautiful afternoon in the spring of that year I was taking my two kids to a Sav-On drugstore to look at some toys. We'd just spent the afternoon at a political fund-raiser for my boss, L.A. district attorney John Van de Kamp. I was driving my Rolls-Royce. My son and daughter, Tiffany, were sitting in the back, and we were on Sunset Boulevard. I looked in my rearview mirror and saw a police squad car coming up fast behind me. I didn't think very much about it, I was the number-three man in the Los Angeles District Attorney's Office, I was the boss. Then the bar lights on the squad car's roof began flashing and his siren started wailing. I still didn't think he was stopping me, I knew I wasn't doing anything wrong. He needs to pass, I figured. As I began moving over . . . "Pull over," he ordered through his loudspeaker.

I pulled over and stopped. Within seconds three other police cars squealed to a halt around me, officers were leaping out of their cars, guns drawn, crouching behind their open doors. The voice ordered me: "Get out of your car and put your hands on top of your head!"

In the backseat my kids were terrified. "It's okay, kids," I tried to calm them, "just sit there. Don't you move."

I put my hands on my head and slowly got out of my car. My heart was pounding. I knew too well how situations just like this one could get out of hand. Even in broad daylight, on one of the busiest street in Los Angeles, on a beautiful spring afternoon. I moved deliberately toward the curb, I was careful not to make any sudden movements. One of the officers approached my car with his gun drawn. "Put that gun away," I told him, "my kids are back there."

He reached into the car and opened my bag, which was sitting on the passenger seat. Probably the first thing he saw was that big gold badge, with the big number three. He immediately waved off everybody else and started apologizing. "Oh no," I told him, "get your sergeant down here right now."

Now that I was safe and my kids were safe, my fear quickly turned into anger. The officer began telling some ridiculous tale about mistaking my car for a stolen vehicle. "Look at that license plate," I snapped at him. My plate read JCJR, the same plate I'd had for years. "Yeah, you saw a black guy driving a Rolls-Royce, that's why you stopped me." My crime was DWB, as it is now commonly known, driving while black.

Chief of Police Darryl Gates personally apologized to me. I never made an issue of it, but I never forgot it. I never forgot that fear, I never forgot that feeling of being totally innocent yet completely powerless.

My kids asked me later, "Daddy, aren't you with the police?"

I had to explain that I was, but that these officers had made a mistake. How could I tell my kids the truth, that this was simply about the color of their skin? They were too young to be so marked for life. There was time enough to teach them the rules for African-Americans.

Even considering the substantial advances made in civil rights in this country, for African-Americans life remains quite different from what it is for white people. While whites can teach their children the basic rules of behavior and safety—don't run with scissors— black parents have to teach their kids how to act when stopped by the police so they don't get shot.

If you're black and you've grown up in America you and every-body you know has been stopped and questioned. Where people don't know who you are, you are identified by who they think you are. It's one of the facts of life. Black people know if you pay cash for an airplane ticket you're probably going to get stopped and questioned because it is assumed that cash came from dealing drugs. Black people in Florida know that some restaurants will add 20 percent to the tip because they assume blacks will not tip well. Blacks know if they go into certain department stores they are going to be followed because it's assumed they're going to steal something, and blacks know if they are driving a nice car there is a substantial chance they will be stopped on the highways of America.

This is called racial profiling. And until four innocent young men got shot on the New Jersey Turnpike one night, most people had never heard that phrase.

A little after ten o'clock the night of April 23, 1998, two New Jersey State Police troopers patrolling the Jersey Turnpike put on their lights and ordered a rented Dodge Caravan to pull to the side of the road. There were four young men in that van, on their way to North Carolina Central University to try out for basketball scholar-ships, and two of them were asleep in the back.

Keshon Moore, the driver of this van, had been very careful to stay within the speed limit; this southern portion of the New Jersey Turnpike was well known among minorities as "White Man's Pass," the stretch in which blacks and Latinos were commonly stopped for the crime of driving on the Jersey Turnpike. For exam-ple, between 1984 and 1988 a black dentist driving his gold BMW through this area of the Jersey Turnpike was stopped almost one hundred times—without receiving a single traffic summons or warning. Years ago Easterners driving south knew all about the small Southern town speed traps that basically extorted money with trumped-up driving violations. But this was much worse; this wasn't economics, this was pure racism.

After Keshon Moore had stopped the van one of the troopers moved cautiously to the front passenger side while the other trooper stayed to the rear. Although both troopers had made numerous stops exactly like this one, they were cautious and drew their guns. Moore was obviously nervous—I know exactly how he felt—and driving a rented vehicle. He tried to put the van in park but instead slipped it into reverse. The van started rolling backward. Forensic experts later estimated the speed at about four miles per hour. But it was enough.

Just like Leonard Deadwyler's car had lurched forward.

The state troopers panicked and started shooting at the van. One of the troopers claimed the van had knocked him down and he was firing from the pavement in self-defense, but forensic examiners determined he had fired five times from "a standing or semi-crouched position." These troopers had no idea who was inside, no crime had been committed, the driver hadn't been speeding or changing lanes without signaling; the only reason they were afraid was that it was a vanload of black and brown people. It was four men, it could have just as easily been a mother and her children. It didn't matter to the troopers, they just kept firing.

The driver tried to duck down between the seats and the van hit the patrol car and veered into traffic. It collided with a Honda Civic, which bounced off a guardrail and burst into flames. By the time it stopped rolling the troopers had fired eleven shots, wounding three of the four men. It was pure luck that no one had died.

The troopers didn't stop there. They pulled these people out of the van, they saw that three of them were bleeding, they hand-cuffed them, strip-searched them, and made them lie facedown in a gully. Then they searched the van—discovering a John Steinbeck novel and a Bible. No drugs, no alcohol, no weapons, just a novel and a Bible. Only then did the troopers call for medical help for the victims. Paramedics arrived and rushed them to the hospital.

The passenger in the front seat, Danny Reyes of Queens, was hit four times in the stomach and the arm. Jarmaine Grant, asleep in a rear seat, was hit three or four times, shattering his kneecap. Rayshawn Brown, also sleeping in the back, was shot once, possibly twice, in the arm and hand. The driver, Keshon Moore, was not physically wounded.

I heard about the shooting on the evening news. I was surprised, not at the shooting, but at the fact that it made the TV news. White cops shoot black kids so often it doesn't even seem like news anymore. What made this case different, I believe, was the fact that this time four innocent people had been shot during a seemingly routine stop on the Jersey Turnpike—while New York was still in an uproar over the Louima and Diallo cases. My phone rang a few days later. A lawyer named David Ironman, who had been hired to represent Danny Reyes, told me, "I need your help on a really bad case . . ." I also was contacted by Jarmaine Grant's family and by African-American religious leaders from New Jersey and New York, including the Reverends Calvin Butts and Al Sharpton.

This was a case in which I really wanted to be involved; there probably isn't an African-American or Latino in the country who wasn't touched by this. We all knew the reality—it could have been any one of us. It almost was me.

I don't know precisely when I first heard the phrase *racial profiling*. It might have been prior to this case, but I don't think so. Certainly it was not commonly used. Instead it was known as *selective enforcement*.

As usual when I got involved in a civil rights case, I called Peter and Barry. At the very beginning of a case like this one, a case that could prove to be really important in terms of changing the way law enforcement works, there's a real surge of excitement that just rockets through your body. I felt that, and I also liked knowing the three of us were working together on another case.

I like to think that I can bring to a case a lifetime of experience, knowledge of the law, compassion...I like to think that, but I know absolutely that the one thing I bring to every case in which I get involved is the media. As arguably America's most controversial lawyer I'm good copy, I can fill a lot of space in newspapers. So I know if I announce a press conference reporters will be there on time. Maybe they still expect me to reveal something about the Simpson case. But the reality is that when I get involved in a case the media is going to shine a bright spotlight it. I like that, it's nice to have that power. I try to use it well. In the case of the New Jersey Turnpike Four, I wanted this story to be on the front page, above the fold. I wanted it to make headlines.

We began by meeting with the victims' families at our office on Hudson Street in lower Manhattan. It was immediately obvious that these young men came from fine families. These were good, hardworking people. Danny Reyes's mother, for example, had been a police officer in Puerto Rico, his father was a truck driver. Jarmaine Grant opened our meeting with a prayer, so you know this was a young man I really liked. We began by telling these people that it was an honor to be asked to participate in this case and assured them we would do everything within our power to make sure justice was done. People in this situation are often confused as to what our role will be; they told us that day that it was very important to them that the two officers be convicted of these shootings.

I had to explain to them the difference between criminal and civil law. We weren't prosecutors, I said, legally we had nothing to do with the criminal case, but I added, as always, "We will work with the prosecutors."

Then we began talking about the whole case. It was important to these families that the troopers be punished for their actions. We wanted that, too, we said, but this is also an opportunity to attack the system that made this crime possible. That if any case was perfect to go after the state for supporting racial profiling, this was it. The families agreed enthusiastically. They quickly became clients who were interested in making certain this didn't happen to anyone else's son or brother. That became very important to them.

Most of the time when attorneys attack an institution it involves a criminal case; for example, a person was illegally searched and the police found drugs. The fact that the suspect was carrying drugs makes it tougher to gain support. But these young men hadn't done one thing wrong, the police found no drugs, no guns, no nothing in their van. These young men were righteous, the perfect plaintiffs.

I don't remember when we started using that phrase, *racial profiling*. I do remember that as soon as we made that accusation New Jersey governor Christy Whitman vehemently denied it existed, stating firmly that there was "no policy of racial profiling in this state."

Her credibility about that was shattered when a photograph taken a few years earlier of her smiling for the cameras while frisking a black man, who had his hands raised and was leaning against a wall, was released. It wasn't so much the actual photograph that bothered people as much as the subtle message it sent: Here was a politician determined to be tough on criminals, a strong law-and-order Republican. There was a big smile on her face—this is some kind of game, right—as she illegally searched a suspect.

Whatever Governor Whitman claimed, there was substantial evidence that for many years state troopers had routinely been stopping minority drivers who were doing absolutely nothing wrong and then conducting illegal searches of their vehicles—with the knowledge and support of the state government. Peter found a four-part series entitled *Without Just Cause* that had been produced in 1989 by WOR-TV in New York. Investigative reporter Joe Collum had uncovered basically irrefutable proof that New Jersey state troopers profiled drivers. But nobody cared, nobody paid any attention. The cops just kept doing it.

At least a few people knew exactly what was going on and were determined to stop it. Three senior attorneys in the Gloucester County State Public Defender's Office—Fred Last, Wayne Natale, and Jeff Wintner—began a major investigation into state police procedures. They conducted a census to determine the racial composition of the drivers stopped by the police; they found that over several weeks police had stopped almost 43,000 drivers—and at the southern end of the turnpike, in White Man's Pass, minority drivers were almost five times more likely to be stopped than white drivers.

They uncovered hard evidence of selective enforcement. During a hearing that lasted almost six months they produced state police officers who admitted being trained to profile drivers. They obtained copies of a handout given to officers telling them to be particularly alert for "possible drug couriers" on the Jersey Turnpike, specifically black and Latino males and "Hispanic males and females posing as a couple."

These were the people they were supposed to stop. "Posing as a couple," isn't that ridiculous. It was also revealed that the federal Drug Enforcement Agency was hiring New Jersey troopers and sending them around the country to teach these "techniques" to other law enforcement agencies. In other words, the federal government was teaching racial profiling techniques to police officers.

That was business as usual. Nobody yelled and screamed at this; nobody bothered to mention little things like "constitutional rights against illegal search and seizures" to these people.

In 1996, in a landmark case known as *State v. Soto*, a Gloucester County judge found the state guilty of "selective enforcement" and threw out nineteen cases in which minority drivers had been arrested on drug or weapons charges. The judge found that police officers had no reason to make most of these stops, that the only violation the driver had committed was being born black or brown. So any evidence the troopers discovered had to be thrown out.

It was a landmark decision. Of course, the state denied it completely and immediately appealed the decision.

So a lot of the groundwork already had been done by attorneys like William Buckman, who filed the case that led to *Soto*, when we got involved. There was absolutely no question that the involvement of three Simpson "dream team" members made this a very high-profile case. What we intended to prove was these young men had been stopped on the turnpike because of their race; that the state knew this was happening and had done absolutely nothing to stop it; and as a result they had suffered injuries that were going to affect them throughout the lives.

For legal reasons the driver of the van, Keshon Moore, was represented by the brilliant New Jersey attorney Linda Kenney, now the wife of pathologist Michael Baden. Rayshawn Brown also was represented by another lawyer. While officially our clients were Danny Reyes and Jarmaine Grant, in many respects we acted for all four men.

One of the first things we did was get the best possible doctors for our clients who had been shot. They had been treated and released from the hospital, but their injuries would require long-term orthopedic therapy. It also pretty much ended their dreams of winning a basketball scholarship to college. We wanted to get a complete assessment of their medical condition, so about three weeks after the shooting Peter went with Danny Reyes to the office of Dr. Stephen Nicholas, one of the top orthopedists in the country. Danny still had a bullet lodged in his spine. But as Dr. Nichols was examining him, Peter spotted a bulge just below the surface of the skin. Incredibly, the bullet had worked its way to the surface. Dr. Nicholas pulled it out of his body right in front of Peter.

Peter immediately started worrying about the chain of evidence. For evidence to be used in court, there has to be a record of each person who handled it. The chain. This bullet was potentially very valuable evidence. As a bullet passes through each surface it often retains some material from that surface; if it passed through seat fabric, for example, some of that fabric might remain on the bullet, if it went through the side of the van there might be some paint on it. It's a good way of determining the path of a bullet. Peter was extremely careful to do nothing that would compromise the integrity of that bullet.

Dr. Nicholas removed it with sterile surgical instruments, dropped it into an envelope, sealed the envelope, and initialed it.

After returning to our office on Hudson Street, Peter called the New Jersey prosecutor's office—who sent a state trooper to New York to pick it up. As Peter handed him the envelope he warned him not to open it, to just deliver it exactly as it was to the New Jersey state crime lab.

No way, the trooper said, I'm not taking anything unless I know exactly what it is.

It's evidence, Peter told him. And unless he signed a document stating that he would not open the envelope he wasn't going to give it to him. The officer refused to sign, so Peter told him to get out of his office.

Finally Peter called the prosecutor's office. "We need to know if there are any fibers, glass, metal, any materials on this bullet before it's examined for DNA or anything else," he said. "So first thing, it has to be examined microscopically." The prosecutor told the trooper to sign the paper, take the envelope, and don't you dare open it. Problem solved.

Almost immediately we started our own investigation. Obviously I am a very strong believer in the tales told by forensic evidence. Even eyewitnesses sometimes make mistakes, but there are facts that can be learned from materials that are irrefutable. Barry and the world renowned criminalist Dr. Henry Lee examined the van to try to plot the path of each bullet. That would allow us to determine exactly where the troopers were standing—or crouching or even knocked to the ground, as one trooper claimed—when they fired. From the trajectory of the bullets it was possible to determine that the trooper who claimed to be on the ground was lying about his position. He definitely was not on the ground; he was standing up and shooting with precision and determination.

We brought in other forensic experts, among them experts on glass and firearms. I had been a prosecutor, I had been a defense attorney, I knew how to prepare a criminal case. We shared the results of our examinations with the prosecutors. We were preparing our case to go to trial. With the prosecutor's office we did three different reenactments of the event. One night the state police shut down that section of the Jersey Turnpike, put the van in position, and we re-created the entire scenario. Our clients willingly cooperated each time.

We also assigned Barry the task of finding out what these two officers had been doing earlier that evening. All too often when prosecutors look at a case involving a cop they deal with it as a single, isolated incident. I'd found that in most situations that if a police officer does engage in some kind of criminal activity—just like someone caught selling drugs—it's probably not the first time he's done it. Or something like it. When a cop plays fast and loose with a citizen's constitutional rights it generally isn't an aberration, it's a behavioral pattern.

At Barry's urging, his insistence really—and Barry can be very insistent—state investigators began examining the behavior of these troopers in the hours before the shooting. Because of the *Soto* case New Jersey state troopers had to record the race of every person they stopped. According to their memo book, these officers had previously stopped several white drivers. Among them were two white males from Camden, New Jersey. The state investigators wanted to interview these men to find out about the stop. They wanted to know if either of the troopers had acted strangely or if these men had smelled liquor on his breath. But when they met these men they noticed one thing very quickly—they were not white. They were black. The trooper had recorded their correct names, but claimed he had accidentally checked the wrong box that described their race.

We suggested that the prosecutor's office go back and examine the stops these officers had made over the last several months. Let's find out if that really was a mistake or if it was a pattern, an attempt to hide the fact that they were out there just looking for black and brown drivers. When the investigators began interviewing people who had been stopped, they discovered that these troopers had been "ghosting" drivers. Usually they simply lied about the race of the drivers they had stopped, describing blacks as white in their records. That happened far too often not to have been a deliberate attempt to hide their actions. There was no reasonable explanation for it; they couldn't claim they were working so fast they continually checked the wrong box.

But we discovered another method they were using to disguise their actions. Rather than writing down the correct license-plate number of the black driver they stopped, they would see a car, preferably from another state, being driven by a white person and record its make, model, and plate number in their memo book, falsely identifying it as the car they had stopped. That lie fell apart when investigators tracked down the plate owners who were incredulous; invariably they admitted they had been on the turnpike that day or night, but claimed they had never been stopped. These officers were stopping black people but recording the plate numbers of white drivers. Either this was the most amazing case of color blindness I had ever seen, or these officers were intentionally lying about their actions. Obviously the only possible reason they would lie consistently about their behavior is that it was illegal.

Even after the *Soto* case they were continuing to profile black and Latino drivers.

It was becoming obvious that there existed a real conspiracy. These two troopers had been the shooters, but I don't think anybody believed they were simply rogue cops, wild men out there on their own. It was apparent that this was institutionalized behavior, that all or most of the troopers were doing this. That these were the methods they had adopted to get around the restrictions instituted after the *Soto* decision. It was sort of a wink-wink deal; on paper they were following the law, in reality they were making up their own laws. Everybody on the force knew about it, but nobody wanted to talk about it.

The state initially had filed a series of charges against the troopers ranging from attempted murder and assault to falsifying traffic stop reports. The troopers faced forty years in prison. When those charges were filed the police union announced, "Today a stake was driven through the hearts of many men and women troopers..." Actually, I thought that was an appropriate metaphor—that's how you kill a vampire who preys on people.

The state's criminal case was moving along in parallel with our civil case. I was in my office one afternoon when a reporter called to ask me, "Did you hear about it?"

A New Jersey judge had thrown out the criminal case for complicated legal reasons. He actually inferred that prosecutors had overcharged the troopers, that their rights had been violated. It was extraordinary. We met later that day with the four victims. They were baffled by this, they were furious about it. Two of them were crying. They didn't understand what had happened. I knew what had happened, believe me, I knew, I'd seen it too often before. We tried to explain it to the four young men, but they didn't understand. We got on the phone with the prosecutor and he told us the state absolutely was appealing the ruling. That ruling was not completely unexpected, he explained, the judge was known to be extremely pro-police. He said he was confident the appellate court would reverse this decision.

That wasn't good enough for me. I was fast losing faith in the New Jersey criminal justice system. Peter, Barry, and I discussed various strategies, but there really was only one thing that made sense. I called U.S. Attorney General Janet Reno to ask her to bring federal charges against the officers for violation of my clients' civil rights.

The attorney general took my call. We had met once, at a meeting of the Congressional Black Caucus. While I certainly hadn't agreed with all her actions in office, I admired the fact that she stood tall and accepted responsibility for the results. I liked that in an attorney general.

There is a good, long history of the federal government becoming involved in local civil rights matters. It began in the 1950s when several Southern governors defied the Supreme Court order in *Brown v. the Board of Education* that schools must be integrated. President Eisenhower had used federal troops to enforce that order. And since then the federal government has actively been involved in a great variety of civil rights cases, ranging from voting rights to murder. Thurgood Marshall showed us how to do it. He understood that sometimes it was necessary to use federal law enforcement officers to implement federal laws on the local level. In those days there just wasn't anybody in Arkansas or Alabama with the power and the courage to challenge people like Governor Orville Faubus or Governor George Wallace. You just couldn't count on the local law enforcement—too often the sheriff or chief of police was at the head of the mob. That's why so many African-Americans are distrustful of the Republican defense of states' rights. We know what happened in the past when law enforcement was left to the states.

When I was working in L.A. I had very rarely reached out to federal prosecutors. There was a tradition in Los Angeles that the police could police themselves. Certainly, I agreed; just like the fox guards the henhouse. From time to time if there was a U.S. attorney we felt we could trust we'd ask for assistance. The one case where the federal government did make a substantial difference was the prosecution of the police officers who had assaulted Rodney King. I give President George H. Bush credit for it. After the jury in Simi Valley had acquitted those officers, the federal government prosecuted and ultimately convicted several of them for violation of Rodney King's civil rights. Meaning they practically beat him to death.

Mostly we've used the threat of federal intervention as a hammer. If local prosecutors felt the federal government might take an interest in a case they immediately became more responsive, they worked a little harder, I think they probably were a little more honest. No local DA wants to close out a case and then have the feds come in behind him and make the case that he failed to win.

It's not a threat I've used often or lightly. I've always, absolutely always, believed in cooperating with local authorities, even when I believed we weren't going to make progress. Because, frankly, they're the best game in town for me. They are the people who will take this case to the grand jury.

Janet Reno seemed extremely concerned. Sit tight, she told me, don't do anything and someone would get back to me very quickly. Within hours Deputy Attorney General Eric Holder called from his office in Washington, D.C. I can't tell you everything that's going on, he said, but we're going to be making an announcement this afternoon. I had met Eric Holder while representing the family of Tyisha Miller, a teenage African-American woman who had been shot and killed by Riverside, California, policemen while sitting in her parked car. The city of Riverside defended the conduct of its officers, and no charges were ever brought against them, but one Latino officer came forward and told us that the cops were practically celebrating, they were high-fiving each other after firing twenty-seven shots at this young lady. Eventually we settled that case with the city of Riverside for $3 mllion. Coming forward had put his life in jeopardy and we appealed to Janet Reno's office for protection. Eric Holder had worked with us to get that protection.

Later that day the Department of Justice announced that it was carefully monitoring the situation. It was a clear message; they were coming in. For all those people who had been screaming loudly about racial profiling, or selective enforcement, or whatever they called it, this was a tremendous victory. It meant the federal government had finally recognized the existence of race-based policing. Racial profiling had become a national issue.

New Jersey got the message loud and clear. The appellate court reinstated the criminal case. More importantly, this case was becoming a political liability for Governor Whitman. It was an embarrassment for her, it had happened on her watch and she had stood in front of the microphones and proclaimed, "No policy of racial profiling [exists] in this state." And she had been proven wrong. She had been forced to fire the head of the state police, Carl Williams, who tried to justify race-based policing by claiming that it was known that different races were responsible for different types of drug trafficking, specifically that minorities were responsible for most of the state's cocaine and marijuana traffic.

Three days before the first anniversary of the shooting the state of New Jersey issued an interim report which acknowledged that "racial profiling is real—not imagined." This was the first such admission ever by a state government. It was the first time a governor and a state's attorney general had admitted a pattern and practice of racial profiling existed anywhere in America. This was really a big deal. But then Governor Whitman added that she believed this was the practice of a few bad cops rather than institutionalized procedure. And instead of admitting she had been wrong and apologizing to the countless victims of this practice, she congratulated her administration for being the first "to fully investigate these allegations."

Peter responded to this report by pointing out that "you'd have to be insane or blind" not to know that racial profiling existed. We eventually learned that certain members of the establishment had set up a pretty sophisticated information network. Owners of hotels and businesses along the turnpike participated in it, alerting the state troopers when a driver fitting the racial profile—for example, a Latino male who paid a large bill in cash—left their premises.

Three days later we filed a lawsuit against the state and state officials asking for "substantial punitive and compensatory damages" in addition to a court order forcing the state police to "change its procedures on car stops and racial interaction."

Rarely do we even begin serious settlement conversations in a civil suit until the criminal case is settled. If there is a conviction in criminal court we begin the civil suit in a much stronger position. But this was an unusual situation. Governor Christy Whitman had been appointed director of the Environmental Protection Agency by President George W. Bush and began making preparations to leave office. It is to her credit that she didn't want to leave the civil resolution of this case to her successor. We were invited to meet with the law firm representing the state.

The first meeting took place at their offices in New Jersey. Sitting on our side of the big glass-topped table were myself, Peter, and Barry, David Ironman, Linda Kenney, who was representing Keshon Moore, and a really fine lawyer named Wayne Greenfeder and his partner, Doug Burns, who were representing Rayshawn Brown. It was a crowded room.

Sitting across from us were seven or eight lawyers representing various defendants. They began by admitting that they would like to get this case resolved within the next thirty days, before Christy Whitman left office. While that meant there probably would be less posturing for position than usual in these negotiations, it cut both ways: It appeared that they were under great pressure to settle this thing before she left, but our knowing that made us at least suspect that this might be the best deal we could make.

I think Christy Whitman overall is a decent person. If, as she claimed, she did not know about the existence of racial profiling, certainly this case convinced her it was real. It was the scandal of her administration—it will be a long time before that photograph of her happily patting down a black man will be forgotten by minorities—and she wanted it finished.

It was a brief moment in time when all of our preparation, all of the legal maneuvering, and all of the passion, met with the reality of politics. It might be called the perfect settlement.

The advantage that we had entering negotiations is that we were ready—and very willing—to take the case to trial. We represented four innocent young men who had been illegally stopped by state troopers, three of them had been shot multiple times, and at least two of them suffered permanent, debilitating injuries. Subsequent to the shooting the state had admitted the existence of racial profiling, meaning we would not have to prove it. We definitely could have proved it, but it would have taken a long time and relied greatly on dry statistics. This was the kind of case you dream about taking into a courtroom.

They asked us to make a demand. How much? What else? Put your cards on the table. That's usually how negotiations begin. We needed to make a demand large enough to give us some room to negotiate. Our goal as always was not to leave any money on the table. That's a cold way of looking at it, but that's reality.

Generally we arrive at a figure by looking at state law to determine what our clients were entitled to recover. If this had been a death case, for example, we would be discussing the value of pre-death pain and suffering. How long did the person live? How badly did he or she suffer? In this case we wanted compensation for permanent injuries, our clients were going to carry the scars of that night forever, we wanted punitive damages and we wanted real steps taken to end racial profiling. Usually we can look to precedents, to previous decisions made in that jurisdiction, to get some idea of how that particular court calculates the value of injuries. A jury can give you a fortune, but the courts almost invariably cut it down, so we had to know what kind of damages New Jersey courts would sustain. How much would they let us keep? But this was an unprecedented case. There had never been anything remotely like it tried before.

We asked for roughly $30 million. Thirty million dollars. If we had said simply, "Thirty million, that's what we want," they would have laughed at us and thought we were crazy. But we didn't, we said, "Thirty million and here's how we figured it. Pain and suffering is worth this . . . mental anguish is worth this much . . ." Maybe the number was high, but we could justify every penny. Thirty million dollars is a lot of money. As a young lawyer it never occurred to me that someday I'd be throwing around numbers like that. Once I'd thought $25,000 was practically a fortune and I was thrilled to settle for it, thrilled that the city of Los Angeles acknowledged responsibility and paid it. Thirty million gave us room to negotiate. It also sent the message that we didn't care if we settled, we were prepared to try this case. Thirty million, and we didn't even blink.

The state's attorneys interpreted the same set of facts very differently. Of course. They began negotiations around $5 million. There was a lot of negotiating room between those two numbers. That opening offer really tells you how serious the other is about settling the case. I've often been disappointed by an opening offer, but only once in my entire career have I been truly surprised. In the Ron Settles case, the city's opening offer was more than half a million dollars, which was actually higher than the amount I had expected to settle for. It was an indication that we really had them and they knew it. I had to sit there calmly and act as if I had expected more. That was high stakes poker.

In this case I thought their opening offer was a reasonable place to start. It was clear they were serious about settling, $5 million is a serious amount of money, and both sides knew that the only way to go was up. Settlement negotiations can get pretty rancorous. Usually when the shouting starts I get up and leave. You don't want to pay my client, see you in court. I know, I absolutely know, that I will get more from a jury than I will in a settlement. But I also know that if I go to trial it will take years before my client sees any money at all, and whatever the jury gives us might well be reduced. So there is a benefit to both sides to settle a case before fighting it out in the courtroom.

The rule I follow is that I never let my opponents dictate which cases I'm going to have to try. If I don't know all the strengths and weaknesses of my case, then I haven't done my job properly. I know which clients are going to be strong in the courtroom and which clients have problems that will be exposed.

We met several times. As we got more serious fewer people were involved in the meetings. Finally Peter and I were meeting with two or three people from the other side. We really hashed it out. Finally they offered $12,950,000. They did everything possible to convince us that $12,950,000 was their best offer. They told us that for reasons they couldn't reveal they were not permitted to go to $13 million.

I wanted $13,500,000. Eventually they convinced us that they were telling us the truth. This was the number. Take it or leave it. "We'll have to discuss it with our clients," we said.

A jury might have awarded us many millions more. The troopers had no defense; the forensic evidence proved they were lying about the shooting and the investigation proved they lied about profiling. Additionally, one of the troopers had actually sued the state, claiming the state had been negligent in letting him work that night. State psychologists should have recognized that he was suffering from posttraumatic stress, he claimed, caused by an incident a month earlier in which he'd shot at a drug suspect trying to steal his car. The state had no defense against our charges; Governor Whitman admitted the existence of racial profiling and we had considerable evidence that it was the long-term law enforcement policy. I have absolutely no doubts that a reasonable jury would have awarded us substantially more than we finally accepted.

But we have a legal obligation to report every offer to our clients. If we don't, and if we go to trial and end up with less, then we're responsible for the difference. So we had several discussions about this offer with our clients. Adding to the complications was the fact that these four people had not suffered equal injury. Keshon Moore hadn't been shot, for example, although certainly he'd suffered. Somehow we had to determine how much each of these people was going to receive. It got pretty complicated.

We settled for $12,950,000.

The state also agreed to make substantial changes in police procedure. By the end of 1999 the state agreed to drop criminal charges against 128 other people who had been stopped and arrested on the Jersey Turnpike, had agreed to drop its appeal of the *Soto* decision, and had signed a consent agreement with the federal government which required them to monitor state police activities and report ethnic arrest statistics every six months. The federal government also mandated that the state make significant reforms in training procedures, as well as its methods for stopping and searching motorists. The state mandated that video cameras be installed in every patrol car.

More than two decades earlier when I was in private practice, we had successfully outlawed the LAPD's use of choke holds to subdue suspects. We did that by publicizing statistics that showed seventeen men had died this way while in police custody—fifteen of them black, the other two Latino. We proved that choke holds weren't a necessary tool for subduing suspects, but that they were still being used as a weapon against blacks and Latinos. Since that moratorium went into effect not a single person, not one, has died in a choke hold in L.A. With this case we wanted to have the same kind of impact nationally; we wanted to stop law enforcement officers from harassing, arresting, and illegally searching people because of the color of their skin. But truthfully, when we started working on this case I don't think any of us realized it would become the poster case for racial profiling. This case firmly put that phrase in the national psyche. It caused a national debate about racial profiling. It precipitated executive orders from President Clinton and legislation throughout the country to end a very old and very entrenched practice.

It hasn't completely stopped racial profiling on the highways, it's still done in many places—maybe even New Jersey. But the process of change has started. I think, interestingly, after the terrorist attack on September 11, 2001, the debate about racial profiling was altered. I travel by airplane a lot and, admittedly, after the attack I found myself looking carefully at my fellow passengers before getting on an airplane; I found myself engaging in racial profiling. Me. It came as a big surprise to me. The difference, I decided, was the difference in the actual threat. People driving on a highway or walking down a street are not posing an immediate threat to anyone. There is no immediate danger that would be alleviated by a race-based policy of stop and search. But as we've all learned, that same thing isn't true about passengers getting on airplanes. One person can destroy that plane and with it hundreds of lives. That's an immediate danger. I think any reasonable person would agree that if the safety of the passengers and crew of that plane during the flight they are about to take can be better assured . . . well, it should be.

In January 2002 the felony charges against the officers were dropped and they pleaded guilty to the misdemeanor charge of obstructing the investigation. They also admitted lying to their superior officers by misrepresenting the race of the drivers they stopped to cover up the fact that they were racially profiling, and they resigned from the force and signed an agreement that they would never again work in law enforcement. This is just another example of the double standard of justice that exists for cops. If someone who was not a cop had shot into a car under these circumstances that person would probably go to prison for life. For life.

Both of the men were fined $280. That was it, they lost their job and paid a $280 fine. Although one of them said to the victims, "I've been thinking about you ever since this occurred. I'm sorry."

I suppose most police officers who shoot innocent people are later sorry about their actions. I don't believe these troopers wanted to shoot those three young men any more than the four cops in the Bronx wanted to shoot Amadou Diallo. But if the victims were white, neither shooting would have happened. And that really is the end result—and the horror—of racial profiling.

Worse, not one of their superior officers, the men who created and supervised this policy, the men who handed out leaflets telling troopers what color skin to look for, were named or penalized in any way.

The victims have moved forward with their lives. Danny Reyes and Jarmaine Grant still have bullets in their bodies. Nobody really knows the long-term damage those bullets might cause. During his rehabilitation Jarmaine Grant became interested in physical therapy and began working as a rehabilitation therapist. Of the four, only Rayshawn Brown fulfilled his goal of playing college basketball. Although two fingers on his right hand remain paralyzed, Brown is on the Bloomfield College team and is working toward a degree in computer science.

I was not at all satisfied with the outcome of the criminal proceedings—those troopers belonged in jail—but ironically, that plea will be beneficial in future cases. While making their pleas the troopers admitted they had been trained to stop and search people based on their race. They admitted it. In another case I represent thirteen black New Jersey state troopers who are suing the state, claiming the state knew that they were being harassed because of their race and did nothing about it. They claim they were forced to participate in racial profiling—just imagine what that must have been like to a black state trooper forced to profile minority drivers— and that they themselves were subjected to racial taunts, things like finding nooses hanging in their lockers and receiving vile letters. In July 2002, we settled this case for $4 million, plus an additional $1 million in attorney's fees. It was poetic justice that the evidence gathered in the shooting case helped us reach this settlement and will inevitably destroy the racist culture inside the New Jersey State Police.

Several months earlier, a study was released which purportedly showed that among all speeding drivers on the turnpike, black motorists were twice as likely to be speeding as white drivers. This is supposedly proof that state troopers were only doing their jobs, that they didn't engage in racial profiling. This is pretty amazing. It conveniently ignores the fact that state troopers admitted being trained to racially profile drivers, admitted making racially based stops, and admitted lying about it. It ignores the handouts issued to troopers informing them that black and Latino drivers were more likely than white motorists to be transporting drugs and it ignores the fact that troopers were alerted by hotel owners to watch for certain vehicles. The report tries to demonstrate that racial profiling didn't exist. It's ridiculous. It's absurd.

This is what it's like to be white in America—when the government makes you a target. Among the cases I was working on at about the same time as the New Jersey Four was one of the longest and strangest cases in which I've been involved, the murder of Donald Scott.

Donald Scott was the sixty-one-year-old heir to a European chemical company fortune. He was living with his third wife, Frances Plante, a much younger woman, on their 250-acre ranch in the Santa Monica Mountains. They weren't bothering a soul; they were actually sort of reclusive. But Scott's land was adjacent to the Santa Monica Mountains National Recreation Area. It is a beautiful piece of property—there's a seventy-five-foot waterfall on it—and someone in the federal government wanted to incorporate it into the recreation area. The National Park Service offered to buy it, but Don Scott was a happy man; he was living there with his wife, he had all the money he needed, he didn't want to sell. He just wanted to be left alone.

Among the truly dangerous government powers is the federal asset forfeiture law, which allows the government to seize and basically keep any property supposedly used in the commission of a crime. Under this law your property is charged with the offense, which makes it a civil action rather than a criminal case. Even if you are never charged with a crime, or are charged and acquitted, it can take years and cost you a fortune to get back your own property. But if you are convicted of the crime the government is entitled to sell your property, with the proceeds divided among all the agencies participating in the original seizure. It's an outrageous program. The L.A. Sheriff's Department, for example, depended on the money raised by selling assets seized and forfeited in drug cases to supplement its inadequate yearly budget.

This isn't racial profiling, it isn't a misidentification in the night, it's protected government theft. An informer supposedly told an L.A. deputy sheriff that Scott was growing four thousand marijuana plants on his ranch. If that information was accurate, it would be sufficient for the government to seize and sell the ranch and split the proceeds, estimated at about $5 million, among all the participating agencies. It was all so neat; the government would get the land and various agencies would be paid for their work.

That deputy, as well as agents from the Border Patrol, Fish and Game Bureau, Coastal Commission, and National Park Service, searched areas of the ranch without spotting a single marijuana plant. While photographs taken by the Air National Guard of the entire property also failed to show any marijuana, a DEA agent fly-ing at about one thousand feet believed he saw about fifty mari-juana plants hidden under trees. But he really wasn't very certain of that and told the sheriff's deputy not to rely on his observation. While the DEA usually takes photographs in this kind of situation, this time nobody took pictures.

They didn't take pictures because there was nothing to see. Whatever the DEA agent believed he spotted, it wasn't marijuana. Donald Scott liked to drink, but all his friends testified he didn't use drugs. And he didn't need the money growing marijuana could bring.

None of this stopped the deputy from obtaining a search war-rant. The government wanted this seizure to be perfectly legal. At 9:00 A.M. the morning of October 2, 1992, Donald Scott and Frances Plante were in bed when their dogs started barking. Frances went to see what was wrong. As she walked into the kitchen the door was smashed open by a battering ram and thirty-one armed men, wear-ing flak jackets, stormed into the house. In addition to the sheriff's deputy, this task force included agents from the National Park Ser-vice, Border Patrol, the L.A. County Sheriff's Department, the Cali-fornia Bureau of Narcotic Enforcement, and the California National Guard. Two members of the raiding party were considered experts in asset forfeiture law. Every agency was going to make money on this one. One of the men carried a map of the ranch on which was a notation that another adjoining property had sold for $800,000, and just before the raid these men were told the ranch could be seized if they found as few as fourteen marijuana plants. Interestingly, there were no local agents from Ventura County—where the ranch was located.

When these men smashed into the house Frances Plante started screaming, "Don't shoot me! Don't kill me!" Donald Scott was in bed, hung over from a drinking bout the night before, recuperating from a recent cataract operation. Now just imagine this: You're in your own home, this is America, you've just woken up, and you hear a crash as someone smashes into your house. Then you hear your wife screaming for her life. Donald Scott grabbed his gun and holding it over his head went to help. When the agents saw him they identified themselves and ordered him to put down the gun. As he started lowering the gun he "kinda" pointed it toward them, according to one of the agents. The deputy sheriff shot Donald Scott to death. In his own house. They ordered him to put down his gun. And as he proceeded to do precisely that, they shot him. They killed him.

After the shooting the deputy and a partner posed outside the house for a photograph. When an agent asked Scott's now-widow, "Where are the plants?" she responded, "I'm the only Plante here—and that's my name."

Every foot of that property was searched, every *foot*—and not a single marijuana plant was found.

I don't remember who referred Frances Plante to my office. In our practice Carl Douglas would work with me on criminal cases and Eric Ferrer would work with me on civil matters. Frances Plante met with Eric and myself. She wanted to sue the county of Los Angeles and the other agencies. A civil matter.

There was no criminal case. Not a single person was indicted or disciplined—including the deputy sheriff—for the death of Donald Scott. Maybe I use the word *outrageous* too often, but that's what it was, an act grossly offensive to decency and morality. Maybe the most surprising thing about this case was that the victim was white and rich. Rich, white people are rarely victims of police brutality. But Donald Scott had something law enforcement agencies wanted, so he died. A case like this is precisely the reason we've fought so hard for so long in so many cases to make law enforcement officers accountable for their actions. It's why I get so angry when the Diallo cops or the New Jersey state troopers walk away free. When you don't make people accountable, it is going to happen again and again and again.

From the minute I met Frances Plante I knew she would be an interesting client. She was in her early thirties, a big, tall, red-headed Texan. She was sitting in a conference room, a beer in her hand, chain-smoking and putting out her cigarettes on the No Smoking signs on the table. And then she told us this horror story.

It was a difficult case. In fact, no laws had been broken. The agencies involved continued to insist that they acted responsibly. It was absurd at the beginning and got more and more absurd as these people tried to defend themselves. The Border Patrol, for example, claimed it participated in a raid taking place in the Santa Monica Mountains because a Forest Service agent had told them that illegal aliens were suspected of being on the prop-erty—and that property was within one hundred miles of the ocean.

Less than a year after the killing, Ventura County DA Michael Bradbury issued a stinging report which concluded that the original search warrant that authorized the raid contained "numerous mis-statements, evasions, and omissions," and "was not supported by probable cause." Among those omissions was that fact that several people had already searched parts of the ranch and found no evi-dence of marijuana plants. Bradbury stated it was his opinion that "the Los Angeles County Sheriff's Department was motivated, at least in part, by a desire to seize and forfeit the ranch . . ." and that the deputy had "lost his moral compass."

The sheriff responded by denouncing that sixty-four-page report and issuing his own report, which completely cleared every-one involved in the planning and carrying out of the raid.

Citing this report, the deputy sheriff who had shot and killed Donald Scott sued the DA for libel, slander, and defamation. That lawsuit was eventually thrown out of court, the deputy was ordered to pay the DA's $50,000 legal fees, and he eventually declared bank-ruptcy. It was later reported that he developed a twitch.

Soon after Donald Scott's death his four children by two previous marriages began fighting Frances Plante for the estate. The first thing we had to do was prove that Frances Plante and Donald Scott had married, making her his legal heir. That began almost eight years of seemingly ceaseless legal battles.

We sued the government for $100 million, claiming wrongful death and violation of Donald Scott's civil rights. The government refused to consider a settlement, claiming that this whole silly operation was perfectly legal. While we were fighting, the ranch house burned down in the Malibu fires of 1996, but rather than moving off the land, Frances Plante erected a tepee over the badminton court, laid expensive rugs on the ground, equipped it with a TV, and lived there.

She just wasn't giving up even though she had absolutely no money. At one point, she told a judge she considered eating road kill but decided against it. As she couldn't pay real estate taxes because the government had killed her husband, the government moved to seize the land for nonpayment of taxes. This was a client . . . well, I had never had another client like Frances Plante. We fought endless legal battles for her and on occasion she would compose songs about the case.

The Donald Scott case started long before the Simpson case and ended after the Louima civil case and the Diallo criminal case. When it began I was thinking about retiring or certainly reducing my caseload in a few years; when it ended I was living part-time in New York and was as busy as I had ever been in my career. At times I thought this case might go on and on forever.

Eventually fifteen different attorneys were involved in the case and the thousands of court documents filled thirty volume binders. I'll never know for certain what caused the county to decide to settle. But the political climate had changed greatly in California since 1992. I think there had been too many highly publicized incidents of law enforcement officers just trampling over the rights of citizens. I don't believe there were any more incidents than there had been previously, but I do think they received a lot more publicity. And after the Rampart scandal proved that police officers lie, fabricate, and plant evidence, the county would have had a particularly tough time convincing a jury that the actions of these law enforcement officers were necessary. There were thirty-one agents and there was Donald Scott. Donald Scott died.

We settled for $5 million, which was split between Frances Plante, Donald Scott's four children, and the estate. We really had to work out some pretty complicated formulas. The lawyers were paid based on the amount of work they did on the case.

Many white people watch quietly as law enforcement officers trample all over the rights of minorities under the guise of crime prevention. And a lot of them are sympathetic, too. They honestly feel sorry for the victims. But they watch from a very safe place, feeling sorry for the victims, but believing as long as they themselves remain law-abiding citizens it can't happen to them.

Donald Scott believed that, too.

NINE

Life evolves. I came to New York City to co-host a television show. Staying there after it went off the air, working there, was not part of any master plan. It never occurred to me that I might settle there. I'm a proud Californian. Los Angeles is my home, I was raised there, it's where my people are. It's where my pro basketball team, the three-time world champion Lakers, play. No matter where I am in the world, I always know what time it is in L.A.

I'd visited New York many times both on business and for pleasure, never for more than a few days. I never really had the opportunity to get the feel of the city. But one day, after I moved there, I remember walking on Fifty-Seventh Street, rushing to a meeting. Now, I'm a pretty fast walker. I like to get where I'm going. But I noticed that as fast as I was walking, people were walking right by me. I liked that, I liked that pace.

The more I learned about New York the more I enjoyed it. The difference between experiencing the city as a visitor and actually living there is probably like the difference between sitting in the audience at a symphony concert or playing the drums. I caught the beat of the city.

But my legal practice remained based in Los Angeles. In New York I worked primarily on high-profile civil rights cases with Peter and Barry. Eventually Dale and I bought an apartment in midtown, I got used to the Carnegie Deli's pastrami sandwiches, I found restaurants I enjoyed, I met all kinds of interesting people, I even started rooting—at least a little—for the Knicks, and I got involved in the politics of the Upper Manhattan Empowerment Zone.

I really enjoyed being in New York. Rather than slowing down, as I had seriously considered before Simpson, I was busier than ever. The phone never stopped ringing. I was being asked to participate in exciting and important civil litigation. It was obvious that if I was going to stay there I needed to establish a complete legal practice. As much as I love Peter and Barry, I needed a larger support staff. I began to think about expanding my Los Angeles practice to New York.

Meanwhile, down in Alabama, three very smart attorneys named Sam Cherry, Keith Givens, and Jock Smith were planning to open a racially mixed plaintiffs' firm, to be based in Atlanta. I met Jock Smith at a book signing. He told me what they were doing and it seemed very interesting to me. Eventually Jock and I met with Keith Givens while we were at the New Orleans Jazz Festival. On a very informal basis, we agreed to try to find a way to expand my Los Angeles–based firm. The most efficient way, it was obvious, was to merge with an existing firm. So Keith set out to find the right situation for me. It was all very informal.

In New York I was involved in a tragic case in which a woman, driving her four children, had collided with an ambulance that had raced through a red light. Three of her children were killed in the accident. Peter and I represented the mother. One of the surviving children, as well as the woman's former husband, were represented by the New York firm Schneider Kleinick Weitz Damashek & Shoot, certainly one of the most successful plaintiff firms in the city. This is one of New York's most respected firms. More than twenty-five lawyers there had won judgments of more than $1 million. I knew Harvey Weitz from The Inner Circle, a prestigious legal organization to which we both belonged.

To protect their clients' rights they filed suit against the driver, the mother. Our client. As harsh as that sounds, in certain situations it is the legally prudent thing to do. But in this case we didn't think that benefited anybody; it accomplished nothing but create an adversarial relationship between us when we should have been working together against the ambulance company. Peter had some pretty hostile conversations with several Schneider Kleinick lawyers. It was potentially a bad situation. Keith Givens happened to be coming to New York and I asked him to meet with Phil Damashek to try to smooth out this conflict. Each side needed to represent its clients interests, but there was nothing to be gained by fighting each other.

Keith met with Phil Damashek and suggested that we focus on what was best for the survivors. Eventually that's exactly what happened. But later in that conversation Keith told him about our plans to expand into New York City. Rather than see that as a threat, Phil Damashek felt that it might be compatible with his firm's plans. That was the first of many conversations. Several months later The Cochran Firm/Schneider Kleinick Weitz Damashek & Shoot was born.

The Cochran Firm. That was quite a compliment to me. I was amazed that they agreed to put my name first on the front door. But that decision had been reached very easily. Lawyers like Ivan Schneider, Harvey Weitz, Phil Damashek, and Brian Shoot are as good as any in the country, but they didn't have as much visibility as I did. They knew it. Actually, Phil Damashek probably understood the value of my name to generate business more than I did. Phil Damashek was one of the first attorneys to do really sophisticated marketing in New York. Nobody in the firm objected to the addition of my name. The lawyers at SKWD&S were successful and secure in their own accomplishments. Keeping the rest of the name made great sense, too; it would allow us to benefit from the almost forty years of goodwill the firm had earned.

The Cochran Firm then expanded rapidly into other cities. Keith Givens set out to build a national law firm with the ability to litigate civil actions, class action lawsuits, and mass torts. He wanted to put together a firm of experienced lawyers able to get involved in major cases anywhere in the country.

I had my own plan. I wanted to bring together attorneys from diverse ethnic and racial groups, men and women, to prove how well we could all work together. I wanted a firm with blacks and browns and whites, Asians, East Indians; men and women; I wanted it to be as diverse as possible—and I wanted to be able to draw cases from every ethnic community in the country, a firm that truly represented the melting pot that is America. That was my plan. Still is.

The Cochran Firm/SKWD&S, located in the classic Woolworth Building in downtown Manhattan, was the foundation.

I was focused on building The Cochran Firm. I wanted to continue working with Peter and Barry on civil rights cases. The one thing I definitely was not looking to do was get involved in another high-profile criminal case. Then Sean "Puffy" Combs called and asked for my help.

Sean "Puffy" Combs is a fascinating young man. He is a really smart kid and very, very talented. He was raised in the suburbs, he wasn't a kid from the streets, but turned himself into "Puff Daddy," an entrepreneur and one of the most successful hip-hop artists. Eventually he founded his own record company, his own clothing company, he published a magazine, made movies, and built himself a $300 million empire. In 1999 he was number nineteen on the *Forbes* magazine list of America's most powerful celebrities. He was also dating the very beautiful Jennifer Lopez. At that time they were probably the most glamorous and publicized couple in the country. On December 27, 1999, they were staying at his home in the Hamptons. The next morning they were leaving for a Caribbean cruise. He'd charted a yacht for them. Apparently not much was happening out there so they decided to drive into the city and go to a club. They weren't bothering anybody, they weren't doing anything wrong, they just wanted to have a good time.

They went to Club New York in Times Square. Puffy and Jennifer stayed in the VIP area. They had some people with them. Among them were a young rap star who recorded for Combs's Bad Boy Records, Jamal Barrow, known as Shyne, and Anthony Jones, Wolf they called him, and he had been Puffy's bodyguard. As this group got ready to leave, one of them apparently bumped into an ex-con named Matthew "Scar" Allen, who was standing at the bar. An argument started. Someone else, I don't know that this person was ever identified, threw a wad of cash at Combs. The message was obvious: It was a way of telling him that he wasn't so big, wasn't so important, that other people had a lot of money, too. You ain't all that. In the hip-hop world that is a challenge, a sign of disrespect. Guns appeared, between three and six shots were fired, three people were hit. Fortunately, none of the wounds were life-threatening.

The whole club was in chaos. Nobody knew what was happening. It was a terrible scene. People dived on the floor. Women were screaming. A lot of people started running for the exits. Puffy, Jennifer, and Jones got out of the club safely and jumped into Combs's Lincoln Navigator. The driver, a man named Wardel Fenderson, took off at high speed. He was probably right to do that. There have been too many killings in the hip-hop world and Puffy Combs certainly could be considered a target. A lot of people resented his success. Fenderson raced up Eighth Avenue; he drove through red lights, he didn't stop until police cars forced him onto the sidewalk.

When the police searched the Navigator they found a nine-millimeter handgun, a semiautomatic Ruger, under the front seat. Supposedly during the chase someone threw a second gun out of the rear window of the vehicle. The four people in the Navigator were arrested. Eventually Puffy Combs and Wolf Jones were indicted for illegal possession of a firearm. Puffy was later indicted for bribery, supposedly offering the driver, Fenderson, $50,000 and a diamond ring Jennifer had given him to claim he owned the Ruger. As evidence of that attempt, prosecutors had a message Combs left on Fenderson's answering machine, in which he told him, "I just wanna make you feel comfortable . . . make your family feel comfortable and let you know everything is gonna be all right." Shyne faced the toughest charges; he was indicted for attempted murder. Supposedly police had found a gun in his waistband when he was arrested and several witnesses inside the club identified him as the shooter.

When all this took place I was at home in Los Angeles with my family. This was Christmas. My phone started ringing that night. I knew Sean Combs, I knew the whole hip-hop scene. In the past I had represented several very prominent rappers. I represented Tupac Shakur. I represented Snoop Doggy Dogg in several minor cases. I knew Shuge Knight. And I knew Puffy. There was a so-called schism, basically a war, between West Coast and East Coast rappers and I was one of the few people who had the respect of both sides. I had represented people from both coasts.

Hip-hop, "gangsta rap," was a violent world, no question about that. It was about as far from the pristine courtrooms and boardrooms and meeting rooms and fancy conference rooms in which I spent a lot of my time as it is possible to get. Hip-hop was the other end of the rainbow. Mix together street kids, guns, drugs, sex, music, ego, and the opportunity to make more money than these kids ever believed possible, and there was no question what the result was going to be. No question at all. People had been killed. Puffy Combs's best friend, Christopher Wallace, better known as Biggie Smalls and Notorious B.I.G., had been murdered. Tupac had been shot and killed in Las Vegas the week we were supposed to go to court to argue a motion concerning a charge that he had violated probation in another case. Pac was such an impressive person, he had a lot to give and he was just beginning to understand his own capabilities and responsibilities. I was crushed when he was killed. I was just devastated. He was my client and also my friend and I saw that he had an opportunity for a productive life.

I became a father figure to several of these young people. These kids knew that I was someone they could come to when they were in trouble, then some of them started coming by when they weren't in trouble. Just to talk. Whether mainstream society likes it or not, these were the people who had the attention and the admiration of a lot of young people in this country. These kids had real power, they had the opportunity to shape lives. So I was pleased to have some influence with them. I definitely tried with Tupac. "You have this wonderful talent," I told him, "you have a magnificent opportunity here. But this violence. You don't need it, Pac. You need to be careful."

He would listen intently. And then he would tell me, "I'm getting my life together." And maybe he was, maybe he was.

I understand rap, I think it has its place, but truthfully, it is not my favorite kind of music. I grew up listening to groups like the Temptations, who sang about love and despair and the tracks of your tears. My oh my. That music seemed so much more relevant to me than rap lyrics, which too often were violent and crude and demeaning to women. To me, there was no comparison. I'd prefer to listen to the Temptations and Luther Vandross any day.

Maybe I didn't really care for a lot of the music, but I had great respect for these kids. Kids like Tupac and Puffy. Kids with talent and promise. I had initially gotten to know Sean Combs through his entertainment lawyer, Kenny Meiselas. Sean had been involved in an alleged assault on Interscope Records executive Steve Stoute, an assault that resulted from Stoute using footage of Combs in a music video, a scene in which he was nailed to a cross, without approval. As Sean admitted, he just lost his cool. He was arrested and was facing seven years in jail. Instead he allegedly paid Stoute $500,000 in producing and management fees and negotiated a guilty plea to second-degree harassment, for which he received one day of anger management counseling.

Several years earlier I'd helped Michael Jackson resolve charges against him so he could resume his career. Everybody in the music industry knew about that, so when Combs was charged with assault, Kenny Meiselas asked for advice. I played the role of the wise counselor. Kenny wanted to know whether his client was being offered a good deal. Should this be resolved? Should he go to trial? It all worked out very well. And I got to know Sean Combs. He even invited Dale and me to his fabulous birthday party in the Hamptons. We were by far the oldest people at that party, but he made sure we were very comfortable. Eventually he started referring to me as "Uncle Johnnie." Uncle Johnnie, well, well, well.

One day he said to me, "I'm not planning to get into any trouble, but I need to have all your numbers."

Call for the right reasons, I told him when I gave him those phone numbers. That's why Kenny Meiselas called me at home the night of December 27th and told me, "Puffy's in jail." My phone rang often the next few days as everybody raced around, trying to figure out what to do. This case made headlines from the night it started. It had all the elements; a beautiful woman, shots fired, a car chase. It was a career maker, a point obviously not missed by the prosecutor, Matthew Bogdanos. This was the case that was going to give him real visibility in New York, this was a headline-making case, the kind of prosecution that could lead to much bigger things. Rudolph Giuliani had very successfully parlayed his tenure in the U.S. Attorney's Office, where he forged a reputation as a real "law and order" crime fighter, into two terms as mayor. Bogdanos once described his case as a "fight against the arrogance of power," but it seemed to me that his motives for spending a million dollars of the people's money to prosecute a gun possession case were obvious.

Bogdanos as quickly as possible put the case in front of the grand jury. He was doing his job, a good prosecutor wants to get people in front of the grand jury as fast as possible, he wants to get their stories locked in concrete before they have time to coordinate a defense. And Bogdanos was a good prosecutor. But he was also an ambitious zealot. There's nothing wrong with that.

Puffy Combs was represented by a Bronx attorney named Harvey Slovis. Slovis had also represented him in the Stoute case. Kenny Meiselas continued to call me for advice. The first major issue concerned whether or not Puffy should testify in front of the grand jury. Most innocent people want to testify in front of the grand jury. Puffy wanted to testify. He thought he'd walk in there, tell the truth, and walk out a free man. He thought being honest would be enough to convince the jurors of his innocence. But what most people don't understand is that the function of the grand jury is simply to determine if there is the legal basis for an indictment, sufficient reason to charge an individual with a crime or crimes. That's all, is there a reasonable possibility this person was involved in this crime? The grand jury doesn't get involved in questions of guilt or innocence. The prosecutors control all the witnesses. There is no cross-examination by defense counsel. Over a period of time prosecutors get familiar with the jurors. And they can pretty much manipulate them to do whatever it is they want. Bogdanos wanted Puffy Combs indicted.

There was absolutely nothing to be gained by Puffy testifying in the grand jury. Nothing. In New York State if a gun is found in a car and no one claims ownership, the law can attribute unlawful possession to anybody in that car. Bogdanos was going to indict Puffy Combs on that charge. That it might be his gun.

So Puffy wasn't going to be able to make the problem disappear by showing up and telling the truth, and there was a lot to be lost by testifying. "Don't talk to anybody," I said. "Don't answer any questions until we know what they're trying to do. All they're trying to do is lock you in to your testimony."

My advice was don't testify. It's a mistake, I said, a grand jury can indict a ham sandwich. But Slovis was Puffy's lawyer at that time and advised him to appear. It turned out to be a disaster. Slovis and Bogdanos both have tempers and they didn't like each other at all. They got into a shouting match. Bogdanos brought up every negative thing in Puffy's life he could find. During his cross-examination, for example, he vigorously questioned him about the assault charge, which we felt impaired the integrity of the grand jury. He did everything possible to prejudice the jury, to convince them that Puffy Combs was a bad guy and capable of committing these "heinous" crimes. The grand jury indicted Puffy Combs, Shyne, and Wolf. The most serious charges, involving the shooting, were filed against Shyne.

If convicted of the charges against him, Puffy was facing fifteen years in jail. It was outrageous. Fifteen years for what was basically a gun possession charge? If the same thing had happened in L.A. it probably would have been treated as a misdemeanor. If found guilty he would have been fined $150, maybe more because he was well known, and warned against doing it again. He wouldn't be facing jail time unless he had actually fired the gun. Before the Combs case in New York, rap artist Queen Latifah was arrested in L.A. for carrying a loaded gun and for possession of a small amount of marijuana. Carl Douglas negotiated with prosecutors, Queen Latifah pleaded guilty for possession of a loaded weapon and was fined $810, and also had to donate an additional $2,500 to disadvantaged youth and was put on two years probation. The whole process took only a few days.

Being a celebrity certainly has its benefits, but it also has a price. In this situation it turned a minor incident into a major case, and what probably would have been a two-day trial into an eight-week ordeal.

Puffy Combs was facing fifteen years. Realistically, if he had been convicted his sentence probably would have been between five and ten years, but it would have also destroyed his Sean John clothing company, his record label, and the other businesses in which he was involved. There was no reason that he faced that, except maybe that it served the needs of an ambitious prosecutor. By the time I got back to New York after the holidays, Puffy Combs had been indicted and I was asked to take charge of his defense. There were a lot of reasons I didn't want to get involved in this case. I just didn't want to do any more criminal cases. I was very happy with the civil cases I was handling. I knew it was going to take at least two months of really intense work; everything else in my life was going to have to wait, I was going to have to cancel everything else on my schedule.

I also had my new partners at The Cochran Firm to consider. I had finished—at least I thought I'd finished—my criminal career with the acquittal in the Simpson case. I'd helped win the case of the century. Now frankly, I've never been afraid of losing a case because I learned early that if you're really going to get down in the legal trenches you're going to win some and lose some. But after the Simpson case a lot of people thought of me as invincible; a lot of people made comments like, "I don't like Johnnie Cochran, I don't like what he did in the Simpson case, but if I had needed a lawyer, he'd be the first person I'd call."

Well, that's pretty good for future business. But what if I fought this case and lost it? It would change the public perception of me. Everybody wants to end their career like Michael Jordan, hitting that last-second shot to win a championship. But when Michael Jordan later came back to play he proved to be very human, getting injured and suffering through some of the worst games of his legendary career.

I remember sitting with Sean Combs and looking at him and thinking that the system is trying to knock out another guy that got too big. If this wasn't Puff Daddy, if he wasn't with Jennifer Lopez, if his businesses hadn't earned nearly $100 million the previous year with music and clothing that kids embraced, there was no way they would be making this case against him. No way. I thought, This kid has so much to offer. He's just beginning to touch his greatness. If I don't step up and get in there and fight, he is going to prison. He's going to get a minimum of five years. I don't think at that time he believed that, but it was true. I didn't want them to take him down. That's why I got involved in the case.

Arguing against a prosecutor like Bogdanos was just a bonus. I'd seen his type all through my career. Another guy trying to make a name for himself at somebody else's expense. "A résumé case," prosecutors called it. He was so confident, so cocky. He was arrogant, full of vitriol, an unpleasant person. At that time he was the rising superstar in the Manhattan DA's Office. He had tried many cases in front of this judge; he knew this judge, he knew the rules, he knew what he could get away with. He knew he had the home court advantage. In my career I don't know that I had ever encountered a prosecutor so much more interested in winning a case than seeking justice.

I told Sean Combs I would work with him, but that I couldn't work with Slovis. He had severely underestimated this case. He'd allowed his client to testify in front of the grand jury. He'd said things in court like, "This is nothing but a gun case." He had to go.

I also knew I couldn't handle this case alone. I needed a tough, experienced New York criminal lawyer. Bogdanos knew the state law. The judge certainly knew the state law. We needed someone equally experienced in the state of New York. When hosting *Johnnie Cochran Tonight* I'd met Ben Brafman. I liked him a lot. I thought he was knowledgeable and tough, tougher than Bogdanos. And I saw in him a real passion for justice. He knew the law, he understood the way the Manhattan District Attorney's Office and the NYPD worked, he had tried many cases in that courthouse, and he had known Judge Charles Solomon most of his professional career. He also knew Bogdanos and respected him. We met over breakfast and I asked him to join me on the defense team. The first decision we made was to limit that team to the two of us. That meant we both would have to do a lot of work, but it also enabled us to make decisions quickly—and unlike the Simpson "dream team," there was never, never a clash of egos.

During the trial Ben Brafman was a warrior. Like Peter and Barry, he was the kind of person you want to have in your foxhole. Totally trustworthy. We didn't always agree on strategy, we had some pretty good debates, but it was never personal, it was always about what was best for our client. Ben also has a great sense of humor. He did similar things to Bogdanos that I had done to Chris Darden, whispering things to him like, "I think you forgot to take your medication today."

The first thing we had to do was understand the case against our client. We needed to know every fact and understand the prosecution's theory, then try to pinpoint those parts of their theory that were suspect or not supported by credible evidence. While it appeared to be a relatively straightforward case, in fact it was very, very complicated. Different aspects of the case had to be dealt with differently. The accusation that Sean had a gun in the club could be defended much more easily, for example, than the charge that he was responsible for the gun in the car. Then we had to refute the charge that he had tried to bribe Fenderson.

The evidence against him would consist primarily of eyewitness testimony. But each of those people, just about every one of them, had also filed a civil suit against him. There were almost a billion dollars' worth of lawsuits filed against him. Some of them had sued him for astronomical amounts of money. Driver Wardel Fenderson, for example, who Combs had supposedly attempted to bribe, sued for $3 million. I believe all three shooting victims sued, and at Ben Brafman's suggestion the position we took was that being a victim doesn't give you the right to become an opportunist. These people had sustained nonlife-threatening injuries, but they hadn't been injured by Sean Combs. Suing him for hundreds of millions of dollars was essentially a fraud. But these people knew, and after we got done so did the jury, that the only person charged with a crime who also had the money to pay large civil judgments was Sean Combs. Unless he was convicted of the criminal charges these people would have a difficult time collecting damages in civil court. They had a motive to lie.

We also were faced with the difficulty of mounting a joint defense with Shyne and Wolf. Shyne's lawyer was very competent, Murray "What? Me Worry Murray" Richman, as he was known. He and Ben had known each other for more than twenty years. But his client's legal problems were very different from ours. Shyne was an aspiring rapper who Sean had signed for his Bad Boy Records label. A month earlier Shyne had been jumped by some people in Brooklyn, his life had been threatened, so he was carrying a gun for protection. It was so silly to be carrying that gun. To carry a gun into a club, so silly. If he was that worried he should have stayed home. If he didn't want to stay home he should have had a body-guard. The result of his decision was this trial. But several witnesses saw him firing inside the club. That was his problem.

Shyne voluntarily signed an affidavit swearing that Sean never had a gun that night. He also was willing to testify to that—if we could get separate trials. For obvious reasons he didn't want to testify to that in front of the jury that would also decide his guilt or innocence. We asked Judge Solomon for separate trials. It was mostly a formality. We were pretty certain he would turn us down, so we were not surprised when he did, but it was the proper request to make. Throughout the trial we shared every bit of information we had with Murray Richman. We gave them all our witnesses, we gave them anything we discovered that might help in Shyne's defense.

Sean Combs paid all the attorneys' fees and from the very beginning he prohibited us from putting any witness on the stand who might give prejudicial evidence against Shyne or Wolf. We had witnesses ready to testify that Puffy was lying on the ground in the club when the shots were fired, we also had a witness who was actually on top of him—but some of these people also would testify that they saw Shyne firing the gun. Puffy would not let us call any of them. I don't think Shyne really understood that. Truthfully, we got into some pretty heated discussions about it, but we never called those witnesses.

In fact, Sean Combs was paying for everything. If he had not been able to afford a credible defense I suspect Bogdanos might still be telling people he had never lost a case. Most of the time criminal defense lawyers want to get paid in advance. Criminal lawyers know that the time to get the fee is when the tears are flowing, when the client really is afraid. If you don't, and you win the case, too often the client will say, "I was innocent anyway, I shouldn't have to pay you." And if you don't and you lose the case, you probably never will get paid.

The fee should always be reasonable, but often lawyers and clients have a different definition of reasonable. We knew it was going to be expensive because we knew there had to be a trial. Puffy wasn't going to plea bargain, he wasn't guilty. Bogdanos wanted the exposure the trial would give him. In this case I knew Puffy Combs, so I wasn't concerned about not getting paid. Including legal fees, investigators, and everything else it took to mount our defense, it cost Puffy Combs more than $1 million. On a gun possession charge.

The other problem we had to deal with was the media. Before the trial Ben Brafman told me he thought he was prepared for that. He'd been involved in several high-profile trials. "Ben," I told him, "believe me, you can't imagine what this is going to be like."

This was the biggest celebrity trial in the country since the Simpson case. This was the biggest gun possession case in history. It was going to sell a lot of newspapers and magazines. It was a trial as entertainment, a forerunner of reality programming, just a few steps away from dramatic series like *Law and Order*. I couldn't complain: It was the kind of trial I would have been talking about if I was still hosting a Court TV show. Johnnie Cochran was once again defending an African-American celebrity, another chance for him to "play the race card." Beautiful singer–movie star Jennifer Lopez was involved, which allowed the newspapers and magazines to run endless sexy pictures of her. The most successful young black entrepreneur in the country, a superstar, was on trial. Scores of reporters covered the case every day. Meanwhile, four terrorists were on trial right down the block. Potential mass murderers, the advance scouts for Osama bin Laden, who were charged with killing 224 people in the bombing of two American embassies in Africa. Our trial got the headlines; the media barely mentioned the other trial.

A few days before the trial was scheduled to begin the *Daily News* ran a front-page story in which one of the victims said flatly, "Puffy Combs shot me in the face." That was exactly the kind of story we didn't want prospective jurors to read, but there was little we could do about it. Sean hired his own public relations company to try to get some sort of balance in the press. The trial became the hottest ticket in town. People would arrive more than two hours early and stand in line behind a velvet rope waiting to get in; there was reserved seating for friends and family.

The judge, Judge Charles Solomon, did not want this case tried in the press. He didn't want to turn the trial into dueling press conferences, so he imposed a gag order on the participants. That meant we weren't allowed to talk to the media. While in theory that seems fair, the reality was very different. The witnesses and victims spoke to the press, in fact one police sergeant even held a press conference after he testified—and yet we couldn't respond. The victims had their own agenda and they didn't hesitate to talk to the media. The government leaked information to reporters, who would cite "unidentified sources close to the prosecution." Bogdanos would stand up in court and claim he had nothing to do with it—and he was probably telling the truth. There was no way of finding the source. "Sources close to Puffy Combs's defense" were limited to three people.

One day I was leaving the courtroom and a reporter asked me how I felt about that day's testimony. I said, "If it doesn't make sense, you must find for the defense." I thought I was being funny, Johnnie Cochran rhyming again. Bogdanos wanted Judge Solomon to hold me in contempt of court for that remark. Ridiculous, absolutely ridiculous.

For the most part, trials are won or lost in preparation and jury selection. Preparing for this trial we once again hired Kevin Hinkson as our investigator and he turned up numerous witnesses. We interviewed between forty and fifty people while putting our case together. Sean was a completely hands-on client. He wanted to know everything. Everything. He worked right along with us. You could see why he had been so successful; he knew everything that was going on around him, he knew how to manage people, he knew how to get things done. His people on the street produced several other witnesses for us that Kevin tracked down. He'd call Kevin three, four times a day to give him information, to pass along names, to set up meetings. We interviewed many of the witnesses he found and learned a tremendous amount about what had happened that night. We had witnesses who had been in the men's room and overheard Scar and his friends complaining about Combs and Jennifer Lopez. They resented his presence, his taking over their club by walking in with a beautiful movie star. One of them supposedly said, "We're gonna pop a cap in that nigger's ass." We knew all about the victim who had been hit in the face by a ricocheting bullet; while she claimed to have been badly hurt and in public walked with a limp, we found a close friend who told us "She told me she didn't see anything," and that rather than walking with a limp, in private she was dancing. We had a list of about twenty people who were in the club that night and were willing to testify that Sean never had a gun and was on the ground covered by other people. We knew we could make a very strong case through eyewitnesses that he had never had a gun inside the club, and then we focused on what had happened in the car and the ensuing bribery charge.

The only people who had been present throughout the entire series of events were Jennifer Lopez and Sean Combs. And they were the only people the media cared about. Would either one testify? Both? If Jennifer testified, what would she say? Just to make the situation a little more media enticing, during this period Sean and Jennifer ended their relationship. Nobody except the two of them knew why or what had happened. It added another element: Would Puff Daddy's ex-girlfriend testify in his behalf?

From the beginning of our preparation, we planned to end the trial with star power; we intended to have both Jennifer and Sean testify. Jennifer was prepared to testify. Ben and I decided that if Jennifer testified I would question her and that he would question Sean. Our thinking was that if I examined Sean the jurors might focus on me as much as him, and we wanted them to really listen to his testimony. My presence might have detracted from that. But we felt that Jennifer was such a superstar, people would hardly even notice I was there.

So I prepared her to testify. We would meet at her lawyer's office and spend hours going over and over the questions Bogdanos likely would ask and the questions I definitely would ask. Jennifer Lopez is a beautiful and astute woman. Jennifer said flatly that she had never seen Sean with a gun in his hand. She never wavered from that. She said she was leaning against him in the car coming into the city, danced close with him in the club, and watched as he danced on a table and his shirt rose up—and never felt a gun or saw a gun. She acknowledged that the police had recovered a gun from the Navigator, but denied that a second gun was thrown out of the car window. She never heard him offer Fenderson a bribe. She was consistent on all the important facts.

The problem we faced with Jennifer was that she had spent three days testifying in front of the grand jury and we couldn't get a transcript of her testimony. In New York the DA doesn't have to give the defense a copy of a witness' grand jury transcript until that witness has finished his or her direct testimony. The theory is that the truth remains the truth; if witnesses could read their grand jury testimony they might tailor their answers to be consistent with it. In California the law is much more fair. The judge would have given us that testimony in advance in the interest of full disclosure. So while Jennifer remembered much of her grand jury testimony, she couldn't possibly recall all of the details. After thirteen months few people could. It's possible to tell the truth differently on two different occasions: Where were you standing? How far from the wall were you? Who was standing on your right? Who was on your left? Without being able to review her testimony in advance, it would be almost impossible for her to be completely consistent with it. If she had made even a slight mistake on a single detail, Bogdanos could have destroyed her credibility. Having her testify would be risky, so Ben and I decided to wait until we presented our case to decide if we needed her testimony.

We knew from the beginning that Sean would have to testify, and I think we suspected that the outcome of the trial would depend on that testimony. If the jurors liked him, if they believed him, they would acquit him.

Often before a trial the DA will offer the defense a deal, a plea bargain, to avoid the time and expense of a lengthy trial and eliminate the risk of defeat. That way he gets his conviction and the defendant gets a better sentence than he might get from a judge after trial. While we never had any formal plea discussions because Sean maintained from the first day that he did not have a gun, did not shoot anybody, and did not try to bribe Fenderson, prior to the trial Bogdanos asked Ben Brafman—hypothetically, of course—if there was any chance Combs would consider pleading guilty to a felony if he didn't have to serve any time. Legally and ethically Ben had to bring the hypothetical question to Sean, but there was no chance of a deal. Sean wasn't going to plead guilty to a crime he didn't commit and even without serving time in jail, being a convicted felon or being on probation carries real penalties, particularly for someone who travels as frequently on business as he does. And, finally, we were confident we were going to win this trial.

Basically, picking a jury is done by just a gut feeling. I like this person. I think this person understands this case. I think this person will be fair to my client. In the Simpson trial we used an expert in picking juries, Jo Ellen Demetrious, but in this case we decided against it.

In picking the jury for the Simpson trial we asked members of the jury panel to fill out an eighty-page, 302-question questionnaire. In addition to including all the basic information—age, race, education, marital status, employment history—this questionnaire also allowed us to learn quite a bit about these people's real feelings. For example, we asked, Do you have the authority at work to hire or fire people? Is this hard or easy for you? Or, Do you agree or disagree with the statement that people who make a lot of money are treated better by our court system than other people? Have you ever asked a celebrity for an autograph? Have you ever experienced fear of a person of another race?

Knowing that a lot of people don't like hip-hop and associate it with violence, we wanted to provide a similar questionnaire to potential jurors in this trial. But Judge Solomon prohibited it. He said he was going to ask his own questions.

One of the things I found out right away is that New York legal procedure is much more formalized than in California. New York has strict guidelines covering just about every aspect of a trial. Fortunately, Ben Brafman was familiar and comfortable with those rules. Even the method used to pick juries in New York is different. It's a somewhat cumbersome system. In California the prosecutor or defense lawyer has to stand up and request that a specific juror be excused; in New York it's done anonymously. Jurors get excused and don't know why or by which side.

We knew the kind of jurors we wanted. We preferred women to men, because we thought they would be less resentful of a young rap star—and because Sean was very close to his mother, Janice Combs, who would be in the courtroom every day. We thought that would play well with all women, but especially black women. We wanted younger people who might understand rap music. We certainly wanted at least a sampling of African-Americans and Latinos. We looked at socioeconomic factors. We looked at the clothes and the jewelry worn by members of the panel. One older white woman, for example, had several earrings in one ear. Looking at her we knew she certainly wasn't conservative; we wanted her. Another middle-aged white woman taught autistic children; that suggested she would be compassionate and would have to be absolutely certain before voting to destroy someone's life; we wanted her.

Definitely we were trying to fill the jury with people who would be sympathetic to our case, there's nothing wrong with that. Bogdanos was trying to seat as many older, white, conservative jurors—who not only didn't know the hip-hop world but probably were even afraid of it—as possible. That's fine, that's the way the system works. The more diverse a jury is the better I like it. When people who come from different places in life collectively bring their wisdom to bear, the system works. It's what you need for a fair trial.

Ben and I took turns questioning potential jurors. Just about all of them knew who I was and were at least somewhat familiar with the Simpson case. We heard from several people, "I didn't agree with the verdict in the Simpson case."

And in return we asked, "Will that affect your ability to be fair in this case?" A few people admitted it would. "You know," I said to them, "I really applaud that kind of courage," and then I had them removed. Among those people was the former wife of Guardian Angels founder and radio talk-show host Curtis Sliwa. On the show Sliwa mentioned that she was on the panel, so we intended to challenge her anyway, but when she volunteered, "I can't be fair in this case," she was gone. There are a lot of people who prejudge a case without knowing all the facts; the problem is that many of those people won't admit it.

During jury selection, Bogdanos tried to create the impression that it was him, just one nice guy all by himself, against an array of highly paid legal talent. Particularly me. So when the very white Ben Brafman stood up for the first time to address the jurors he said, "I'm not Johnnie Cochran. But just in case you get confused, I always wear a pin in my collar and he doesn't. The guy without the pin in his collar is Cochran."

At another point Bogdanos said, "I'm wearing a blue tie. If Mr. Cochran or Mr. Brafman got up and tried to convince you that this tie was not blue, you would maintain that it was blue regardless of how talented or persuasive they might be, isn't that right?" The jurors agreed.

The only problem with that was that Bogdanos wasn't wearing a blue tie. Ben and I love ties. We know ties, I probably own five hundred ties and Ben has at least that many. So we could state with a high degree of expertise that this was definitely not a blue tie. It was blue and green and yellow in a paisley design. When Ben pointed out, "That is not a blue tie..." people actually started laughing.

We ended up with a racially and economically diverse jury. It was an excellent jury. We had seven men, five women; seven African-Americans, five whites—although two of the black men were corrections officers and one black woman worked as a peace officer at a library. We took a chance on those three, hoping that people in law enforcement would understand a bad case better than civilians.

The trial lasted almost eight weeks. The transcript ran six-thousand pages long. There were sixty witnesses and 126 court exhibits. For a gun possession case. During this trial "against the arrogance of power," Bogdanos sat alone, all by himself at the prosecution table, the supposed underdog charged with protecting the common man against the rich and powerful and therefore probably evil. It looked silly. When Giuliani was in the U.S. Attorney's Office he and then-Senator Al D'Amato had put on leather jackets and participated in a drug bust, playing the role of tough guys for the newspaper photographers who just happened to be there. This was Bogdanos's leather-jacket drug bust. Obviously he didn't work alone. I'm sure most people knew that he was being supported by the Manhattan DA's Office, which included a complete support staff, as many investigators as he needed whenever he needed them, dozens of people, all working for him and being paid from his large taxpayer-supplied budget.

His opening argument made it clear he was playing the class card. "I can't go to jail," he practically sneered, making fun of Sean, "I'm Puff Daddy."

The defense strategy is pretty much always the same; destroy the credibility of the prosecution's witness and then present evidence that your client is not guilty. There were a lot of exhibits, but no physical evidence that proved anything as far as Sean Combs was concerned. Bogdanos put five witnesses on the stand to testify that Sean Combs had a gun in the club that night—but their testimony was immediately tainted by the fact that four of them had filed multimillion-dollar lawsuits against Sean.

Ben Brafman and I split the cross-examination. A real trial is usually nothing like a television drama. It doesn't build toward a climax. It has endless ups and downs, peaks and valleys; the most important thing for an attorney is to remain even, calm, and not to react to every high or low. You never know when during a trial the key testimony is going to be given. It can just as easily come from the first witness as the last. One of the first witnesses Bogdanos called was perhaps the most dangerous to our case. This was a very attractive young African-American woman who had been in the club that night with some friends, who testified that she saw Puffy Combs with a gun. She was prim and proper, nicely dressed, with no criminal record and a good job. Most important, she was the only person claiming that Combs had a gun who was not suing him. She had absolutely nothing to gain with her testimony. The only reason she had to give this testimony is that this is what she believed she saw that night.

These are the kind of witnesses jurors remember and believe. Bogdanos was smart putting her on the stand early because his other witnesses each had problems.

We received a transcript of her grand jury testimony just before she got on the stand, which didn't give us a lot of time to figure out how to deal with her. Her testimony was straightforward and believable. She stated what she believed she saw. We had to convince her and the jury that maybe she wasn't exactly certain what it was that she had seen.

To begin with she was small, only about five feet tall. The club was packed, hundreds of people were there—most of them taller than she was. It was hard to believe, with people moving around, with the lights in the club kind of dim, that she really saw Sean holding a gun. Ben did the cross-examination. He didn't challenge her so much as lead her to doubt her own statements to the grand jury. He asked her if she had watched news reports on television, spoken to friends about the case, spoken to other people who were in the club that night about what they saw. She admitted that all of that was true. Then Ben took a gamble and asked her if her grand jury testimony was based completely on what she had seen, partly on what she had seen, partly on what she thought she saw, partly on what she saw on television or heard on the radio or read in the newspapers.

A combination of everything, she admitted.

We then did a demonstration. Ben positioned himself about as far away from her as she claimed Combs had been. He held a black cell phone in his hand, pressed against his thigh just as she had described. How many people were running around at that moment, he asked.

Hundreds, she admitted.

From your position could you really see a gun? She just disintegrated as a witness. When Ben reread her grand jury statement to her, that she had seen Sean Combs running out of the club with a gun, she said, "That's what I thought I saw."

In a criminal case jurors do not convict anyone based on that testimony. "I thought I saw" just isn't sufficient, particularly when that's the prosecution's strongest witness. We were elated. The only witness without a real agenda had been compromised.

Several days later the young woman who had been hit in the face by a bullet and who still had bullet fragments in her skull testified. She had a motive to claim she had seen Sean Combs holding a gun—she was suing him for $150 million. Her testimony was very dramatic and potentially very damaging. She said she saw Combs reach his right hand across his body, pull out a weapon, and fire. "It felt like a sledgehammer hitting me in the face," she said. "Blood began pouring out of my face and I said, 'Oh God, please don't take me.'"

Obviously we were sorry she had been shot, but we knew our client hadn't shot her. By the time she took the stand we'd developed quite a bit of information about her background. Some of it Judge Solomon would not allow us to use; for example, the fact that she had also been present at another shooting. Our strategy was to portray her to the jury as an opportunist and someone who exaggerates the truth. She was tough; she stuck to her testimony. We couldn't shake her that way. But she got some facts wrong and that tended to destroy her credibility.

For example, she testified that Sean was wearing a silver parka over his shoulders inside the club. We knew that wasn't true. While he was being booked at the precinct one of his assistants had gone back to his apartment and gotten the silver parka, which Sean then used to cover his face as he left the police station. Every newspaper photograph showed him holding this parka. That's where she saw it. But she insisted he was wearing it in the club. No other witness would corroborate her testimony. We also put on the stand the young man who actually retrieved the jacket.

We asked her how he could be wearing the parka around his shoulders and firing the gun. The way she described it made little sense to anyone.

Kevin Hinkson tracked down several people who had worked with her in a beauty salon. One of her best friends testified that the victim had severely exaggerated her wounds by wearing big bandages for the cameras, later taking them off in private; and in the hospital the night of the shooting she admitted, "I don't know who shot me." She told her friends that she was suing Puffy because he was the money at the end of the tunnel.

As much as anything else, I don't think the jury liked her very much. She was arrogant on the stand, even when it was clear her testimony was not accurate. Jurors will give witnesses some room for error; they will accept the fact that a good lawyer can confuse a witness, but only if they feel sympathy for the witness. This young woman was a victim, and had she been mostly truthful and just exaggerated or made up a few facts, she might have gotten away with her deception. But by the time she left the stand, I doubt very many jurors believed her testimony.

One of the victims, a man who had been shot in the shoulder, was suing for $700 million. At one point, I remember, I suggested to

Ben that the theme of this trial should be "Who wants to be a millionaire?" Well, this witness certainly did. After he testified that he had seen Sean with a gun I cross-examined him. We knew as much as we needed to know about his personal life before he took the stand, information that we knew he couldn't admit. The thing I had to be careful about was not bullying him, not maligning him. It was a very conversational cross-examination, not at all confrontational. He was a victim.

We just wanted to prove to the jury that his testimony wasn't believable. During his testimony I asked him several questions about his personal life. He claimed he had gone to the club with his "home girl." How long have you known her, I asked. Twelve years. Where does she live? In the building next door to me; we grew up together. What is her name? He gave her first name. What is her last name? He didn't know. What does your home girl do for a living? He didn't know.

Then I asked him about his personal life. You were wearing a leather jacket and leather pants at the club, you paid the forty-dollar admission fee, you were drinking champagne, what do you do for a living? I don't do anything.

There were enough streetwise people on the jury to understand what "I don't do anything but I've got plenty of money" really meant.

When I asked him how much he was suing for he claimed not to know, explaining, "I leave that stuff to my lawyer."

I think most jurors believed that anyone suing for $700 million would know it; they probably would lay in bed at night thinking about what they would do with the money. By the time we were finished he admitted that he had been smoking pot that night, and said, "I just wanted someone to pay my medical bills."

"Is that your final answer?" I asked. No one gets convicted of a crime based on this type of testimony.

Our strongest witness was an African-American woman, a single parent who was working at the club as a security guard. That was her second job, during the day she was a supervisor at the Department of Social Services. She was a bright, responsible woman working a second job to help pay her daughter's school tuition. She had tried to end the confrontation before any shooting began, tapping Sean on the shoulder and telling him, "You don't need to be part of this." When the shooting started she fell on top of him, allowing her to say, "I was on top of him when the shots went off, so I'm absolutely positive he didn't have a gun."

She was the perfect witness. She was a college graduate. Her only encounters with law enforcement had been two parking tickets. There was no way for Bogdanos to attack her credibility. The only problem we had was she didn't want to testify. She didn't want to get involved. She wanted to protect her privacy. But Kevin stayed in contact with her. I met with her several times, then Ben met with her. She just didn't think her testimony was necessary; he was innocent and therefore wasn't going to be convicted. Finally Kevin told her, "If you don't come and tell the truth, he'll go to jail. Can you honestly sleep at night knowing that an innocent man is in jail because you didn't testify?"

Reluctantly, she agreed. She was a great witness for us. When she left the courthouse reporters surrounded her. And just as she got into a car she turned and said bluntly, "Puffy is innocent. He didn't have a gun that night." It played on every TV newscast that night. It was a very strong day for us.

We felt we had effectively dealt with the events inside the club, so that left what happened in the car. The only witness who claimed Sean had a gun in the car was the driver, Wardel Fenderson, who also claimed that Sean had tried to bribe him. Fenderson was suing Combs for $3 million. Bogdanos tried to corroborate his testimony with the answering machine message, which we believed was too ambiguous to support the bribery charge.

This is where Fenderson's grand jury testimony hurt the prosecution's case; in his grand jury testimony Fenderson said—as we reminded the jury—that he thought Combs's answering machine message was an attempt to comfort him about losing his day job. In addition to his $3 million lawsuit, Fenderson had a second strong motive for accusing Combs of bribery: initially he'd told police it was his gun in the SUV, but after he agreed to testify against Combs all charges against him were dropped.

To support our contention that Fenderson was simply going after money, that Fenderson was trying to extract money from Combs for accepting responsibility for the gun, we introduced evidence that he was deeply in debt, that he hadn't paid child support in years. The single mothers on the jury definitely responded to that information.

The prosecution did introduce one surprise witness, a very public person who had once been close to Sean and claimed to have inside information. I'm not surprised too often in a courtroom, but this time I was really surprised. And really angry. Someone on our staff spoke bluntly to this person's lawyer and told him bluntly, your client is a heavy cocaine user and if he gets up there and makes wild claims, we're going to prove that he's an addict and that his judgment and memory are impaired—and that'll be the end of his career.

A trial is a war. That was a battle we won.

There is no such thing as normal life during a trial. It's life lived at full speed. Every second, every minute, every day counts. There's no time to do anything except work—no television, no newspapers, no casual conversations. I was usually up by 6:00 A.M., I'd work out if possible because it's vital to stay healthy and keep your energy up. Before court we'd meet and review the day. Judge Solomon was a hard worker, the people got their money's worth with him; we'd be in the courtroom from 9:00 A.M. to about 5:30. Midday we'd get exactly one hour for lunch, but we'd stay inside— Sean had food delivered—working. During the entire trial I think

I went out for lunch once, with Murray Richman. Reporters and cameramen followed us into the restaurant. By the time we got served we had to get back to court. At the end of the day we'd meet to discuss strategy or interview the next day's witnesses. When we were all done with that I'd have to do some work on my other cases. We were preparing the Patrick Dorismond case, for example, which took a lot of time. I had my whole practice in Los Angeles. Sometimes I had as many as fifty phone calls that seemed urgent. At times I'd be working until one o'clock in the morning. I'd sleep in the office. Ben was working the same crazy hours as I was; in fact, neither one of us would hesitate to call the other at 1:00 A.M., both knowing for sure the other would be awake and working.

Sean Combs also had to run his various businesses. Fashion Week, the week that all the clothing companies display their designs for the next season and take orders from stores, took place toward the end of the trial. So while he was fighting for his freedom all day, at night he was producing the fashion show that would pretty much determine the immediate future of Sean John. These aren't small shows—they're extravaganzas competing for media attention. Obviously there was tremendous pressure on him; on a Saturday night near the end of the trial we attended his show. It was magnificent. I have strong feelings about Sean, in many respects I consider him like a son. And I was so proud of him that night. To be able to pull off this show in the middle of a trial was incredible and he did it. Sean John got great reviews—except from the antifur people, who were outraged that he used some fur in his designs.

There are times when I think he enjoys the controversy.

Now, I do take great pride in the way I dress. I like well-made, stylish suits. And ties, I like to wear ties that make a statement. In L.A. I tended to wear much brighter colors. The reporters used to joke that they had to buy the big pack of Crayola crayons so they could correctly identify the colors I was wearing. During the Simpson trial on several occasions I wore a beautiful white suit; Chris

Darden used to tease me about it. "Nice," he'd say, "nice, you're wearing your ice-cream man suit."

In New York I dressed more conservatively—darker suits, blues and grays. But one day, I remember I was wearing a mauve suit and a reporter asked me, "Johnnie, what's with the mauve suit?" I told him, "It's a mauve kind of day."

Ben wore dark suits, mostly navy blue, but he, too, took great pride in his ties. Sean wore lighter-colored suits, grays and off-whites. We suggested that he not wear earrings, chains, or jewelry; he was entitled to his lifestyle but we didn't want him to flaunt it in front of the jury. Most days he looked like a well-dressed college student or a very well-dressed young businessman.

There was one day when we all looked pretty sharp and Sean decided, "Okay, tomorrow we're gonna have a lawyer-off?"

"What the hell is a lawyer-off?" Ben asked.

"Tomorrow, depending on who comes in dressed the sharpest—but like a lawyer—someone will get some kind of prize."

I took some time picking out my clothing the next day. I wore a double-breasted navy suit with pinstripes, a white shirt, and colorful tie. Ben came in wearing a navy blue chalk-striped suit and a white shirt with fine blue pinstripes. We looked almost identical. Then Sean came in—wearing a navy blue suit. Appropriately, we decided it was a three-way tie.

Several weeks later, while the jury was deliberating, the reporters who had covered the trial held their own pool. Among all the participants, they selected me "worst dressed." Now some people who take pride in the way they dress might take that as an insult, but all I had to do was look at those reporters and see how they dressed . . . and it didn't bother me at all.

I don't believe in lucky charms and I'm not usually superstitious during a trial, but one morning Ben came in wearing a red fabric bracelet. Sean asked him about it. "It's called a bendel," Ben said, explaining that it was an ancient Hebrew charm which supposedly warded off the evil eye and deflected envy. The theory was that evil people would be attracted to the bright red band rather than the beauty or good fortune of the person wearing it. Sean decided he wanted to wear one.

Ben agreed to get a bracelet for him, but pointed out, "Once you put it on you have to wear it until it falls off. You can't take it off yourself." So Sean put on his red band—and then insisted that I wear one, too. So for most of the last month of the trial we all wore these red wristbands. But one day toward the end Sean took me aside and asked, "You still wearing your red band?" When I told him I was he nodded in agreement and said, "Me, too. I'm afraid if I take it off I'll fall in the shower and kill myself or something."

Not that I actually believed in this charm—but I didn't remove it, and after several weeks it just fell off.

Eventually we had to decide if Jennifer Lopez and/or Sean Combs would testify. That was a very tough decision to make. Very tough. Although they'd split up, during the trial Sean tried to win her back. He was often on the phone with her. Just after the trial started Jennifer had left the country, going to Australia for a concert, although some people speculated she'd left to make sure she didn't get involved in a scandal. That wasn't true at all—those people didn't know what they were talking about. We were in continuous contact with her and she told us that if we wanted her to testify she would be there. She didn't equivocate; if her testimony would help him, she would testify.

Ben and I discussed it a lot. I was in favor of her testifying, he was against it. Even if her testimony was not entirely consistent with her grand jury testimony, I thought the jury really needed to see her on the stand. She was there that night, every minute, she knew what happened. She would support the big picture, even if she remembered minor details differently fourteen months after the incident. I was a lot more concerned about what jurors might speculate if she didn't take the stand. The media had created an expectation that I believed we needed to fulfill.

Ben Brafman felt the fact that we didn't have the transcript of her testimony made it much too risky. If her testimony was not consistent it could really hurt the case. Finally, we agreed that Jennifer Lopez would not testify—but that Sean Combs would have to take the stand, look directly at the jury, and tell them the truth. If he did that, we believed, it wouldn't matter whether or not she had testified. But he had to testify; he had to withstand Bogdanos's cross-examination; the jury had to see him, the jury had to like him. They had to understand who he really was rather than the person the newspapers and TV portrayed him to be.

The trial was rough on Sean Combs. He probably lost about fifteen pounds. But he was anxious to finally tell the real story. We knew that Bogdanos would try very hard to provoke him, to get him angry, to prove to the jury that he was just another dangerous street guy wearing nice clothes. We spent hours and hours preparing Sean to testify. Ben went over in excruciating detail the kind of questions he would ask on direct examination. We went through thousands of possible questions to prepare him for a withering cross-examination.

Just be yourself, I told him, don't be afraid to show a little of your personality. Don't try to be something you aren't. Most important of all, try not to lose your temper. This guy will do anything to get under your skin. He's gonna try to catch you in some kind of mistake. You just have to stay consistent with your grand jury testimony. Anything you want to change, anything you remember differently, we'll bring it out during your direct testimony.

Don't try to play with Bogdanos, I warned him. He's really good at this, it's something you've never done before. You know he wants to get you, he wants to make you mad. You can disarm him by being your usual charming self.

I told him that numerous times in a lot of different ways. I had known Sean Combs for a long time, I knew what kind of person he was. As long as he didn't get caught up in the excitement of the moment, I thought he would do a wonderful job.

On direct examination Ben led him through the whole night, practically minute by minute. We knew we were going to have a problem with the answering machine tape; not so much what he said, but how he said it. There was a lot of street language on that tape. We played that tape during direct examination in order to show the jury we weren't afraid of it and could explain it. Sean explained exactly what he meant. Also we warned him to be very careful about using curse words on the stand. In fact, when he was with us he rarely used street language. In his setting he plays the bad guy; with us he was just a scared—and *scared* is precisely the right word—kid.

During the cross-examination Bogdanos tried every possible way to lure Sean into a confrontation. He was desperate for the jury to see Puff Daddy, the street guy, the rap star, the kind of person who would be carrying a gun into a crowded club. What he never understood, I think, is that this was the real Sean Combs on the stand, a bright, extraordinarily successful, college-educated young man. Sean answered every question directly and never wavered, never lost his temper. He was one of the best witnesses I have ever seen.

When Bogdanos walked back to his seat after finishing I thought he looked defeated. That's just my opinion. But he had failed completely to make even a small crack in Sean's demeanor. Sean got off the stand and we embraced each other. I was exhausted, but confident.

I wanted Ben Brafman to do the closing argument. The closing argument is the big finish, the time you present your entire case to the jury; the prosecutor failed to prove this, we proved that. It's a showcase for a lawyer, the soliloquy, the grand climax. It may well be my greatest strength in the courtroom. I think pretty much everybody expected me to make this argument, but I decided to step aside and remind the jurors that this case wasn't about me, it wasn't about my ego, it was about justice. I went to Puffy and explained it to him and he agreed with me. We both had complete confidence in Ben Brafman and I thought he had earned the right to do it. We worked together to prepare his closing argument. And he was perfect; he rhapsodized, he rapped to that jury. He is a great lawyer and this was a national stage for him.

Then we began waiting for the verdict. And waiting. It's the toughest part of every case, the waiting, the wondering if there was something else we might have done. While we were waiting Sean took a program from his fashion show and wrote on it, "Uncle Johnnie, my Uncle Johnnie, the fliest motherf—in' lawyer on the planet."

Thank you, I told him, but I don't think I can hang this on my wall. That was Sean as Puff Daddy, or Puffy, or P. Diddy, as he was soon to become known.

The jury had deliberated twenty-two hours. Judge Solomon ordered everyone to stay in the courthouse. I sat out in the hallway, trying to work. Occasionally I'd hear some sound from the jury room; on Friday afternoon about four o'clock, for example, we heard a shout. We didn't know what it meant. We hoped it meant they'd gotten over a hump and acquitted somebody, but we really didn't know anything.

The jury sent several notes to the judge. Sometimes you can figure out what's going on in the jury room based on those requests. This time the notes made little sense.

As it got to be late Friday afternoon we began to think that the jury was not going to bring back a verdict that day. About five o'clock the judge announced he was going to stop deliberations and send the jury to a hotel for the weekend. That meant we'd have to wait through the weekend, an excruciating prospect. But unexpectedly, only a few minutes later, the jury informed the judge it had reached its verdicts. The judge notified both sides as well as the media and gave everyone an hour to get back into the courtroom.

In preparation for the verdict a platoon of armed officers wearing riot gear took positions all around the courtroom. These people were prepared for real trouble. It was pretty unsettling. The wait for the jury to return was interminable. I'd been practicing law for thirty-eight years but I still wasn't prepared for this hour. You can feel your heart thumping through your chest. I looked at Puffy and I could see he was extremely anxious. In only a few minutes the jury was going to tell him his future. At moments like these you go back to your faith, go back to the basic things. We're gonna be fine, I told him, but no matter what happens you've got to keep your composure. Remember who you are. Expect the best, prepare for the worst.

Sean was holding his Bible in his hand and together we read the Twenty-third Psalm as the jury began filing back in. I glanced at them as they took their seats. None of them made eye contact with me, which made me uncomfortable. Worse, a few of the jurors that we believed would be favorable to us were crying.

The jury had to go through seventeen different counts. Shyne was first; he was acquitted of attempted murder, but convicted of the other charges. That didn't surprise me. There was substantial evidence against him and this was just not the kind of jury that was going to decide, "Not guilty, everybody go home."

Anthony Jones, Wolf, was next. He was acquitted of all charges. There was little evidence presented against him, so his acquittal was not a surprise. But when they acquitted him of possessing the gun in the car I suspected we were going to be all right on that charge. I was probably most concerned at that point by the final charge, the bribery charge.

There were five charges against Sean Combs. As Ben often said, we had to sweep. If we had been acquitted on four, but convicted on one, it was a complete loss. A terrible loss. One by one the verdicts were read: Not guilty. Not guilty. Not guilty. Not guilty.

And finally, not guilty. We shouted, we embraced. The release of emotion was unbelievable. Then I said to Sean, "You got your life back. Do the best with it."

Those jurors were crying, I realized, because they had voted to put Shyne in prison.

I don't remember even glancing at Bogdanos. This had to be a devastating loss for him. He is an extremely intense person. He had a bad temper when things didn't go his way. Now I don't know if this verdict put him into therapy, but if it didn't he probably got pretty close to it. His problem, Ben and I both believed, was that he had overtried the case. He had turned what was basically a gun possession charge into a crime rivaling the Lindbergh kidnapping. He had asked too much of the jurors and they wouldn't go along with him.

After the verdict Sean told reporters, "Every day people would come into the trial and testify and I was in disbelief. To me, the whole thing was a nightmare and every day it seemed to be getting worse. . . . This has been a life-changing experience. I'm going to take time off to make sure I evaluate everything and get my priorities straight. I've done a lot of things and I have to see what's important: my family, my children, my faith in God."

That was Sean Combs as himself.

Bogdanos's boss, Manhattan DA Robert Morgenthau said, "The system is supposed to work . . . perhaps cases like this—the exceptions—are reminders of how well the system works. Or maybe not."

I didn't read or hear any immediate comment from Bogdanos.

There was a subdued party later that night. No one forgot that Shyne had been convicted. I know Sean called Jennifer right after the verdict to tell her all about it, but by that time their relationship was done.

Ben Brafman went to his synagogue and I went home. I was

much too exhausted to go to a party. But as I walked down Fifty-Seventh Street, on the way to my apartment, people noticed me and stopped and actually started applauding. That was a very good feeling.

It would not have been normal unless some people accused me of playing the race card; this time I supposedly made sure that there were enough African-Americans on the jury to guarantee Puffy Combs would not be convicted. The difficulty with that charge, obviously, was the same jurors who acquitted Puffy Combs convicted another young African-American who was sitting right next to him.

I didn't even get to take time off, and instead spent the weekend trying to catch up on my other cases. But during the trial I had made an important decision. I realized I just didn't want to go through all the anxiety and stress of a criminal trial ever again. I'd done it too many times. Whatever the outcome, I decided this would be my last criminal trial. I was going to concentrate on civil cases and class actions, where my work might affect the lives of thousands of people. I wanted to get involved with issues that mattered to me, some of them quite controversial, reparations for slavery for example. I wanted to be able to speak out against injustice when and wherever I felt like 'it. Those thoughts just reenergized me. The possibilities excited me. Knowing my career as a criminal lawyer was finished, I actually felt just a little like a kid going off to college.

But if a really important criminal case came along, I . . .

TEN

My love for the promise of justice has never wavered, never, but a lifetime working in the legal system has forced me to deal with reality. What we have in this country is the appearance of justice. Inside the courtroom everybody is dressed properly and stands respectfully in the correct place and uses the correct legal language and files the right papers, and it seems like justice is being done. But it's all a charade. What happens in a courtroom has little to do with real justice for defendants. As a criminal defense lawyer I understood the system, I knew it well, and I used it for my client's benefit. That was my job and I did it.

In the criminal justice system the presumption that you are innocent until proven guilty just doesn't exist, particularly if a suspect is black or Latino. But if a defendant—a black, brown, or white defendant—has enough money, if he can afford a competent lawyer, if he is fortunate enough to find a judge who understands what the Constitution means, if he is innocent—he might be acquitted, although there is no guarantee of that. It's all about money.

I have absolutely no doubt in my mind that the outcome of a trial depends substantially on economic factors. Given exactly the same set of circumstances money will determine whether the accused goes to prison or walks out of the courtroom a free man. I think pretty much everybody understands that—and yet society accepts it. Oddly enough, the first real cry for change that I've heard took place after the Simpson trial. So many people were so outraged that a man they believed to be guilty of two brutal murders was acquitted that there were calls that all sorts of changes be made. They suggested the size of juries in criminal trials be reduced, they wanted the rules of evidence to be changed, they wanted rights taken away from the defendant. But that was pretty much the last time people got upset about the inadequacies of the criminal justice system.

It probably isn't even accurate to use the word *justice* to describe the system. Too many prosecutors think that their job is to win, period. Not to find justice, but to get convictions. They treat it like a sport where the only goal is winning, rather than an attempt to assure that each citizen receives the full benefits of his rights. In their Innocence Project, for example, Peter and Barry have found that almost half of all prosecutors will fight in court to prevent DNA evidence from being examined in old cases. That's amazing. They don't want wrongly convicted people to go free—because every time someone in prison is exonerated, people are going to want to know where the system broke down; how could an innocent person be arrested, prosecuted, and convicted—and in many cases sentenced to life imprisonment or even given the death penalty.

When people do start looking, too often they find overzealous prosecutors who failed to disclose vital evidence that might have led to an acquittal, or they find a cop who gave false or misleading testimony. In half—*half*—of all the cases in which a person was found guilty of a crime and was later proved to be innocent, there has been evidence of police or prosecutorial misconduct. If a defendant had an alibi the prosecutor changed the theory of the case; they changed the time it happened or they convinced witnesses to change testimony.

It's the system that makes this possible. And it starts at the very top. The chief justice of the Supreme Court, William Rehnquist, has said that due process only entitles a person to a fair trial. If an innocent person is found guilty after a fair trial and spends the rest of his life in prison, that's the way it is. Both Rehnquist and Antonin Scalia have said that a claim of actual innocence is not constitutionally significant.

Just imagine that.

It isn't only the prosecutors; I was a prosecutor, I've known and worked with many able and dedicated prosecutors, so I know the difficulties and frustrations of the job. It's also the judges who are beholden to the political interests that got them their jobs—and who want to keep those jobs. And it's the defense attorneys who have accepted the system as it is and have lost their passion for justice— the people who sleep through trials or refuse to do the extra work that might make the difference between conviction and acquittal.

Not surprisingly, many of the same people complaining about the system that allowed O. J. Simpson to be acquitted remain supporters of the death penalty. I'm against the death penalty for a lot of reasons, but certainly one of my primary objections to capital punishment is that we have executed innocent people. I believe that to be true as I know the sun rises in the morning and sets in the evening. People who doubt that must have been living in a foreign country. While governor of Texas, President George W. Bush presided over 152 executions, "and every one of those people was guilty." But at the same time he made that statement, a forensic scientist in Oklahoma who had served for years as a key prosecution witness in numerous trials admitted that she had lied in her testimony. In Chicago a man named Anthony Porter was sentenced to death for two 1983 murders. He had already ordered his last meal. He had been measured for his coffin. He had made his funeral arrangements. Then a group of students at Northwestern University's Medill School of Journalism not only proved he was innocent, they managed to get the actual murderer to confess on videotape. Two years earlier other students in that same class had proved four men convicted of murder—two of them on death row—were innocent.

It's hard for me to accept the fact that our system allows innocent people to be killed by the state and there isn't an uprising. Yet George Bush can remain certain that every person executed in Texas during his term as governor was guilty. I wish that I could be so certain that justice was done.

In a perfect world, a world in which everyone is treated fairly by the system, I recognize I would not have as much right to complain about the death penalty. I don't agree with it, I don't think it does any good, and I believe it diminishes us as a society, but I accept the fact that it is the will of the majority. It just seems logical to me that everyone should be complaining loudly when this ultimate penalty is not fairly and appropriately applied. For example, when police coerce testimony to create "eyewitnesses," as I have seen done in several cases. Or when evidence is fabricated and planted. When minorities aren't called for juries. When cases are moved to different jurisdictions to increase the likelihood of a conviction. When the state refuses to provide an adequate defense for people who can't afford one. Our system relies on human beings, on judges and juries, and human beings make mistakes. There are people who believe these mistakes are the price for a system that protects the majority of the people, the cost of doing business. Obviously, I disagree.

The only way to make the state pay attention is to make it pay. For example, my firm in Chicago, Cochran Cherry Givens Smith & Montgomery, is representing Anthony Porter in his case against the city of Chicago. But with Peter and Barry, we've carved out a whole new area of federal civil rights litigation, called unjust conviction. We're filing these cases in federal court because the federal government's rules of discovery—the ability to uncover evidence—are much more liberal than in local jurisdictions. Under these laws we're entitled to a lot more information. Basically we're going to sue to find out what went wrong, why innocent people were convicted of serious crimes. Usually when an innocent person is freed the prosecutors and police basically say, whoops, our mistake, and bury the reasons the mistake was made. They don't want the people of their jurisdictions to know what crimes were committed in their name. This is our attempt to find out. And we're going to allow the press to write about it. So far we've identified seven states in which we either have or intend to file these federal civil rights lawsuits. Nobody has ever attempted to do anything like this before.

It's going to shake things up. It's going to cause people to be a lot more careful when lives are at stake.

I'm qualified to criticize the legal system because I am a product of it. I grew up in it. I'm a veteran of it. I have four decades of experience to know where the system fails.

Because I have such a high public profile I get asked to become involved in all kinds of issues. People know that I can help them get attention for their cause. So I have to pick and choose carefully. I'm usually pretty sensitive to issues of race-based unfairness in the legal system. It is not the same system for African-Americans as it is for whites and anybody who believes differently is simply wrong. As wrong as they can be. I've seen minorities being abused by the system my entire career. It infuriates me.

That's why I got involved with Harvard Law professor Charles Ogletree and John Floyd, chairman of the National Bar Association's criminal law section, in trying to overturn federal mandatory sentencing provisions for possession or distribution of crack cocaine.

I am not protecting drug dealers. I despise drugs and drug dealers. I don't use drugs. My brother used drugs and they practically destroyed his life. My brother was a wonderful person, but drugs ended his dreams and eventually contributed to his death. So please believe me when I say I am *not* protecting drug dealers. What we did claim in this lawsuit was that the sentencing laws were discriminatory. Black people who use cocaine mostly use crack, while white people who use cocaine mostly use powdered cocaine. But a first-time offender arrested with five grams of crack—basically five doses—faces a federally mandated five-year sentence, while a first-time offender using powdered cocaine would have to be convicted of possessing five hundred grams to receive the same five year sentence.

The sentencing law passed by Congress in 1986 stated that because crack was more potent than powdered cocaine it was more addictive, thus leading to more violence than powdered cocaine. But medical researchers found that the 100-to-1 disparity in sentencing just wasn't justified by the small scientific difference between crack and powdered cocaine. Writing in the *Journal of American Medicine* these researchers suggested that a 2-to-1 disparity would be more appropriate.

This law impacted primarily the African-American community. White people don't go to jail for possession of five grams of powdered cocaine. Minorities go to jail for five years for possessing five grams of crack. And judges have no discretion in sentencing. Even the U.S. Sentencing Commission urged Congress to change this sentencing disparity. To me, this was racist law, aimed primarily at blacks, which is why I got involved in the lawsuit.

But in 1997, to the surprise of no one familiar with the politics of the Supreme Court, our argument was rejected. This mandatory sentencing remains the law of the land. In March 2002, Deputy Attorney General Larry Thompson, an African-American, announced that after studying fifty thousand cases, the Justice Department had determined that crack conviction sentences are *only* four or five times harsher than convictions involving powdered cocaine. That is absurd. This disparity is wrong. Period. It is simply another example of how the system is racist. Not mentioned is the fact that prosecutors have the discretion of whether to charge a defendant in state court—where you can get a more reasonable sentence—or federal court. Which cases go to federal court? It's not hard to guess. More than 70 percent of the people who get a mandatory five-year sentence are black. So a young black kid who has no previous record will go to jail for five years for possession. It's an unfair sentence. It's wrong. Many judges know it's wrong, but there isn't anything they can do about it.

Thompson argued that in upholding this disparity the Justice Department was simply being extra protective of minority communities, not being biased. That is so paternalistic. I'm sure the African-American community is grateful to the government for being so concerned about its well-being, particularly when it has fallen so short of that in so many other areas. That statement is an outrage, an absolute outrage. But it certainly doesn't surprise me.

I often tell a story about a wonderful black woman named Sojouner Truth. She was a free black woman, an abolitionist. She was a strong woman, she couldn't read, but she had righteous indignation and the pride we have seen for so long in African-American women. You just couldn't keep her quiet. One day she was giving an antislavery speech and an old white man sitting way in the back shouted at her, "Woman, I don't care as much as a little-bitty flea about your antislavery talk."

"That may be true, sir," she said to him, "but the Lord willing, I'll keep you scratching."

That's what I really see my job as now, I'm a legal agitator, I'm an irritant, a pain to the establishment. It would be very easy now for me to settle into the comfortable role of an elder statesman of the legal profession. I can afford to do that. But while the scope of criminal law has remained relatively stable, the possible applications of civil law have exploded. When I became a lawyer the real action was in criminal law; everybody wanted to be Perry Mason. Civil law was basically personal injury law, it was business law, it was suing for damages, everyday problem-solving law. Only on rare occasions was it applied successfully to significant societal issues.

Maybe the scope of civil law really began to change when civil rights leaders moved from the streets into the courtroom. *Brown v. the Board of Education*, which ended legal school segregation, marked a real turning point in the use of class action lawsuits. After that came the barrage of class action lawsuits in civil rights and, more recently, consumer rights. Americans actually began using the civil legal system in new and creative ways to assert their rights against the government and large corporations. For decades corporate America had done pretty much whatever it wanted to do, where and when it wanted to do it. Issues that no one ever would have thought about before are being contested in courtrooms every single day. Civil law is definitely where the action is, where I want to be.

I set out as a young lawyer to change the world. The fact is that lawyers—for all the shark jokes, for all the ambulance chasers promising fortunes to people who slip on sidewalks—are doing exactly that. Lawyers are making multibillion-dollar corporations responsible for their actions. Lawyers are saving lives by forcing companies to clean up the poisonous mess they've made of our environment. They are forcing companies to admit the products they market can be deadly. They are forcing manufacturers to add safety devices and do the extra testing necessary to ensure that their products can be used safely. And lawyers are holding entire industries, like big tobacco, accountable for hiding devastating information about the dangers of their products from consumers.

I've gotten myself involved in cases that have the potential to change thousands of lives. I've joined with one of the most successful class action lawyers, Michael Hausfeld, to sue cigarette manufacturers for targeting young people with their advertising. What age group do you think the cartoon character Joe Camel was created to attract? The Joe Camel campaign was very successful—and as a result we now have all these sixteen- and seventeen-year-old kids addicted to nicotine. That's a potentially deadly addiction. We want the tobacco companies to pay for programs to help kids kick this habit, and we want to make sure that they don't do it again.

I'm also among a group of lawyers representing Korean women allegedly forced into prostitution by the Japanese during World War

II. Many of these former "comfort women," that's what they were called, had their lives destroyed. Our suit is aimed at making Japan pay for that.

The lives of just about all the families living in the small town of Anniston, Alabama, have been ripped apart by the Monsanto chemical plant, which dumped highly toxic chemicals into the land and waterways for decades. There isn't a family in that town who hasn't suffered some personal loss. I went down there to meet with potential clients and more than seven thousand people showed up. We didn't have enough room in the auditorium. What happened to the people of this small American town wasn't the result of some tragic accident; this was done by a corporation that, as we contend in our lawsuit, knew exactly what it was doing and thought it could get away with it. When I walked down the street with a resident of the town, he pointed out house after house to me, saying, "Over there is the so-and-so house, he's thirty-four years old and dying of cancer. The kid who lives in that house across the street has lymphoma. Down the block three people in that family have cancer . . ." Listening to these stories makes me feel that an economic penalty isn't enough—but it is a way of making sure other companies don't do the same thing.

But undoubtedly the most controversial class action lawsuit in which I'm participating is a class action lawsuit against the federal government and presumably some private corporations for reparations, payment in some form, for perpetuating and profiting from black slavery. There are people who have tried to talk me out of getting involved in this lawsuit. There is no way you're going to win this one, I've been told, you, you don't need this. There is some truth to that, I don't need it at all—in economic terms. But as an African-American I think this country needs this very badly. I can't even imagine being property, I can't even visualize it. I like to believe that if I had lived in the time of slavery I would have spoken out against it then, whatever the consequences. So it would be impossible for me not to speak out against it now.

"Johnnie Cochran is about to play the race card once again," wrote conservative columnist Linda Chavez, head of the U.S. Commission on Civil Rights under Ronald Reagan, and George W. Bush's choice for Secretary of Labor—until she withdrew from consideration when it was discovered that she had employed an illegal alien as a housekeeper. ". . . (D)o Johnnie Cochran and his fellow trial lawyers really believe that the problems that still plague the black community will in any way be solved by reparations? Will reparations find responsible, loving fathers for the 70 percent of black babies born out of wedlock each year? Will they close the skills gap between black and white high school graduates or help a single black child to read?

"Or will the talk of reparations simply pump up more business for a group of already successful and wealthy lawyers like Johnnie Cochran?"

The answer is that I believe with all my heart that reparations will help us attack—if not solve—the mammoth problems that still plague the black community. And it seems obvious to me that anybody who doesn't understand that simply hasn't done enough research. We are at the very beginning of this class action lawsuit; there are countless legal questions to be answered before we can move forward. But right now I know one thing for certain: There is an easily identifiable cause and effect. Black slaves helped build this country—they literally helped build Washington, D.C. Slaves were denied basic human rights. Their families were ripped apart to be sold. Slaves were forbidden by law to learn how to read. After the slaves were freed, black people became second-class citizens. They were prohibited from participating in the most basic forms of American society, they were denied the opportunities available to whites, forced into segregated communities and inferior schools. So given that history it shouldn't be surprising to anyone that the black family structure is weak or that black children do not have a strong educational foundation. Modern black American culture is the direct descendant of the slave culture.

Affirmative action programs were an attempt to recognize that minorities, among them African-Americans, were disadvantaged and needed additional benefits to compete in education and in business. Affirmative action became a major political issue, and attacks by Republicans and conservative groups have pretty much gutted it. One of the first major legal challenges was brought against law schools for setting aside a certain number of slots for minority students whose overall qualifications were not equal to whites. As a result fewer African-American students are attending the best law schools, meaning that they're not going to get jobs at the most prestigious law firms. In 1996 more than half of the nation's top 250 law firms had at most one black partner. That's a disgrace, and it is directly attributable to the difficulty young African-American kids still face in getting a good education.

I happen to be a big supporter of affirmative action, which is why I have to wonder about the motives of people like Supreme Court Justice Clarence Thomas, who benefited tremendously from affirmative action in getting into college and law school and yet now opposes it. Clarence Thomas is a charming man, he's very engaging, but I believe he has become a barrier to black progress in this country. The fact that George H. Bush nominated him for the Supreme Court seat once held by Thurgood Marshall was shocking. It was frightening. The only thing that qualified him for that seat was the color of his skin, which combined with his conservative politics guaranteed his admission. His was an incredibly cynical nomination, a political appointment. It allowed George H. Bush to boast that he had put an African-American on the Supreme Court while at the same time he was adding a conservative vote.

I just don't understand Clarence Thomas. He took advantage of affirmative action programs, he got admitted to college under affirmative action quotas, and later voted to do away with the program. He crossed the bridge and now he wants to burn it. I just don't understand thinking like that.

The foundation of any reparations lawsuit has to be the acknowledgment that we have a permanent underclass in this country, and that it is a direct result of slavery and the ensuing racial discrimination. We no longer have slave labor; instead, we have minimum wage labor to do the menial jobs in society. Who's doing those jobs? Maybe the majority of people in America are satisfied with this situation, but I would hope not. I would hope people realize that for the future of this country—not just for African-Americans, but for America—it is vital we find a way to provide the tools young African-Americans need to succeed. I think reparations is the most direct means to accomplish that.

My great-grandfathers were slaves. They worked in the Louisiana cotton fields. The fact that I'm a product of slavery obviously is proof that even given the realities of life in segregated America, some families prospered. But many more did not. Many more families have lived in poverty for generations, people whose children don't have a chance for success. The legal questions about reparations are very complicated: What is the basis for a lawsuit? Who are the plaintiffs? Who are the defendants? What remedy do we propose? Is there a statute of limitations?

I don't know the answers to all of these questions. Yet. But in time I will. We all will. A group of extraordinary lawyers have volunteered to do the basic work on this case. To create the legal structure necessary to proceed with this lawsuit. I do know that there are precedents for paying reparations to a class of people; the United States government has paid more than a billion dollars to Japanese-Americans illegally interned during World War II. European governments have paid reparations to Holocaust victims. European corporations have paid reparations to World War II slave laborers. So the concept of paying reparations isn't so far-fetched.

Obviously what makes our case so different than these others is that those plaintiffs are alive. These are living people who had been deprived of their rights and property, and they wanted to be paid for it. These were the victims. Every former slave is dead, an estimated 25 million died in slavery in the United States. But there are still millions of victims of American slavery and the subjugation of blacks. Their families are still suffering the consequences.

Most people don't know that this is not a new effort. This isn't something that some smart lawyer thought up one day. The quest for reparations is much more than a century old. The first slave reparations bill was introduced in Congress in 1867, only two years after the end of the Civil War. This bill guaranteed each freed slave forty acres of land and $100 "to build a dwelling." It didn't pass.

In 1915, a suit filed against the Treasury Department asking for $68 million in remuneration for slave labor was dismissed on the grounds of sovereign immunity—you can only sue the federal government in very specific situations. And in 1962 the Reparations Committee of Descendants of United States Slaves filed a claim in California.

So this campaign started more than a century ago. This is simply a new strategy to achieve an old objective. As a nation we need to confront the issue of slavery to understand why we have this massive economic and educational gap between black and white Americans. The most difficult question to answer is what do we want from the government. I'm not particularly interested in seeing every African-American whose ancestors were enslaved receive a check. Just distributing money would create unsolvable problems and enduring animosities without accomplishing the overall objective. That seems to me to be an impossible task. What I would like to see is recognition from the United States government that this atrocity occurred, that the country benefited from slave labor, and an apology for it. An acknowledgment that it happened, that it was absolutely wrong, and a commitment that it will never happen again. That may not seem like a big deal, but to me it is extremely important. It would be the beginning of giving back to us the pride that was robbed by the institution of slavery.

An educational benefit would have to be the primary aspect of any settlement. That would be the appropriate place to start. An investment by America in its African-American young people. This might include remedial courses, tutors, tuition, all the educational tools that children who are behind need in order to catch up. Statistically, an estimated 80 percent of all young white people have access to computers, compared to only 20 percent of young blacks. That is simply a guarantee that the racial divisions in this country will get worse in the future; it will be compounded by the digital divide. Any child who is not computer-literate will not be able to compete. It really is that simple.

I also would like to see a serious effort to educate the majority community about the history of blacks in America. It's a compelling story that hasn't been told. I would like to make sure that it becomes a standard part of the curriculum. Young people of all races should know about the contributions that African-Americans have made to this nation—and they don't. I think that would be a very important step toward giving young African-Americans the self-esteem which they so often seem to lack.

Not everyone involved in this process agrees with me. It has been said that if you want three opinions, ask two lawyers. There are a lot of different opinions about how to proceed with the legal case and what our settlement goals should be. In April 2002, for example, another group of attorneys filed a lawsuit against three private corporations, claiming that each of these companies had profited greatly from slave labor. I understand they have a right to do this and that their suit is much more limited than ours. We believe, clearly, that in addition to private companies and institutions, the government has to be a defendant. Our lawsuit will be much more comprehensive, much more detailed, and hopefully much more instructive. What is troubling to us is that other lawyers bringing suits could get a bad decision that might impact upon our case. But we are united with this other group in the belief that reparations are owed, and we are united in the belief that settling this case would benefit the entire nation.

There also are some critics of our lawsuit who believe that we would benefit personally from this. That is completely untrue. Without qualification, neither I nor any member of our team will ever see a penny from our work. Not one penny. This is being done for the descendants of slaves and the good of the nation, and hopefully will result in an educational benefit which will help bridge the economic gap between blacks and whites.

What is so difficult to accept is that slavery still exists in the modern world. I mean actual slavery. In 2001 I joined with Ken Starr, the special prosecutor in the Clinton matters, to defend three activists who were arrested for protesting against slavery in the nation of Sudan. The Sudanese government is enslaving or killing by starvation millions of its people, primarily black Sudanese in the south of that country. To raise attention to the issue, our clients chained themselves to the building housing the Sudanese Embassy and were arrested for unlawful entry. It was a misdemeanor case, a very minor charge involving a very major issue.

I was asked to get involved because my presence, particularly standing alongside Ken Starr, would bring out reporters and photographers. This wasn't so much a legal case as a publicity effort. The real intent was to put the government of Sudan on trial, to make people aware of the atrocities. What's going on in that country is barbaric; the intentional starvation of people, genital mutilation, and enslavement. The prosecutor eventually dismissed the charges against our clients due to a lack of evidence. We did attract a lot of attention. The story appeared in every major newspaper and Ken Starr and I made several joint television appearances. We succeeded, I think, in making people aware of this incredible human tragedy, but the potential to have a real impact was lost in the wake of the terrorist attacks on the United States. The situation became even more complex when Sudan was accused of harboring terrorists. No one can predict what's going to happen there, but it is a bad situation that undoubtedly is going to get worse.

The day I became a lawyer I accepted the fact that I wasn't going to be successful in every case; knowing that has never stopped me from at least trying. After moving to New York and establishing The Cochran Firm, I've gotten involved in several class action discrimination lawsuits against major corporations. Class action discrimination law is extremely complex, made even more difficult by judges who refuse to recognize, or certify, a class. To make it extremely simple, a group of people with a common legal complaint can be considered a class for purposes of legal action. That means that all the members of a class have the same reason to file a lawsuit. A thousand citizens of Anniston, Alabama, for example, would be considered a class. They've all suffered because of the actions of a single company. It's a way of consolidating what would otherwise be a large number of individual lawsuits.

What we've been trying to do is represent a group of people who have been held down by the big corporations because of their racial or ethnic background or even their gender. But to file a class action lawsuit a judge has to agree that a class of people exists, and a lot of judges don't want to do that. They put big roadblocks in the legal path. The courts have made it extremely difficult for working people to get justice against big corporations.

That isn't just me making that claim. We've actually proven statistically that the courts do as much as possible to protect corporations against employee discrimination lawsuits. Cyrus Mehri, one of America's leading employee discrimination attorneys, and I commissioned two Cornell Law School professors to examine the actions of the federal court of appeals in employment discrimination cases. And we found out something pretty remarkable. If a plaintiff—an employee—manages to fight through the entire legal process and actually win a jury verdict, almost half the time the federal appellate court will overturn that verdict; but when the employer wins they just about never reverse it. Here's the way it works: If an employee wins there is a 43 percent chance the court will overturn that victory; but if the employer wins there is only a 5 percent chance of reversing that decision.

That's the overall statistic covering all twelve federal districts. Certain districts are much worse. In 60 percent of cases won by plaintiffs in the Fifth Circuit in states like Mississippi and Louisiana, for example, the decision has been reversed—while there has *never* been a reversal when the corporation has won. How curious.

Those statistics send this message to employers: You can discriminate against your employees and not worry about it. The courts are going to protect you.

A lot of people believe that racial discrimination in business and society, the so-called Jim Crow laws, ended a long time ago. That under the law everybody now has an equal opportunity for promotion and benefits. But that is just not true. What actually exists in many companies is a discriminatory culture, call it Jim Crow Jr., an unwritten way of doing business that prevents African-American employees from getting the same pay and opportunities for advancement as the white people working right next to them.

Beginning in the 1960s the big companies finally started hiring African-Americans. It was only a hundred years after the end of the Civil War, but finally we got our foot in some doors. That was unprecedented. But over time the people who got an opportunity to work began finding out that they were not making as much money as their white counterparts, that they were not being considered for promotion, that they weren't moving into management. They found themselves getting passed over by the same people they had originally trained. It wasn't that these people were always better, but they were always white.

We're representing a class consisting of 2,400 past and present African-American employees of the Georgia Power Company, for example. This is one of the leading energy companies in America. For decades no one complained about discrimination. So when we went to Atlanta and joined with the Bondurant Firm to accuse the company of a decades-long pattern of job discrimination and racial harassment, people believed this was just an example of some big-shot lawyers coming to town to stir up trouble and make some money. That's the perception.

The reality is that this company has a long tradition of discriminating against its black employees. A man named Cornelius Cooper has worked there almost thirty years, most of those years as a lineman. He's a hardworking man, his performance reviews were excellent, yet he has applied for and been turned down for about fifteen different jobs. Jobs with better salaries. The people who turned him down kept telling him he had to do this or that to advance in this company, and when he did whatever was suggested they found other reasons to give the job to a white employee. He even took a company course on interviewing techniques that taught him to project more confidence; but when he did that at an interview he was turned down because, "I was told I acted like I walked on water."

When Cornelius Cooper began talking about it with other long-time African-Americans employees at Georgia Power he realized it wasn't him, it was the company. Almost 20 percent of Georgia Southern's employees are African-American, yet out of 272 foremen only fifteen—6 percent—are black. Not only are blacks routinely passed over for promotion throughout the company, they are paid less than their white counterparts for doing the same job; one woman, for example, was earning $4,000 less than the white employee she had trained while they did the same job. The exact same job. In several cases black employees doing the same job as white employees earned 20 percent less.

Discrimination was part of the corporate culture. Racially offensive jokes were tacked up on company bulletin boards. A supposedly humorous Ku Klux Klan recruitment letter was sent through company mail. African-Americans were subject to racist comments from coworkers, and in eight different plants thirteen hangman's nooses were hung—and left hanging for months or years. Hangman's nooses. When the former CEO and president of the Southern Company, which owned Georgia Power, was asked about these nooses, he said, "I had no earthly idea that anybody today would consider that to be a racial symbol."

Well, where on earth had he been living? Finally, in 2001, we filed a class action lawsuit for the 2,400 past and present African-American Georgia Power employees. The biggest hurdle we faced was being certified by a judge as a class, as a group in which all the workers were subjected to the same patterns of discrimination. Once you get that certification the case can go forward. It seemed obvious that there was a company-wide policy of keeping blacks in their places. Those nooses were hung in eight different plants. But a judge turned us down, refusing to allow us to proceed with a class action lawsuit. The system has been carefully built to protect corporations against judgments.

The reality is we can still proceed with 2,400 individual lawsuits, but as a practical matter the discriminatory practices of the company have been protected.

We encountered the same problem when we tried to bring a class action lawsuit against Lockheed Martin, the aerospace company. We had substantial evidence that they had discriminated against African-American employees in pay, promotions, in determining who would be laid off, and in granting leaves of absence. Black employees there encountered the same insensitive culture, including invitations to join the Ku Klux Klan and the presence of the hangman's noose and Confederate flags. If they complained they were fired or otherwise penalized. But again, in this case the judge refused to certify the entire class. So we either have to fight a thousand individual lawsuits or a single class action lawsuit.

In certain circuits it is nearly impossible to get class certifications. The judges just refuse to do it. Like everything else, politics figures into it. We know, for example, that most judges appointed by Presidents Reagan or George H. Bush are not going to certify a class. In both Georgia Power and Lockheed we had extremely conservative judges. One of those judges actually tried to explain in his decision why nooses weren't evidence of discrimination. Reading it made me sick to my stomach. We could appeal—but the statistics we compiled demonstrate the futility of that.

Presenting these cases is expensive; in one of our arguments we paid an expert almost $200,000 for his research. Now what we have to do is disburse the individual cases among various lawyers and try them one by one by one.

The only way to fight is to persevere. We've filed class action discrimination cases against Microsoft, Johnson & Johnson, Alcoa, and Bellsouth. Look, Microsoft's Bill Gates is a very decent man; he gave a billion dollars to the United Negro College Fund. Microsoft does hire minorities—but, as I was told by many people, when African-Americans and women get in the door they are denied the same promotional opportunities as white men. And while they get paid well, they don't get paid the same as white males. It's the result of a system in which managers exercise tremendous discretion, and the managers are all white men. The statistics prove it; we're not claiming that this is the result of some diabolical plot, but we have strong anecdotal evidence that it exists. What we have had difficulty doing is getting a class certified.

I've stood in front of a thousand judges; more even. I've called every single one of them "Your Honor." Sometimes I've had to practically swallow my tongue after I'd said it because I certainly didn't mean it. With some judges the decision is preordained before the trial starts. The judge knows what he wants the result to be. In the Old South, for example, a trial was a brief stop on the way to the lynch mob. They just wanted things to look correct. In some parts of the country we still have that mentality. There are bad federal judges. They have biases, they don't even attempt to be fair. Everybody knows who they are, even the other judges know, but there is nothing that can be done about them. Federal judges serve for life. You can't remove them with a crane.

There is nothing more frustrating, nothing, than walking into a courtroom representing a client with whom you have identified or a case that you have a real passion about, and watching a judge gut that case, just throw it out. Or watching that judge overturn a jury verdict to reach his own conclusion. It is so hard for me to watch a judge manipulate the law to his own ends—and still have to be respectful to him, to have to call him "Your Honor."

There is nothing more depressing than to believe in our system of justice and not be able to go into a courtroom and get that justice.

But you can't quit trying. You can't give up. You have to see these people as small pawns in a much bigger picture called justice. You have to utilize everything that you have learned in your career; you have to hope that the bright lights of publicity will prevent that judge from acting without reason.

There are so many good judges and I have been privileged to stand in front of many of them. A good judge is simply a person knowledgeable about the law and who applies it evenly and without bias. A good judge has courage and integrity, and understands that ambition should not be part of the job description.

Maybe that's why I put so much faith in the wisdom of juries. I know that if I can get my case in front of a jury I've got a real chance of winning. Maybe because jurors haven't spent their lives inside the courthouse, they don't take the justice system for granted; instead, they tend to treat it with respect. While a jury's decision can be manipulated by a judge, most often it will return a decision based squarely on the evidence presented in the case.

Probably the most courageous jury I ever tried a case in front of was the six-member panel who sat in judgment of the Walt Disney Company in Orlando, Florida. Disney had turned Orlando from a small aging Southern town to one of the major tourist destinations in the world when it built Disney World there, followed by Epcot Center. The economy of the city depends heavily on Disney. Either directly or indirectly a large percentage of people living there are employed by Disney or companies dependent on Disney. You really don't want to sue Mickey Mouse in Orlando, Florida.

My involvement in this case began with another letter that intrigued Carl Douglas, who brought it to my attention. In this letter two men, a former baseball umpire named Nick Stracick and an architect named Ed Russell, claimed they had conceived and designed a multisport amusement complex and had approached Disney with their idea and plans. They wanted Disney to build it in Orlando. Disney discussed the concept seriously with the two men for almost three years, then told them it had decided against proceeding. But four years later Disney announced plans to build a $100 million sports complex, Wide World of Sports. The sports-themed amusement park opened in 1997. Stracick and Russell claimed that Disney had violated their copyright by stealing their idea—and most importantly, that they could prove it.

As I read more of their material, the more interested I got. This was a pure business case. At the end of it nobody was going to go to prison, but it was about things that mattered: ethics and honesty. It was just another example of a giant corporation stomping on an ordinary person and—unless an attorney agreed to do something about it—getting away with it.

I had a lot of respect for Disney dating back to 1955. I was right there when Disneyland opened in Anaheim. For a time, my best friend, Ron Sunderland, had worked for Disney and spoke well of the company. In the past I'd had a couple of cases against them and found them tough but reasonable opponents. And I did enjoy a lot of their movies. But if this claim was true, Disney had stolen a very valuable idea and had to pay for that.

I met with Stracick and Russell and they had an abundance of evidence. Without question they had been involved in a development arrangement with Disney. Disney had ended that relationship and proceeded without them. I was confident we could prove that; however, I was less confident we could get a jury in Orlando—where the case would have to be tried—to make Disney pay for it. A large decision against that company could hurt their community.

I'd never tried a copyright infringement case or, as it later became, a trade secrets case. It's interesting law. I knew I would need a Florida attorney to work with me, as I had worked with Brafman in New York, and I had just the right person. Willie Gary is the child of sharecroppers, growing up in a house without plumbing and moving across the South following the harvests to pick crops. He became one of America's best and most successful personal injury lawyers, flying above those same fields in which he once picked fruit in one of his two private jets, which he has named "The Wings of Justice," living in a fifty-room house near Palm Beach. For this case there wasn't a better lawyer in the country. "Let's do it together," I suggested. "I don't know that we can win it, but we definitely can send them a loud message."

We worked out of Willie's large law office. I don't believe too many people thought we had a real chance to beat the Disney empire. Most entertainment companies are used to being sued by people who claim that their idea has been stolen. Rarely do these cases ever get into a courtroom and the plaintiff almost never wins.

Disney denied completely that it had stolen any ideas from anyone. For a time we were treated like a minor irritation that would soon go away—even though we sued for $1.4 billion dollars, a figure we based on the success of the sports theme park. Initially we sued in federal court for copyright infringement. When that suit was thrown out we filed in state court, claiming fraud, misappropriation of trade secrets, and breach of confidentiality. I knew we were right, our clients had brought their concept to Disney, they had even worked for three years with the same man who later headed the project for Disney; but I also knew that Disney had the home team advantage and I'd seen too often that the courts are generally sympathetic to large corporations. So I wasn't optimistic. That was okay; Willie Gary was optimistic enough for both of us.

The state appellate court ruled we had a cause of action and that our clients were entitled to have it decided by a jury. At least we were going to have our days in court.

Willie and I both deposed Disney chairman Michael Eisner. Willie started the videotaped deposition in a conference room on the Disney studio lot, but things fell apart after a few hours when he practically got into a fight with one of their lawyers. They were literally about to hit each other. Eisner finally got up and left.

I had to finish the deposition another day. Eisner seemed irritated, his attitude was simply: We didn't do anything wrong, why am I even here wasting my time? I didn't mind that, I suspected the jurors would think he was awfully arrogant. When I was preparing to question Eisner I read his book, which basically explained that his job was to make lots of money and keep his shareholders happy. I just used his own words to draw a portrait of a company desperate for earnings. I thought jurors would get the message: desperate enough to steal a potentially very valuable idea. Eisner claimed that nothing important happened in that company that he didn't know about and approve—but that he knew absolutely nothing about our clients, their work, and the development process. He also confirmed that he worked very closely with Disney's top architect, Wing Chao, who had been present at several meetings with Stracick and Russell. The overall impression, I thought, was that he was trying to be evasive and actually knew a lot more about this project than he admitted.

The six-person jury consisted of five whites and one African-

American, three men and three women. Ordinary people, one of them a truck driver, another a house cleaner. During the twenty-five-day trial some of the testimony from Disney executives was pretty difficult to believe, particularly that of Wing Chao, who claimed he knew absolutely nothing about Stracick and Russell's plans. In an organization as tightly run as Disney, it just didn't seem likely that one executive would spend three years dealing with our clients without the decision makers above him knowing all about it.

Willie Gary presented our summation. "There is a mountain of evidence in this case," he told the jurors, asking them to return "not half justice, but full justice."

Finally he concluded, summing up our case, but also summing up the essence of our entire legal system. More than anyone else, he said, "You have the power to see wrong and make it right."

Judge Ted Olson was tough but fair. He instructed the jurors that the only thing they were allowed to consider were the conceptual similarities between Stracick and Russell's plans and the Disney sports complex. We pointed out eighty-eight of those similarities.

The jury deliberated most of two days. The waiting was pleasurable compared to waiting for the jury in Puffy Combs trial, or pretty much in any criminal trial. The pressure was completely different; this was about money, not someone's life.

When the jury finally returned I didn't have the slightest idea how these people had decided. I thought we'd done a good job presenting our case, but I knew that these people would have to show great courage to deliver a verdict for us in Orlando. The first question the judge asked was, "Have you reached a verdict?"

"We have, Your Honor," the jury foreman replied. "We find for the plaintiff." Yes! I leaned back in my chair and took a deep breath. We'd won the case; now we were going to find out exactly how much. ". . . and we assess damages at $240 million."

Two hundred and forty million dollars. It was unbelievable. Astonishing. We had beaten Disney in Orlando. We'd proved that it was possible for David to beat Goliath. We'd proved that the system can work. The jury found that Disney had acted with malicious intent, meaning they knew what they were doing was illegal and did it anyway. Disney was being punished for its greed. An alternate juror, released when deliberations began because he wasn't needed, told reporters he would have awarded us the entire $1.4 billion we'd requested.

Willie Gary had previously won huge verdicts, hundreds of millions of dollars, but for me, for someone who once had been thrilled with a $25,000 settlement from the city of Los Angeles, this was almost beyond comprehension. I felt like shouting out loud in joy. Fortunately, I didn't. The judge also awarded us $1, one dollar, in punitive damages and, of course, Disney has appealed the verdict. With the accruing interest, that verdict has now reached $300 million.

Appellate judges certainly can ignore the will of the jury and throw out the verdict. But knowing that those six individuals who became one jury had the courage to follow the truth—even when it could not have been comfortable for them—is a pretty wonderful thought.

It may well be years before this case is finally settled. No case simply ends; rather, the river of legal paperwork eventually becomes a trickle and finally stops. Most cases last years. Some cases I became involved in before the Disney case will continue long after that case is finished. I've got my class action discrimination cases. I'm representing the family of Gideon Busch, an Orthodox Jewish man with mental problems who was shot to death by police officers in Brooklyn when he supposedly raised a small hammer above his head in a threatening manner. Peter, Barry, and I are in the pretrial phase of the case of African-American teenager Dantae Johnson, who was shot in the back by a New York City policeman for running away when stopped for no apparent reason. We're representing the family of Thomas Pizzuto, a recovering heroin addict serving a ninety-day sentence in a Nassau County, New York, jail for traffic violations. He was beaten to death in jail, left to suffer with a ruptured spleen for five days by three police officers when he complained too loudly that he needed his methadone. We represent members of the family of four people, one of them a baby born prematurely upon his mother's death but who didn't survive, killed when a drunk NYPD police officer ran over them. I represent 16-year-old Donovan Johnson, who was handcuffed by Inglewood policemen, who smashed his head against his car and punched him in the face—for riding in a car with expired license plates. I represent . . .

. . . so many people who have been injured through the negligence or anger of others or have been discriminated against because of their skin color or have been abused by corporate America. I have represented people who have suffered and have no other voice but mine. I represent a voice of calm in international disputes. The phone continues to ring, the cases continue to fascinate me, the horizon just seems a little farther and farther away.

There are still many days when the injustice I see makes me angry. Days when the racial injustice and politically conservative nature of the system frustrates me. And fortunately, days when the system works just exactly the way it was designed, and provides justice for the people.

I loved it the first day I went to work as a lawyer. I love it still. And I know without any doubt that I will love it always. I have heard all the jokes, I laughed at many of them myself—and I am so proud to have spent my life as a lawyer.

I rest my case.

ACKNOWLEDGMENTS

It is impossible to complete a book—or live my life—without the support and assistance of so many people. I have been fortunate to have had many wonderful secretaries and assistants throughout my career, including my special assistant, Sonia Davis. I want these people to know how much I appreciate what they have done for me.

I have a wonderful family, and I want them to know how much I appreciate their support, especially my beloved wife, Dale; my wise father, Johnnie Cochran, Sr.; my wonderful children, Melodie, Tiffany, and Jonathan; and my always inspiring sisters, Pearl Baker and Martha Jean Sherrad.

I also have partners in the practice of law whom I greatly appreciate: Messrs Sam Cherry, Keith Givens, Jock Smith, Jim Montgomery, Julian Bolton, Hezekiah Sistrunk, Cameron Stewart, Eric Ferrer, and Derek Sells.

And finally, I have been fortunate to have the full support of my publisher, Tom Dunne at St. Martin's Press, and my diligent and always smiling editor, Sean Desmond.

INDEX